Tales from the 'Pool

A Collection of Liverpool Stories

MIKE ROYDEN

Best Wishes

Mike Royden

First Published 2017 by Creative Dreams Publishing (UK)
an imprint of World of Creative Dreams

54 St James Street
Liverpool
L1 0AB

worldofcreativedreams.co.uk

British Library Cataloguing in Publication Data.
A catalogue record for this book is available from the British Library.

ISBN 978 0 9935524 1 0

Cover illustrations:
Portraits – (L-R) Dr William Duncan, Captain Noel Chavasse VC & Bar, MC, Julia Wallace.
Background: 'Liverpool South Shore 1797' (H.Greenwood (lithograph)/William G.Herdman (on stone) (c.1856) [looking towards Liverpool from the Dingle area]

In memory of my parents

William Henry 'Bill' Royden
(1929-1998)

Hazel Royden
(1931-2013)

THE AUTHOR

Mike Royden has taught History for over 30 years, and has also lectured on numerous courses in local history in the Centre for Continuing Education at the University of Liverpool. He has written several books, and has made regular appearances on radio and television including Radio 4's *Making History* and BBC's *Heirhunters,* as well as filming with Hollywood star Kim Cattrall discussing her Liverpool roots for *Who Do You Think You Are?* He also appeared on the programme featuring Gareth Malone in the same series, and with Ricky Tomlinson in *Blitz Cities.* Mike Royden also runs several history websites at www.roydenhistory.co.uk.

He has two sons, Lewis, who is a photographer, and Liam, a musician.

TITLES BY MIKE ROYDEN

Village at War – The Cheshire Village of Farndon During the First World War (2016)

Liverpool Then and Now (2012, 2nd edition 2015)

Tracing Your Liverpool Ancestors (2010, 2nd edition 2014)

Pioneers and Perseverance: A History of the Royal School for the Blind, Liverpool, 1791-1991 (1991)

A History of Liverpool Maternity Hospital and the Women's Hospital (1995)

A History of Mill Road Hospital, Liverpool (1993)

'The 19th Century Poor Law in Liverpool and its Hinterland: Towards the Origins of the Workhouse Infirmary' *Journal of the Liverpool Medical History Society* (vol 11. 2000)

'The Roots of the New Liverpool Women's Hospital: 'The early medical care of women and babies in the late 18th/early 19th century' *Journal of the Liverpool Medical History Society* (vol 10. 1999)

The Impact of the Coming of the Railway on 19th Century Halewood (1989)

The Effects of Enclosure: Halewood Township by the Mid Nineteenth Century (1989)

Did Adolf Hitler visit Liverpool in 1912/13? - bbc.co.uk website (Legacies)

Forthcoming:

A History of Thomas Royden & Sons, Liverpool, Shipbuilders
(due 2017)

Merseyside at War 1939-45 (Pen & Sword) (due 2018)

Plus a variety of articles published on:
www.roydenhistory.co.uk

Some of the web sites designed and maintained by Mike Royden include:

'Mike Royden's Local History Pages'
Halewood Local History Pages www.halewood.org.uk
Farndon Local History Pages www.farndon.org.uk
Ellesmere Port War memorial www.eportwarmemorial.org.uk

CONTENTS

Page

1 Liverpool Castle and the Foundation of a Medieval Town   9

2 Edward Rushton - The Life and Times of an 18th Century   33
   Radical and Poet

3 Dr. W.M. Duncan and Public Health in Liverpool   51

4 The Leveson Street Murder of 1849   65

5 The Poor Law and Workhouse in Liverpool   97

6 Lewis's of Liverpool – The Story of an Iconic Store   129

7 The Docker's Umberlla - Liverpool's Overhead Railway   161

8 Ruth Harwood Bowker – Titanic Survivor   179

9 Liverpool Old Pals Regiment   201

10 Captain Noel Godfrey Chavasse VC & Bar, MC   231

11 The Liverpool Police Strike of 1919   255

12 Frank Hornby and his Factory of Dreams   279

13 The Murder of Julia Wallace 1931   297

14 Exploding Munitions - Captain Kinley and the May Blitz 1941   311

15 The Hitler Family of Liverpool   335

Artist impression of Liverpool Castle From Cox, E. W. 'An Attempt to Recover the Plans of the Castle of Liverpool from Authentic records; Considered in Connection with Medieval Principles of Defence and Construction' in *Transactions of the Historic Society of Lancashire and Cheshire*, vol. 42 (1892)

1

Liverpool Castle and the Foundation of a Medieval Town

For over four hundred years, Liverpool Castle dominated the town and the old pool from its prominent site at the top of Lord Street overlooking the Mersey, but today there is nothing left of the structure, and only the name 'Castle Street' gives any suggestion that the building ever existed. The castle was demolished by 1720 and no satisfactory views or plans of it survive. There are many estimations, but none are wholly accurate. Yet, for much of its existence it was the main seat of administration for the area and was controlled by the most powerful local lords.

Such a dominant structure is difficult to imagine today – easy of course in those towns where castle remains still exist as heritage attractions – but in Liverpool, on a site now swallowed up by a combination of urban retail and the judiciary, it would be a lost medieval island within a high-rise sea of glass and concrete. To many local people therefore, it often comes as a complete surprise to learn of what did actually exist on the site, and to those who are aware of its existence, most tend to know little of its history. In fact, at the time of the building of the castle, Liverpool was undergoing a crucial transition, and the new structure effectively confirmed the transfer of local government to the new town from West Derby, the original centre for local bureaucracy, pre-dating the Norman Conquest of 1066.

In 1066 West Derby was a royal manor held by the last Saxon King of England, Edward the Confessor, and probably contained a fortified manor house, a royal hunting lodge (as West Derby was a hunting ground of the Saxon kings), three eyries of hawks and extensive woodlands. By 1086, after the Normans had established control - Domesday Book records that an early form of feudalism had been put into place, and that six 'hundreds' stretched from the Mersey to the Ribble in the north. Each hundred had its own chief centre for local administration and West Derby was the capital manor of the 'Hundred of West Derby', which stretched from Hale in the south to the Crossens area in the North.

[In England a 'hundred' was the division of a shire for administrative, military and judicial purposes under the common law. Originally, when introduced by the Saxons between 613 and 1017, a 'hundred' had enough land to sustain approximately one hundred households headed by a hundred-man or hundred *eolder*. He was responsible for administration, justice, and supplying military troops, as well as leading its forces. Therefore, a 'hundred' sometimes later referred to the amount of land sufficient to sustain one hundred families, defined as the land covered by one hundred 'hides'.]

The future royal borough of Liverpool meanwhile, was a mere farming settlement based around a small, tidal creek of the River Mersey, and was so insignificant it wasn't even mentioned by name in the Doomsday survey of 1086. The story of how Liverpool came to rise to prominence over it's parent manor is one of economics and royal politics, plus one key figure, King John of England, who succeeded his brother, Richard the Lionheart on the throne of England, in 1199. But this transition would take another century and a half, and dominance for now would lie at West Derby.

Domesday records that control of West Derby had been given to the Norman, Roger of Poitou. It was probably Roger who built the castle of West Derby, a regular Norman motte and bailey design, approximately 40 metres wide, a wooden tower most likely on the motte, and surrounded by a moat. To the south was a bailey, around which there was another moat, completing the structure in a figure of eight pattern, and here local matters of court, law and government were dealt with. The exact date of the construction of the castle is unknown, but it was probably erected before the end of the 11th century. West Derby was now on a par with Lancaster as a local centre of feudal administration. The local Saxon population were now under subjugation at the hands of their Norman masters, who controlled the application of law and collection of taxes and fines. Norman feudalism had begun to tighten its grip here too in this seemingly unimportant, sparsely populated backwater.

Although Liverpool is not named in Domesday, it is thought to have been one of the six unnamed berewicks (barley farms) or 'outliers' belonging to this superior royal manor of West Derby. Once the named local areas in Domesday are accounted for, there are several omissions which have Saxon or Norse origins and would, therefore, be expected to feature. These sites were most likely the six outliers held by Edward the Confessor in 1066 which were directly dependant on the West Derby estate, and probably included Thingwall, Garston, Aigburth, Hale/Halewood, Everton and the fishing hamlet at Liverpool.

The earliest mention of the place-name of Liverpool appears as 'Liuerpul' in a grant to Henry Fitzwarine of Lancaster by John, Count of Mortmain, (later King John), in 1190-94. This was confirmation of possession of the lands in South Lancashire originally granted to Warine's father by Henry II. A few years later, John, now King of England, was eager to mount a conquest of the Welsh and Irish and needed a new naval base as an alternative to Chester, which was at that time was under the control of the powerful Earl of Chester. He was advised that the most suitable site in the area was that of the small sheltered creek of 'Liuerpul'. Consequently, lands were exchanged with Warine and on 23

August 1207, Liuerpul came into direct ownership of the Crown.

John wasted little time, as five days later he issued a Letters Patent (a grant of a holding, or privilege). By this action Liverpool became a royal borough, with John promising to the burgesses *'all the liberties and free customs which any free borough on the sea has within our land'*. The document was actually rather vague, as it mentioned no specific rights, but it did include exemption from taxes levied in the markets and fairs, and freedom from forced service on their superior lord's land. To become a freeman of the borough was an attractive proposition for those tied to a feudal lord, and there was probably no shortage of applicants. The 'burgage' comprised sufficient land to build a house facing the street, and enough for a garden plot behind, plus an allocation of strips in the common fields and common rights. For this they would be required to pay an annual rent of one shilling and appear regularly at the local court. Further rights, concessions and restrictions were added through the passage of time. [The original King John's Letters Patent of 1207 still exists in Liverpool Record Office]

A significant change came in 1229, when Henry III granted a charter stating that Liverpool should be a free borough for ever. More specific about rights that than the charter of 1207, independent jurisdiction was given to the borough court, burgesses were exempted from attendance at the shire and hundred courts, and possibly most important of all, the burgesses gained the right to operate merchant guilds. This, the burgesses hoped, would permit and encourage growth on a grander scale.

John's original charter though had given the impetus for the minor fishing hamlet to develop into a town. Precise planning laid down a grid plan of streets laid out around an 'H' shape. The seven original streets have actually survived, although much altered in width: Dale Street, Chapel Street, Juggler Street, Castle Street, More (now Tithebarn) Street, Mill/Whiteacre (now Old Hall)

Street, Bank (now Water) Street. Most of the notable buildings in the small town had been erected within a century or so of the 1207 charter. The Chapel of St Mary del Key was constructed in the early 13th century, (although Liverpool was still not a parish in its own right, remaining part of the parish of Walton-on-the-Hill until 1699); Moore Hall was built in the 13th century; the Chapel of St Nicholas in 1355; and the Tower of Liverpool during the late 14th century. A granary owned by The Prior of Birkenhead existed in the Chapel street area and the Liverpool Townfield was also laid out during the 13th century. (The Townfield was the agricultural lands shared between the burgesses).

One of the earliest buildings in the new town was the castle. The date of commencement has long been a matter of contention, since very little documentary evidence exists. The issue is further compounded by the fact that it is rarely clear in these early records as to which castle reference is being made, whether Liverpool or West Derby. It is possible, and most likely, that it was part of John's original plan for the town, and was completed some years after his death, probably in the 1230s. This is reasonable, given that a castle was a usual feature of the majority of similarly planned medieval towns.

However, documents do exist which record that William de Ferrers, who succeeded to the Lancashire estates of his brother-in-law, Randle, Earl of Chester, acquired the castle of West Derby (no mention of Liverpool) in 1232 - but by William's death in 1247 his son inherited both the castles of West Derby and Liverpool. Of course, the obvious deduction here is that Liverpool Castle was built in the intervening years, sometime between 1232 and 1247. It is not quite this cut and dried. The 'spanner in the works' is a document of 1235 which states;

> 'William, Earl of Ferrers has letters directed to his knights and free men, requesting them to make him an aid for the strengthening of his castle of Leverepul'

This was not to construct a castle but to strengthen. The crux of the problem is in the interpretation of 'strengthen'. If it does actually refer to the construction, these dates are fine. It has also been suggested that it may have been built in an earlier period prior to John's reign, leading to the need for strengthening in 1235 after many years of wear and tear, but this is unlikely as there seems to be no reason to construct a castle in such a minor backwater as Liverpool prior to the charter of 1207, when, until then, West Derby was in the ascendancy.

There has been mention of the possibility of inadequate design. Could the castle defences have been felt to be to insufficient *during* its construction, say between 1232 and 1235, leading to a directive to improve the design as the work progressed? In a charter of William Earl of Ferrers of 1237, the witnesses named on the bottom of the document - William de Wayle - is recorded as castlellanus ('of the fortress') in Liverpool. This would suggest that the castle was completed by that year.

There is inadequate evidence to make a case for the construction of the castle during John's reign. But with regard to documents of his son's reign, the Great Pipe Roll of 1226 records rents of £9 received in that year by William, Earl of Ferrers in respect of assizes in Liverpool, in contrast with £8. 7s received a century later in 1325. Rob Philpott, (former Field Archaeologist for National Museums on Merseyside) believes that the discrepancy may have been due to the destruction of several burgages to make way for the construction of the castle. The same document records the farm rent of a burgage *at the castle gate* of 4s.

To summarise, John probably had plans for a castle but did not live to see construction begin. Efforts were made sometime after 1226 to clear an adequate site, although work is unlikely to have commenced until Henry off-loaded his Crown lands in Liverpool in 1229. (Randle Earl of Chester held them until his death in

1232). When in the hands of William, Earl of Ferrers in 1232, work was begun but it was decided there were shortcomings in the defensive structure and he was directed in 1235 to strengthen it, with the total work being completed by 1237.

The castle was usually the focus of attack whenever violence was visited upon the town, and in 1315 it experienced the first siege in its history when a rising broke out, known as the Banastre Revolt. Led by Adam Banastre assisted by Henry Lea, William Lea and William Bradshaw, their intention was to take control of the county of Lancashire from the powerful Holland family. This was essentially a feud between the families, but soon developed into a frightening local civil war, with many of the local population being drawn into the conflict. In Liverpool, it cumulated in the castle siege, which saw Banastre fail in his attempt and being driven back, until he retreated to capture the relatively defenceless and now ruined motte and bailey at West Derby. The transfer of power from West Derby to Liverpool had long since been completed, and although there had been 'considerable additions and repairs in 1201' to the motte and bailey, plus a sizeable garrison of '140 foot-soldiers and ten knights and crossbowmen' stationed there in 1213, by 1298 it was described as *the old castle* and as the *site of a ruined castle in West Derby* in 1326. Banastre's personal crusade had petered out.

[Regarding its later history, part of the West Derby site was still being recorded in local tax returns in the late 16th century, and the castle ruins were shown as a mound marked *Castle Hill* on Yates and Perry's map of 1786, but by 1817 it had been levelled. The site continued to be shown on maps down to the 20th century, but was destroyed in the late 1980s to make way for a modern housing estate].

Mentions of Liverpool Castle in documents are sparse. Between 1315 and 1323 the Borough was under the direct control of the crown, and £1,323 was spent repairing the damage to the roof of the Great Hall in preparation of the visit of Edward II, who stayed at the castle in 1323. Damage, no doubt, sustained during the Banastre siege. An inventory of 1323 listed the contents of the castle, which included 186 pallet beds, 107 spears, 39 lances, 15 great catapults for hurling stones and several other defence engines. There was a vat for brewing, two tables, one large and two small brass pots, and one ewer with a basin for washing. The most detailed medieval account was made in 1347, which described the castle as having 'four towers, a hall, chamber, chapel, brewhouse and bakehouse, with a well therein, a certain orchard and a dovecot'. It was surrounded by a fosse, or a dry moat, cut from solid sandstone.

The main fabric of the castle consisted of a great gatehouse surmounted by two small towers, which stood at the north-eastern corner and looked down Castle Street, with three circular towers at each of the other corners linked by a curtain wall. One of the towers, probably at the south-east corner, was built later than the rest of castle in 1442. The south-western tower operated as the keep of the fortress, and a wall running from north to south divided the courtyard. In the north-west angle, there was a postern gate which led to an underground passage from the moat to the edge of the river, which at that time lapped up to the bottom of the slope of the street now known as James Street. This still lies below street level.

In 1446, the castle came under the control of the powerful Molyneux family, when Sir Richard Molyneux and his son Richard were appointed to office of Constable of the Castle. From this time onward, their successors claimed hereditary office, lasting for over two centuries. Their land ownership was extensive and they also held stewardship of West Derbyshire and Salfordshire, mastership of the Forest of Simmonswood, together with the parks of Croxteth and Toxteth.

PLATE II.

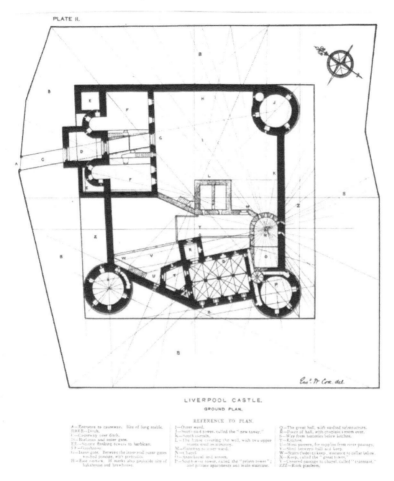

LIVERPOOL CASTLE.

GROUND PLAN.

REFERENCE TO PLAN.

A—Entrance to causeway. Site of long stable.
BBBB—Ditch.
C—Causeway over ditch.
D—Barbican and outer gate.
EE—Square flanking towers to barbican.
FF—Guardhouse.
G—Inner gate. Between the inner and outer gates a walled passage, with portcullis.
H—East curtain. H marks also probable site of bakehouse and brewhouse.

I—Outer ward.
J—South-east tower, called the "new tower."
k—South curtain.
L—The house covering the well, with two upper rooms used as armoury.
M—Gateway to inner ward.
N—Chapel.
N—Abbot level and screen.
P—South-west tower, called the "prison tower"; and private apartments and main staircase.

Q—The great hall, with vaulted substructure.
R—Tower of hall, with spacious a room over.
S—Key from butteries below kitchen.
T—Kitchen.
U—Stone pantries, for supplies from river passage.
V—Step between hall and keep.
W—Stairs (tower) to keep, entrance to cellar below.
X—Keep, called the "great tower."
Y—Covered passage to chapel, called "transmutt."
ZZZ—Rock platform.

In the early 1890s, local historian Edward W. Cox made a study to try to piece together how the grand plan of the castle may have looked. His work was published in the Transactions of the Historic Society of Lancashire and Cheshire, volume 42 (1892), entitled 'An Attempt to Recover the Plans of the Castle of Liverpool from Authentic records; Considered in Connection with Medieval Principles of Defence and Construction'.

Yet, the town had witnessed little growth from the time of the borough foundation down to the mid-seventeenth century. Liverpool, as in common with the surrounding townships, was mainly dependant on agriculture, though there was always fishing and some maritime trade. The same seven streets continued to appear in the taxation lists, and even as late as 1660 there were only around 190 houses covering these main routes. Throughout much of the fifteenth and sixteenth centuries, Liverpool was in a state of economic hardship, even decay. The population was ravaged by disease in the 1540s and 50s and a storm did serious damage to the haven in 1561.

Only two years earlier the Castle was recorded as being in a poor state and a survey of 2 October 1559 declared that it was *in utter ruin and decay* and there having been no lead on any of the buildings within living memory;

'First the said castell is scituate [situated] upon a rokk of stone and joyneth harde to the towne of Litherpole, being a port towne, in so much that the castell yate [gate] is full into the face of our street of the said towne. And also the said castell is scytuate near upon the heaven ther, in which haven, by reporte of honeste marchauntes of the said towne, ther may lye at harbour three hundred sayle of shipps. The said castell is but a smale thinge, beinge in manner square, and the longeste waye within the same by estimacione not 1x [60] yards, having three rounde towres of stone scytuate at thre severall corners thereof. And the gatehowse, beyinge mayde tower fasshyone sware [square], serveth for the forth corner. All which said towers, with the gatehowse, ar in utter rwyne [ruin] and decay, so that there remayneth neither tymbre or lead, other then [than] such as hereafter is expressed, for that ther was no lead at any tyme in the remembeaunce of man remayninge upon any buyldyhge within the said castell'.

Yet despite the dilapidated condition, the commissioners felt it was not beyond hope. Furthermore, they also suggested that the great south west tower, if it had its slate roof repaired, could be used for the keeping of the Queen's local record office, and for the storage of the court rolls. The curtain wall and the masonry of the towers seem to have been fairly sound, only needing protection from the weather, while the commissioners strongly advised spending at least £100 on a substantial repair, *'otherwaies it were a grate defacement unto the said towne of Litherpole.'*

'Also ther is one tower of the three rounde towers which is the greatest of them all, which towre hath hadd a rooffe of tymbre and coverede with slate, as it appereth, now utterlie decayede. And within the said towre ther is too [two] flowres [floors] of tymbre much in decaye, for that the rayne doth contynuallie fall upon the said flowres to the great consummacion [consumption] and waste of them, which is a great pytie. Nevertheless, if the said rouffe of the towre were newe made agayne, and well coverede with slate, and some lead to make the gutters, the said towre would be made for to contynewe a long tyme, wherein the Quenes Majesties courtes for Her Graces Wappentaecke of West Derbyshire, beinge a very greate soken, may be for tyme to tyme therin kept; and also a convevent place may also be made for the salfe [safe] custodie of the Quenes Majesties courte rollees [court rolls] touching the said Wappentack, with others, beinge great in numbre'

It might have been no use defending the river from invasion, but it could still play a role as a safe haven for those seeking refuge.

'Furthermore, the said castell is of little effecte for the defence of the haven, for that the entre [entry] into the said havyn is so daungerous that ther is no navye that will gyve the attempte to entre therin endomage [and damage] the countrie theraboute, in asmuch as yf they shuld comme in, they cannot quyetlie get owt agyne, for that both Worrall [Wirral], Lancashyre, and also Walles [Wales], do back and also adjoyne unto both sides of-- the said havyne, by reason whereof hit is thought in the countrie ther the said haven is sure [secure] inough for any invasione therin to be made by the adverserie. Otherwyse if need shuld so require that the inhabitauntes of the countrie thereaboute shulde for salfgarde of themselves be enforcede to secke [seek] succour at the said castell, it would for a tyme preserve them until such tyme as they may be rescwede by the inhabitauntes of the hole countrie theraboute, which is very populus'.

But little help was forthcoming, and local M.P., Rauff Sekerston, petitioned Elizabeth I in 1571 from the *'decayed town of Liverpoole'*, stating,

'Liverpole is your owne towne. Your majestie hath a castell and two chauntries... the fee fermes of the towne, the ferrie boot, twoe wyndmylnes, the custome of the duchie, the new custome off tonnage and pondage which was never paid in Liverpole before your tyme, you have a gud haven, and all the hole towne and the comoditie thereoff is your majesties. For your own sake suffre us not utterlie to be caste awaye in your graces tyme but relief us like a mother'

- Liverpool Town Books, vol.1 fol.157r. Liverpool Record Office.

This too fell on deaf ears, yet towards the end of the century, she did grant letters of marque and privateering statutes to Liverpool sailors which despite being licenced piracy, brought a great improvement to the local economy.

But it was the conflict between King and Parliament in the following century that would see the castle play its most prominent role, and would also see the second siege in its long history. The town was divided from the outset – most of the burgesses were Puritan Parliamentarians, while the powerful landed families of Molyneux, Stanley and Norris, were firmly in the Royalist camp. The latter controlled the town for the King, the Mayor being a Royalist, and Colonel Edward Norris of Speke Hall governor of the castle, plus Lord Derby of the Stanley family controlled South West Lancashire.

It was soon realised by both sides that Liverpool and its castle were integral to the war effort in maintaining an essential supply route from North Wales and Ireland – that is, for whoever had control of the port. By early 1643, Parliament were gaining the upper hand, and April saw the first local hostilities when Colonel Assheton attacked the Royalist held castle in pursuit of Colonel Tyldesley, who had arrived with his troops to garrison the town. The town was routed by the Parliamentary forces, and after two days of fighting throughout the town streets, thirty lay dead with 300 Royalists taken prisoner.

There followed a frenetic period of activity where temporary ditched earth defences were constructed encircling the town, with cannons positioned throughout the length of the makeshift garrison. The castle, town hall and the pool all lay within its protection. It wasn't enough to prevent a reversal however, when in May the following year the Royalist forces under Prince Rupert, were poised for revenge from their vantage point on Beacon Hill in Everton, above the town. Despite stubborn resistance, they took both the castle and the town. In the early hours of 13 June 1644, Rupert's troops forced an entry to the north, around present-day Old Hall Street. Meanwhile, the Parliamentarian troops, now under the command of Colonel John Moore, had given up the cause, and had quietly embarked upon their vessels and left Liverpool via the Pool, without telling the burgesses and people, leaving the town completely defenceless. Despite Moore's treachery, the citizens continued to fight through the night without support, and put up fierce resistance, forcing the Royalists to take Liverpool street by street. But as daylight came, bodies lay everywhere, after the most terrifying night Liverpool had yet seen. Rupert's men had stormed in, and, showing little mercy, massacred around 400 of the townsfolk, many of whom were unarmed. Eventually, the town's population surrendered at the High Cross, today the site of the Town Hall. Survivors were imprisoned in the Tower at the bottom of Water Street, and when this was full, prisoners were kept in St Nicholas' Church. Meanwhile, Rupert's troops were allowed to ransack the town.

Determined to hold on to Liverpool, Rupert engaged Bernard de Gomme, military engineer to King Charles I, to draw up plans to fortify the castle and create impregnable defences around the town. Such plans, however, were shelved when Rupert and his forces headed to battle at Marston Moor in July. It was a turning point. The Royalists were defeated and Parliament again took the upper hand in Lancashire. Surrounding the town under the command of Sir John Meldrum, Parliament dug in for little more than three months before castle force mutinied and the rest of the garrison surrendered without a fight. By early November, Liverpool was again in Parliament's hands, and would remain so for the remainder of the war.

Liverpool Castle c.1680
A close up of the castle extracted from the Peter's Painting. This is the only known contemporary view, although some of the castle structure would have been demolished shortly before this was painted

Liverpool c.1680

Known as the Peter's Painting, this is the earliest known view of Liverpool, possibly by an unknown Dutch artist, late seventeenth century. This painting inspired many prints, drawings and watercolours over the next two centuries

Liverpool c.1682

Known as the Peter's Panel Painting, this is thought to be a later copy of the Peter's Painting, possibly mid eighteenth century or even later. There is clearly a discrepancy regarding the depiction of the castle, probable long gone when this was painted

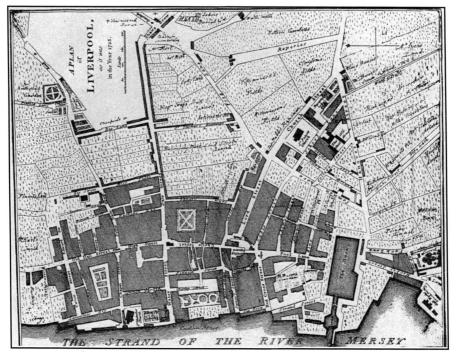

A Plan of Liverpool as it was in 1725

By this date, pool has now been filled in and the Old Dock constructed in its place. In the centre, the castle has been swept away and Derby Square and Preesons Row laid out in a circular fashion, with the tidal river still lapping up to the Strand

Liverpool was the sole port on the west coast which had remained loyal to the Parliament cause, and the victorious Protectorate were consequently well disposed to aid the town in its post war rebuilding programme. The required five hundred tons of timber were granted, giving orders that the wood would come from the local estates of the defeated aristocracy and landed gentry. In addition, Lord Molyneux's rights over the town were transferred to the Common Council, a move which effectively removed the last vestiges of feudalism from the town, at least until the time of the Restoration in 1660. Meanwhile, the town remained under military occupation for the same duration, an expensive necessity paid for by local taxes, which also saw the removal of the civil war defences, as life began to return to normal. A further order was given to remove the castle in 1659, still felt to be a reminder of Royalist domination over the town, but only the gatehouse and part of the walls were destroyed.

Forty years later, this dilapidated stronghold was still the focus for political dominance in 1689, when local protestants in support of William of Orange took up occupation, but this soon ended following the conclusion of the Glorious Revolution. But by the end of the seventeenth century the castle had become an eyesore and was clearly a thorn in the side of the Corporation. Through most of its existence it was under the control of the Crown and was always outside of the jurisdiction and liberties of the town. Consequently, its occupants were never subjected to local laws and customs, nor to the control of the town authorities. The hereditary Constableship of the Castle, awarded to the Molyneux family in 1446, had been lost to them in 1672 and once the last Constable had died in 1701 (the Earl of Macclesfield), the Corporation felt the opportunity was ripe to be rid of it for good.

Since the Civil War, the port and town had begun to expand with an impetus not witnessed for centuries. A key development came in 1647 when Liverpool was made a free and independent port, no longer subject to the Port of Chester. Rapid expansion was encouraged and in the 1660s and 1670s the principal landowners laid out several new streets, including Lord Street, Moor Street, Fenwick Street, Red Cross Street and St James's Street. The town's growing status was reflected in many of the new buildings constructed during the period, such as the Town Hall (1673-4) Bluecoat School (1721), the Custom House (1721) and St Peter's (1704). Such growth was matched by the sweeping away of many of the buildings which had served the town since the medieval period, notably the old Tithebarn, the Crosse Hall, and the Townsend Mill, although the ancient chapel of St Mary del Quay lasted until 1814 while the Tower of Liverpool was demolished four years later.

The old Pool, which had acted as a magnet to King John's advisors, the early settlers, and generations of merchants and seafarers (not forgetting a mythical bird), was now being reclaimed by the end of the seventeenth century, although not totally, as it would provide the site for the towns' first wet dock designed by Thomas Steers which opened in 1715. The Pool, now known as the 'Common Sewer', had become an eyesore, it was in need of dredging to make it fully navigable, and was probably empty at low water. A programme of draining and dumping of earth and rubbish was mounted to create valuable building land on the site.

The opportunity to develop the area had been assisted in 1671, when the Corporation secured rights to the foreshore of the Pool and other privileges from the lord of the Borough, Lord Molyneux. In return, he was granted freedom to build a bridge across the Pool from Liverpool Heath to his new street in Castle Hey ('Lord' Street).

In such a drive for mercantile modernisation, the castle was doomed. Soon after the death of the Constable in November 1701, the Corporation petitioned Queen Anne for the lease, with a request to use the site for a church (originally, when Liverpool broke away from Walton Parish in 1699, the site was intended to be used for the Parish Church. Matters clearly couldn't wait and St Peters was erected in Church Street in 1704). In a final appeal they described the castle as an eyesore, 'Which is long since demolished and only one ruinous tower remains standing'.

But as a last throw of the dice, Lord Molyneux, still claiming hereditary right which he had lost in 1672, contested the application, and under his influence a number of squatters, traders and vagrants occupied the castle refusing to move. Eventually, the

Mayor and his bailiffs succeeded in forcibly evicting them, but the matter dragged on in the courts. By 1715, the case had been settled in favour of the town, and three years later the Corporation secured the deed for the site. Meanwhile, from 1715 to 1720 a crescent of new housing was constructed on the west side of Derby Square facing the castle, in preparation for the complete modernisation of the site. Work began to level the area, and the last vestiges of the Castle had disappeared by 1726 when it was ordered that the old castle wall at the top of Lord Street be immediately pulled down and the ground cleared for contractors to build.

The new church of St George, designed by Thomas Steers, engineer of the first enclosed wet dock in the world just yards below the site in the Old Pool, was constructed on the castle plateau and consecrated in 1734. Originally, it had an elegant terrace, supported by rustic arches, on one side under which were occupied the Red Cross market, while at one end of the terrace was the office of the clerk of the market, and at the other that of the night watch. Below ground there was a vault for interments. But within twenty-five years however, the spire developed major structural problems, and a pronounced lean could clearly be seen. Frequent repairs took place and by 1789 a survey revealed it was 3'2" out of perpendicular, although seven architects reported no danger! Yet, in 1809 a rent appeared between the tower and body of the church. The Mayor had the spire examined by two London architects and Corporation surveyor, who all agreed it was beyond repair, and it was demolished shortly afterwards. In 1819, a new foundation stone for the tower was laid, but as work progressed, further defects in the church structure were discovered, and it proved necessary to rebuild the whole church.

Old St George church
*The original church of St George - begun in 1726 and
completed in 1734 to the design of Thomas Steers*

The second St George's was designed by John Foster jnr. who also designed St George's Crescent, erected around the perimeter of Derby Square four years later (demolished 1941). The entire church was rebuilt piecemeal between 1819 and 1825 after structural problems had become apparent, and a new spire, reduced in height, was finally added in 1833.

The church was both owned and maintained by the City Council, and it was the place of worship for the mayor, the council and the judiciary. In 1863, the council elected a Jewish mayor, Mr. Charles Mozley, following which the incumbent of St George's preached a sermon denouncing the choice. From that time the Corporation ceased to attend St George's. Loss of status, coupled with local residents gradually migrating away from the centre of town, resulted in dwindling congregations. As a consequence, the church closed in 1897 and was demolished two years later. Following the death of Queen Victoria in 1901, the former castle site was chosen for the new memorial, and the Victoria Monument, which still stands today, was erected in 1902.

Two archaeological excavations of the site took place in the 20th century. The first, by F. Charles Larkin in 1927, was of the castle moat site, prior to the construction of underground public conveniences in front of the Monument. This work enabled the course of the west moat to be determined more accurately. The north moat was found during the building excavations immediately preceding the construction of the Midland Bank on the corner of Castle Street in 1928. Some twenty feet from the south west corner of the bank, the subterranean tunnel running in a southerly direction below James Street was re-discovered, having been uncovered by Borough Engineer James Newlands' men in the 1860s when digging a drain for the basements of buildings on the corner of Castle Street and James Street. Archaeologists believed that it connected the moat or ditch with the old tower or some defences on the shore. A sewer has now been constructed along the tunnel. The second dig took place in 1976 led by Peter Davey, in anticipation of the construction of the Crown Courts in the late seventies. A ditch was uncovered which is likely to have formed part of the Civil War defences.

In 1941 the site experienced warfare to an extent never witnessed, nor imagined in the days of the Castle, when almost the entire area was decimated by blanket bombing during the Blitz. From that time to the present, the site has been completely redeveloped and has changed so much that it is difficult to picture the feudal structure that once dominated the borough and the pool below for almost five hundred years.

The Queen Victoria Memorial on the former castle site

Further Reading

Most general works on the history of Liverpool refer to the Castle, below is a list of the most useful specific studies.

Hand, C.R. *Liverpool Castle and its Builders* (1909)

Hand, C.R. *Notes respecting the Annals of Liverpool Castle* (1910)

Touzeau, J. 'The Castle of Liverpool' *in The Rise and Progress of Liverpool;* Vol. 1 (1910) p349-358

Larkin, F. C. 'Excavations on the Site of Liverpool Castle, 1927' *Transactions of the Historic Society of Lancashire and Cheshire;* Vol. 79, p175-197

Cox, E. W. 'An Attempt to Recover the Plans of the Castle of Liverpool from Authentic records; Considered in Connection with Medieval Principles of Defence and Construction', *T.H.S.L.C;* Vol. 42 (1892) p195-254

Davey, P. 'South Castle Street 1976: Interim Report' *Journal of the Merseyside Archaeological Society;* Vol. 1 (1977) p13-15

Davey, P.J. & McNeil, R. 'Excavations in South Castle Street, Liverpool 1976 and 1977' in *J.M.A.S;* Vol. 4 for 1980-81 (1985)

Belcham, J. ed., *Liverpool 800: Introduction* p9-57 – general overview, p59-60 – West Derby, p59-72 – 'Small Beginnings'

Guy, Neil, 'Liverpool Castle' *Castle Studies Group Bulletin;* Vol. 18 p188-201 (2005)

Edward Rushton (1756-1814)

2

Edward Rushton

The Life and Times of an 18th Century Radical and Poet

Edward Rushton, poet, anti-slavery campaigner and co-founder of the first School for the Blind in the country, was born in John Street, Liverpool on the 13th November 1756, the son of Thomas Rushton a Liverpool victualler. As a teenager, while away at sea, he lost his sight after contracting a disease and later showed strong character, pursuing radical causes, often in the face of local adversity. At six he began his education at Liverpool Free School and by the age of eleven he was apprenticed to Messrs. Watt and Gregson, a Liverpool shipping company with West Indian interests. His experience at sea was full of incidents which must have had considerable effect on his character. At the age of sixteen he showed great courage while still an apprentice, when he took the helm of the ship in bad weather which the captain and crew were about to abandon. He guided the vessel back into the safety of the port of Liverpool, saving the lives of all on board. This act of bravery was endorsed on his indenture of apprenticeship, and he was promoted to second mate. As an adult, among his intimate friends were many of the respected thinkers of local Liverpool societies and clubs, such as William Roscoe. He also became a poet and his subjects were frequently the controversial issues of his day.

By the end of the eighteenth century, his home town of Liverpool had become the nation's second port after London. Built largely on the profits of the slave-trade, the rate of expansion had been remarkable. The new age of the port had begun with the completion of the first wet dock in the modern world in 1715. The building of more docks soon followed, and in the town, fine houses stood in both Duke Street and Hanover Street, while Mount Pleasant was lined with impressive terraces with large gardens. To the north, the urban sprawl had extended as far as the new Leeds and Liverpool Canal basin, with a much larger mass of labourer's housing in the south. However, overcrowding was already becoming a problem. The 1700 population of 5,000 had increased to 25,000 by 1760. Shipbuilding yards lined the north and south shore, rope yards were numerous, as too were windmills. The increase in population grew in tandem with the expansion in world wide trade; in 1700 there were around 70 port owned vessels employing about 800 seamen, but by 1751 these figures had increased to 220 vessels and 3,319 seamen. The port was also benefiting from the silting of the River Dee and the consequent decline of Chester; the bulk of the Irish trade now moved through Liverpool docks, and Scotland and Wales were also commercially dependant on Liverpool, now cemented as Britain's central port.

It was trade with the Americas and the West Indies which had become the most profitable, supplying the main staples of sugar, tobacco and cotton. At the beginning of the eighteenth century, Bristol had the greatest share of this traffic, but by the mid century Liverpool was well to the fore, bringing in an annual profit of around £250,000. Growing industrialization in the cotton towns of Lancashire and West Yorkshire increased their role as an integral link in the triangular trade, placing unceasing demands on Liverpool merchants and vessels more than any other for more supplies.

It was on a Liverpool merchant slave ship to Guinea in 1773 that Edward Rushton almost lost his life. During the passage, he formed a friendship with a young Negro boy by the name of Quamina, to whom he gave a few reading lessons. Shortly afterwards, while both were part of the crew of a small boat despatched to the shore, the vessel capsized. Rushton swam towards a small water cask where Quamina was already safely holding on. Quamina, seeing that his friend was too exhausted to reach him, bravely jeopardized his own safety, and pushed the cask towards Rushton, saving his life. Quamina was never seen again. Later that same year, while working as Second Mate on a slaver bound for Dominica, Rushton became so sickened with the brutality meted out to the slaves by the captain, that he remonstrated with him so forcefully that he was charged with mutiny and threatened with the irons. Almost all of the slaves had fallen victim to contagious ophthalmia, which in the appalling conditions below, had spread like wildfire. Only Rushton took pity on them, and he tried to bring what relief he could. His actions resulted in his own personal tragedy, as he too caught the disease. His left eye was completely destroyed and the right so badly damaged that he became blind. Given the horrendous conditions on slave ships, such a disease was not uncommon. Indeed, the great abolitionist, Thomas Clarkson, in his book 'The Cries of Africa', tells a story of a French slaver on which thirty-nine Africans became infected and lost their sight. Being of no commercial value they were contemptuously tossed overboard.

When Rushton arrived home, his father took him to several of the leading medical men of the day, even the King's oculist, all to no avail. To compound his plight, after his father remarried, the relationship between son and step-mother was never a good one, and inevitably he was turned out of the family home. He was fortunate to be taken in by an aunt, and Rushton was to stay there for seven years. Nevertheless, his father still cared for him, and supported him with an allowance of four shillings a week. Keen to keep up with the news and politics of the day, he paid a young boy threepence a week to read to him.

Rushton was becoming increasingly interested in politics and philosophy. The last quarter of the eighteenth century was the height of the Enlightenment, which drew its strength and development from a cumulation of interlinking factors a such as growth in human knowledge, civilisation and rationality; man's increasing control over nature; the progress of trade, production and wealth. The leading exponents were the progressive classes - the mercantile circles, financiers, manufacturers, entrepreneurs and the educated middle class. In England, numerous provincial societies were formed, from which advances came in scientific, industrial and political arenas. The Lunar Society in Birmingham for example, included Josiah Wedgewood the potter, James Watt, inventor of the modern steam engine, and biologist Erasmus Darwin (grandfather of Charles).

To many, Enlightenment was a revolutionary ideology, and although until the 1780s much of it was still moderate, this was now the time of political and social upheaval. America had gained independence in 1776, the elites in Paris were overthrown in 1789, while in England unrest increased among the rural poor and those in the squalor of the industrial towns. Public opinion regarding the slave-trade was also beginning to change in England around this time, especially after the abolition movement had been established in London. Naturally, there was little turn around in Liverpool where the movement was received with much hostility. The Corporation even went to the trouble of paying a Jesuit, Reverend Raymond Harris, £100 for his pamphlet which confirmed the scriptural approval of the slave-trade, of which he assured readers of 'its conformity with the principles of natural and revealed religion delineated in the sacred writings of the Word of God'. His work did not go unanswered in Liverpool, as a direct attack came from the Reverend Henry Dannett, minister of St

Johns, (the church site was immediately to the rear of St George's Hall) who published a brave, yet scathing reply in 1788 entitled *'A Particular Examination of Mr. Harris's Scriptural Researches on the Licitness of the Slave-trade'*. (Not only did he attack Harris, but those involved in the trade, some of whom attended his church).

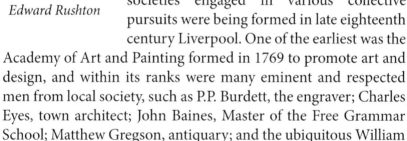

Although there were only two Liverpool members of the London based abolition movement, William Rathbone and Doctor Jonathan Binns, there were other sympathisers living in the town now recognised as the centre of the trade, who did not wish to openly declare their beliefs for fear of reprisals. Most of these men were already friends and associates, and had come together in the various societies formed in the previous two decades. In common with other towns, societies engaged in various collective pursuits were being formed in late eighteenth century Liverpool. One of the earliest was the Academy of Art and Painting formed in 1769 to promote art and design, and within its ranks were many eminent and respected men from local society, such as P.P. Burdett, the engraver; Charles Eyes, town architect; John Baines, Master of the Free Grammar School; Matthew Gregson, antiquary; and the ubiquitous William Roscoe.

Edward Rushton

But other societies that followed, were often more concerned with politics. The Conversation Club, formed as early as 1768, met at George's Coffee House, and debated such radical topics as voting by secret ballot. However, it was the French Revolution and the subsequent suppressive policy of Pitt's Government that was to arouse the most widespread debating in Liverpool. Societies were formed with both conservative and radical foundations. In support of the government, for example, were the Association for King and Constitution, which met at The Buck and Vine in Hackins Hey, and the Friends to the King and Constitution, which met at The Eagle and Child in Redcross Street.

Far more formidable was the fellowship formed by Dr James Currie and William Roscoe in 1795; the Debating Society, which met weekly in the Long Room, Marble Street, attracted large audiences, but soon fell foul of the oppressive Seditious Meetings Act of December 1795 and was forced to dissolve shortly afterwards.

Other societies were formed with philosophical and literary interests to the fore, often a front for more radical leanings. One such society, which name has now been lost, had a small membership of around a dozen individuals which met weekly in a local hostelry. Rushton was among its members.

It was from this small intellectual gathering that in 1790 the idea for a much-needed institution was born. Rushton described later how the idea originated;

> 'Early in the year 1790, I regularly attended an association consisting of ten or a dozen individuals who assembled weekly for the purpose of weekly discussion; and one evening, the conversation having turned on the recently established Marine Society, it was observed by a member of that body, Captain W. Ward, that the committee for the management of the Marine Fund had declined the acceptance of small donations. It immediately occurred to me that if an institution could be formed, in Liverpool, for the relief of its numerous and indigent blind, the small donations thus declined by the Marine Committee might be brought to flow in a channel, not less benevolent, and prove of essential service in the establishment of a fund for the benefit of that unfortunate description of the community'.

Rushton swiftly produced two letters on the loss of sight. The first of these bemoaned the plight of the blind person and the second, according to Rushton, 'contained an outline of an institution, by which it was hoped that the pecuniary distress, and consequently the gloom of the sightless, might in some degree, be alleviated'. Rushton planned that,

> '...an association should be formed consisting entirely of blind persons; that the names of females as well as males, should be registered and that each individual should contribute a small matter weekly, or monthly, with which, and the benefactions of the humane, such a fund might speedily be established, as would afford to each a weekly allowance in cases of sickness, superannuation etc.'

Encouraged by the backing of the Society, Rushton began to circulate his letters and gradually gained support from wealthy and influential locals who would be able to bring his plan to fruition. He was aided in his efforts by an acquaintance, a blind musician by the name of John Christie of 46 Church Street. Their friendship had been formed some years earlier in what Rushton termed *a fellowship in misfortune* (with respect to their sightless plight). Rushton was boosted by his friend's reaction, who joined him in his cause and suggested the idea of,

> '...having a place appropriated to the use of the blind, wherein, by gratuitous musical instruction, they might soon be enabled to provide for themselves, which, to a well-disposed mind, must ever prove a source of the highest satisfaction.'

In September 1790, both men were invited to dine with the Reverend Henry Dannett of St John's. Dannett was an influential figure, St John's was attended by many wealthy merchants, men of the medical profession and other influential figures. Dannett had also invited a such a diverse group to join them. Also present were local philanthropists Richard Carson and William Roscoe; the Reverend John Smyth, incumbent of St Anne's; and their friend Robert Lowe. Two other men were also invited; the well known local surgeon Edward Alanson, who was indisposed, and a Mr Sutton, who, not having made Mr Dannett's acquaintance, thought it to be a mistake and did not attend, but like Alanson would become part of the founding party. Immediately after dinner, Mr Dannett commenced business by reading Rushton's two letters, and then those of Christie. By the end of the evening, there was full agreement to make plans for the establishment of an institution to care for the indigent blind.

Further meetings took place and a list of regulations was crafted into an official press announcement as 'A *Plan for Affording Relief to the Indigent Blind*' which was inserted in *Williamson's Liverpool Advertiser* on Monday 22 November 1790. It was ambitious from the very beginning. Not only did they intend to teach a member of the blind persons' family to write and read music so as to help in the pupils' studies, but they also hoped to be so successful in their overall achievements as to be a model for other towns to follow suit and care for their blind in a similar manner.

A further article appeared in *Williamson's Advertiser* on 3 January 1791 announcing the intended opening of the School in the second week of January. The notice advised how to subscribe to the charity, what would be taught, and brief answers to the main criticisms already voiced. This was the first institution of its kind in the world to cater for blind persons of almost any age, to educate, and provide some form of training to enable them to support themselves when they left. In less than a year, the ideas of Rushton and Christie had come to fruition, when the School for the Indigent Blind opened on 10 January 1791.

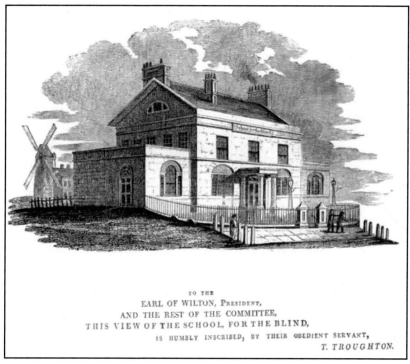

School for the blind
The purpose-built school (designed by John Foster) situated on the site later occupied by the Odeon cinema on the corner of London Road and Pudsey Street

However, the first building to be used by the school was a temporary affair and quite unsuitable. Situated at 6 Commutation Row, opposite the potteries of Shaw's Brow (now William Brown Street), two adjoining terraced houses recently erected, were rented by the charity for the sole use of the school. They were much too small, and by 1800 enough money had been raised through subscription and donations, to erect a purpose-built school (designed by John Foster) nearby on the site later occupied by the Odeon cinema on the corner of London Road and Pudsey Street (the street was named after Pudsey Dawson who was a major benefactor of the school in the early 1800s). The school was now well and truly established and would stay on this site for the next 50 years.

Much of the initial day to day running was carried out by Dannett. There is no surviving evidence of any further assistance from Rushton, although Christie taught music to the pupils for many years. The lack of involvement by Rushton was likely due to practical reasons relating to his own blindness, furthermore, he wasn't a musician. Yet, he may also have fallen out with Dannett, who, from the opening, claimed sole responsibility for the founding of the School. By 1804, his claim had become more public, and had come to Rushton's notice. Clearly furious, he reacted swiftly by drawing up a detailed account of the early stages and developments to 'set the record straight', and a spat began in the local press. Severely critical of Dannett's claims, he rebuked him for trying to rewrite history by erasing the role played by himself and Christie altogether.

Rushton was scathing;

> '...Mr Dannett has also deposed that in originating the Liverpool Institution for the Blind he had no assistance from any being on earth. Now if this statement be not the result of mental imbecility I will venture to say it is one of the most singular and shameless that ever was made... thus in a brief, unvarnished way I have given the origin of the Liverpool Institute for the Blind. If I have stated falsehoods, those falsehoods may readily be refuted by an appeal to living testimony... [Roscoe and Christie, for example, were still alive] ...if I have adhered to the truth, the deposition recently made by the Rev. H. Dannett, whether proceeding from forgetfulness or design, must necessarily be erroneous...'

Shamefully, Dannett even tried to secure the support of the Committee of the School for the Blind to back up his claims regarding the foundation of the School, but to their credit, they were unwilling to become embroiled in what they regarded as a private matter between Rushton and himself. The dispute came to an end in 1804, when Dannett moved to a new appointment in Hopton Wafers in Shropshire.

Nevertheless, it is certain that the founding of the institution cannot be attributed to one man alone. Rushton had the idea for a benevolent fund, which came from his discussions in the philosophical society; Christie, the idea for a kind of institution where the inmates could be taught music, therefore having a chance to make life more tolerable and to be able to support themselves; and Robert Lowe, who spent much time and effort circulating the letters. Roscoe, Smyth, and Carson played their part at the meetings, and Dannett brought together these men who were likely to make a significant contribution, and also put his name to the public announcements to give them credence. Alanson too played a small role in an advisory capacity. In addition, most of the group were known to continue their support during the early years of its establishment, though Rushton appears to be a notable exception - (in his incapacitated state and lack of musical talent this is not surprising). It is unknown if he had any later involvement - his name is not mentioned in any of the School Committee notes or reports. The original founders therefore, are these eight men who all played a significant role in the early pioneering days of the School. Rushton may have had the original idea of wanting to help alleviate the plight of the blind in some way, but Christies' expansion of this plan was closer to the actual manifestation of the Institution.

Before the founding of the Blind School, general attitudes towards human affliction had begun to change in the later eighteenth century and this too owed much to the development in philosophical thought of the Enlightenment and progress in medical science. In Liverpool, institutions began to be founded on private charity, an early example being the Bluecoat School (Grade 1 listed Queen Anne architecture which still stands today in School Lane). Established by Bryan Blundell, it was begun in 1708 and completed ten years later. Blundell had been master and owner of a vessel employed in transporting young paupers to the New World, often with the pretext of seeking a new life, but usually to get them off the streets or out of the workhouse. He was so moved by their condition that he resolved to give up his life at sea and devote his time to the running of a new school. He had not just been affected by the transportation of these street urchins, his vessel had also been involved in the Slave-trade.

**Bust of Edward Rushton
by Liverpool sculptor
John Gibson R.A.**

This rare artwork went missing from the Hardman Street school during military sequestration in WWII

The workhouse infirmary had to cope with the sick and diseased of the labouring poor until the 1740s when the council granted a site for an infirmary. Completed in 1748 through charitable donations, it was an imposing building, with a large courtyard and extensive rear garden on the site now occupied by St George's Hall. Alongside in 1752, was erected the Seamen's Hospital, for seamen and their families. Every mariner of the port had paid a compulsory contribution of 6d a month towards its support. In 1778 a dispensary was established in North John Street which provided medical advice and medicine to the poor, again supported by voluntary subscriptions.

Yet, despite such positive steps in a port increasingly influenced by its diverse cultural influx, by the end of the eighteenth century, it had become a town of much pauperism, appalling housing conditions and frequent violence. Only a small minority of men had benefited from the great wealth of the port, the majority eking out an existence in sordid conditions and miserable degradation. An American loyalist exile, Samuel Curwen, on visiting Liverpool in 1780 wrote that,

> '...the streets were long, narrow, crooked and dirty...We scarcely saw a well dressed person...The whole complexion of the place was nautical and so infinitely below all our expectations that nought but the thoughts of the few hours we had to pass here rendered it tolerable...'

Public houses stood at the end of most street corners in the town, supplied by thirty-seven large local breweries, and cargoes of rum were regularly brought back on the return leg of the triangular trade from the West Indies. The streets were frequently scenes of drunkenness, fighting, riots and press-gangs. Local politics were constantly anarchical and corrupt. The Improvement Act for Liverpool in the late eighteenth century did see spacious transformations to Castle Street, Dale Street and Water Street, but further opportunity to continue such fine moves was wasted. Nevertheless, the period saw increased attempts by enthusiastic, intelligent men to improve the conditions of all members of society. Most of the credit for this can undoubtedly be centred on the radical liberal factions who, with their frequently unpopular politics, tended to be looked upon with scorn and suspicion by fellow citizens. Vigorous advocates of political and social reform, their opposition to the slave-trade, on which the ports' wealth and prosperity was largely based, frequently earned a hostile reception from the mercantile ranks.

Among these reformers were such notable local men as William Rathbone (the fourth, 1758-1809), James Currie (a Scottish doctor, biographer of Burns, author of several political pamphlets and the man largely responsible for the efficient administration of the Poor Law), Doctor Traill (a founder of the Royal Institution), the Reverend William Shepherd (Unitarian minister of Renshaw Street), and a man who is frequently alluded to as being one of Liverpool's greatest citizens, William Roscoe.

Born in 1753, William Roscoe was the son of an innkeeper of Mount Pleasant, and was articled to a Liverpool solicitor in 1769. A man of high intellect and wide reputation, he was nationally famous for his poetry and verses set to music. At the age of only 19, several years before the abolition movement commenced, he dared to publish his views in verse. Later, in 1787, once the movement had been established, he produced a long work entitled 'The Wrongs of Africa', following it up a year later with 'A General View of the African Slave Traffic'. Throughout his life he was to continue this approach and frequently spoke out about the injustices and corruption that he saw around him, especially those in his home town.

Edward Rushton, who had formed a friendship with Roscoe, spent much of his time studying literature, politics and philosophy. He especially loved to read the plays of Shakespeare and found additional inspiration in the prose and achievements of the sightless Milton. The experience of his travels and the injustices he had witnessed, led to the publication of his first poem The Dismembered Empire in 1782, a condemnation of the American War. In 1797, he wrote to former President George Washington questioning his blatant hypocrisy in retaining slaves for his own use, while fighting for liberty and independence. He wrote in similar fashion to the radical Thomas Paine, author of The Rights of Man and Common Sense, questioning the confinement of his libertarian ideals to 'white slaves' only. But both turned a deaf ear and did not reply. His abhorrence of the slave-trade was reflected in *The West Indian Eclogues*, the first of his poems on the subject published in 1787. So well-known had Rushton's reputation and views became, that Thomas Clarkson sought him out while on a visit to Liverpool to credit his contribution to the abolitionist cause.

Around this time, his father established Edward and his sister in a tavern at 19 Crooked Lane, Liverpool. Unsuited to the work, and now with his new wife Isabella, he moved on to become the editor of the *Liverpool Herald*. This was also to be short lived. Concerned with the excessive barbarism of the press-gang he attacked the practice in the pages of the *Herald*. His partner, worried about a local backlash resulting from Rushton's allegations, suggested a retraction, but Rushton resigned rather than compromise. His views on press-gang brutality inspired his poem *Will Clewline* published in 1806.

A short while later, he became a bookseller at 44 Paradise Street, but yet again his outspoken views made him enemies and lost him valued custom. Rushton was a man of principle and no matter how fool hardy this appeared to some in the atmosphere of war with France he made no attempt to moderate his radical thoughts. At length, his business recovered, and he was able to live out his life in relative comfort while raising a family. Edward junior, the eldest of four, was born on 22 September 1795 and became a prominent figure in Liverpool politics. He was called to the Bar on 18 November 1831 and was appointed Stipendiary Magistrate of Liverpool on 17 May 1839. He was an ardent social reformer, advocating Catholic emancipation, prison reform, humane treatment of juvenille offenders, and opposition to capital punishment. He died on 4 April 1851 aged 55 at his home Parkside House in Liverpool and was buried in St James' Cemetery, Liverpool.

Edward Rushton senior partially regained his sight in his right eye in 1807 following an operation by Manchester surgeon Benjamin Gibson, thus enabling him to see again after thirty-three years of blindness, and to see his wife and children for the first time. In the days before anaesthetic he had to endure the surgeon's knife without sedation. The Reverend Thomas Lund, minister of the Chapel of the School for the Blind, later described his courage;

> 'It was characteristic of the man's fortitude that he refused to be bound for the operation, a process deemed to be quite necessary before the use of anaesthetics; and he wrung from the operator expression of amazement at the absolute control he exerted over himself while the most sensitive organ was being attacked'.

Sadly, his wife Isabella died a short time later in 1811 as well as one of his daughters. Three months before his own death Rushton wrote to his friend Samuel Ryley about the loss of a mutual friend.

> 'Why friend Ryley are you so much afraid of dying seeing that it will come when it will come? If there be another world, let us do well here, and we shall do well there; and if there be not another world, there is a vast consolation in acting our part well in this.'

Rushton died on 22nd November 1814 of 'paralysis' and was buried in St James' Churchyard (now St James' Gardens, below the Anglican Cathedral). Although not a great poet or a man of advanced political opinions, he was still a remarkable man for his time and a fighter for the under-dog and for freedom in its many forms. A contemporary called him, *A man of high moral qualities, of great intellectual endowments and of the most inflexible strength of principle*'.

His lasting legacy, The Royal School for the Blind, Liverpool, celebrated its bi-centennial in 1991 with a visit from the Queen, and today still continues to provide outstanding education and residential care for pupils aged from 2-19 years.

Further Reading

Thomas, Mary G., *Edward Rushton* – N.I.B. Biographies No.1 (1949)

Royden, Michael W. *Pioneers and Perseverance – A History of the Royal School for the Blind, Liverpool* (1991)

Royden, Michael,W. Edward Rushton 1756-1814, entry in the revised *Oxford Dictionary of National Biography* (2004)

Rushton Jnr, Edward *'Biographical Sketch of Edward Rushton',* Belfast *Magazine* (Dec 1814)

Lund, T.W.M. *Blindness, or Some Thoughts for Sighted People* (Sermon preached in the Chapel of the Royal School for the Blind Liverpool, Feb 20th 1887) (includes Appendix A – *A Sketch of the Life of Edward Rushton, the Blind Poet* (1887)

Hunter, Bill, *Forgotten Hero - The Life and Times of Edward Rushton* (2002)

Rushton, Edward – published writings 1782-1806 notably:
The Dismembered Empire (1782)
West Indian Eclogues (1787)
Will Clewline (1806)
contained in two collections of verses:
Rushton, E., *Fugitive Pieces in Verse* (1806)
Shepherd, ed. W. *Edward Rushton - Poems and other writings - with a sketch of a life of the Author'* (1824) (a second edition of the 1806 work, plus other writings such as his letter to Washington and an 'Essay on the Causes of the Dissimilarity of Colour in the Human Species')

Doctor William Duncan

3

Dr. W.M. Duncan and Public Health in Liverpool

For the nineteenth century poor, housing conditions in the dockland courts were horrific, and living in the slums meant a constant struggle to survive in overcrowded, damp, poorly ventilated buildings with no private toilet or washing facilities. Sewage ran through the streets and polluted the wells from which people collected their drinking water. Disease was widespread, and epidemics of cholera, typhus, and typhoid decimated the population during the early to mid-nineteenth century. The first outbreak of Asiatic cholera in Britain was in Sunderland on the Durham coast, during the autumn of 1831. From there the disease made its way northward into Scotland, and southward towards London. Before it had run its course, it claimed 52,000 lives, the main epidemic occurring during 1832. The disease caused profuse diarrhoea, severe dehydration, collapse, and often death. There was widespread public fear, and the political and medical response to this new disease was variable and inadequate. In the summer of 1832, a series of 'cholera riots' occurred in various towns and cities throughout Britain, frequently directed against the authorities, doctors, or both.

Liverpool experienced more riots than elsewhere. Between 29 May and 10 June 1832, eight major street riots occurred, with several other minor disturbances. The object of the crowd's anger was the local medical fraternity. The public perception was that cholera victims were being removed to the hospital to be killed by doctors in order to use them for anatomical dissection. '*Bring out the Burkers*' was one cry of the Liverpool mobs, referring to the Burke and Hare scandal four years earlier, when two men had murdered people in Edinburgh in order to sell their bodies for dissection to the local anatomy school. This issue was of special concern to the Liverpool citizens because in 1826, thirty-three bodies had been discovered on the Liverpool docks, about to be shipped to Scotland for dissection. Two years later a local surgeon, William Gill, was tried and found guilty of running an extensive local grave-robbing system to supply corpses for his dissection rooms.

The widespread cholera rioting in Liverpool was thus as much related to local anatomical issues as it was to the national epidemic. There was a distinct lack of trust between the local population and the medical profession regarding the rumour and counter-rumour over what was causing the disease and what was happening to the bodies when in the possession of the coroner. The riots ended relatively abruptly, largely in response to an appeal by the Roman Catholic clergy published in the local press, but also being read from church pulpits. In addition, a respected local doctor, James Collins, published a passionate appeal for calm. The Liverpool Cholera Riots of 1832 demonstrated the complex social responses to epidemic disease, as well as the fragile relationship between the public and the medical profession. Letters from other doctors printed in the local press did little to alleviate the situation, when declaring that the reasons that victims were affected by the disease was down to 'depressing passions' and 'terror'. Tobacco enemas recommended by some doctors no doubt cleared the wards as quickly as dying victims.

It was into this volatile environment that William Duncan returned to his birthplace, after graduating in Medicine in Edinburgh in 1829, to start his professional career as a doctor in Rodney Street – 'the Harley Street of Liverpool'. Within months he was also working as a physician at one of the town's dispensaries, establishments set up by charities to provide medical services for the poor. A few years later he was appointed as a physician at Liverpool's Northern Hospital from 1837 to 1838, and at Liverpool Infirmary from 1843 to 1848. During this period he also lectured at the Liverpool Royal Institution school of medicine and surgery (from 1844 known as the Liverpool Infirmary medical school) from 1835 to 1848, and was the school's secretary in 1844–5. Duncan also helped to establish the Liverpool Medical Society (he was secretary from 1833 and president from 1836 to 1838) and also the Liverpool Medical Institution (he became its first secretary in 1840). He was an active member of the Literary and Philosophical Society of Liverpool from 1837 onwards and served as its treasurer.

But it was during the cholera epidemic of 1832, that he saw at first hand the conditions which soon led him to put the causes firmly at the door of poverty and overcrowding, both rife in the squalid housing of the poor in the streets below his practices. It was so serious that emergency epidemic sheds had to be opened in Lime Street and Toxteth Park. Working at the northern dispensary in Vauxhall Road, he was shocked at what his researches into their lives revealed, and so began a lifelong campaign to improve their housing conditions and sanitation. His early theories were published in the *Liverpool Medical Gazette in 1833,* where Duncan wrote and analysed the 216 cases he had attended of which 56 had died. The vast majority were living in courts and cellars, where a quarter of those deaths had occurred, while only a seventh of the deaths were in the minority of those cases living in decent housing. He talked of the need for community strategies to fight disease and how private health was not enough. Then after a decade of experience in the field and collecting information through his practice at the Liverpool

Dispensaries, he gave lectures on his findings which he published in a pamphlet entitled 'The Physical Causes of the High Mortality Rate in Liverpool in 1843'. Duncan was astute in not confining his lectures to a narrow band within the profession. He delivered his talks to notable bodies, such as the Literary and Philosophical Society, ensuring a broader dispersal of his work across the town.

When officials from the House of Commons Select Committee on the Health of Towns visited Liverpool in 1840 to gather evidence for their inquiry, Duncan was called to appear before them. He delivered a damning report on some of the worst housing conditions and overcrowding in the country, informing them that a third of the working class lived in the narrow, crowded courts among which another eighth of the population dwelt in underground windowless cellars. There were hundreds of packed lodging houses, often with up to thirty occupying the cellar. Out of the twenty miles of streets in these deprived labouring areas there were only a total of four miles of sewers. Even vessels entering the port had to be carefully vetted before passengers were allowed to disembark. In one instance in the early 1830s, cholera had broken out on board ship, which was quarantined with all passengers onboard, and there they would stay anchored in the Mersey, until cases began to dry up. Out of a full passenger list of 349, 83 succumbed to disease. His reports were supplied to Edwin Chadwick for his national Parliamentary enquiries into his 'Report on the Sanitary Condition of the Labouring Population of Great Britain'.

Chadwick may have been running the Parliamentary inquiry, but it was his New Poor Law Act which was a major contributing factor to the despair of the working classes. Outdoor relief was swept away and his new workhouses operated on a system making them more miserable than the lot of the lowliest labourer on the outside. As a consequence, many of those formerly cared for under the Poor Law were now in acute poverty in the courts and cellars in the north and south dockland areas of the town. As the population doubled within twenty years, unscrupulous landlords had little care for the quality of housing. Builders were unconcerned about privies, sewers, drainage and fresh running water. There was even less interest in cleaning the streets and removing domestic rubbish. In his *Report*, Edwin Chadwick showed that in 1839 for every person who died of old age or violence, eight died of specific diseases. This helps explain why during the second and third decades of the nineteenth century nearly one infant in three in England failed to reach the age of five. By the 1840s, one in three infants in Liverpool died in their *first year*.

Generally throughout the 1830s and the 1840s, trade nationally was experiencing a lull and food prices were high. The poorer classes, being underfed, were less resistant to contagion. Furthermore, during the more catastrophic years the weather was extremely variable, with heavy rains following prolonged droughts. Population, especially in the Midlands and in some seaport cities and towns like Liverpool, was growing rapidly without a concurrent expansion in new housing. Crowding contributed to the relatively fast spread of disease in these places. The Registrar General reported in 1841 that while average life expectancy in Surrey was forty-five years, it was only thirty-seven in expectancy in London and twenty-six in Liverpool. The average age of 'labourers, mechanics, and servants', at times of death was only fifteen. Mortality figures for crowded districts surrounding the docks were lower still.

With cholera sweeping its way through the slums of the great towns of the period, Chadwick concluded that the most important measures which could be taken to improve the health of the public were 'drainage, removal of all refuse from habitations, streets and roads and the improvements of the supplies of water'. But water companies were reluctant to take measures to ensure the purity of their product, however, public pressure was stronger than their resistance, and the first of the Public Health Acts was introduced in 1848 to enable local authorities to take control of their environmental health.

Liverpool authorities however had already made moves, and in April 1845 the Health of Towns Association in Liverpool was established with Duncan a key member, and they helped to create Liverpool's first Sanitary Act in 1846. The following year on 1 January 1847, Liverpool Town Council finally acted on Chadwick's 1842 *Report* on the sanitary conditions, when they appointed William Duncan as the country's first Medical Officer of Health under the terms of a special local Act of Parliament:

> 'That for the general means necessary to prevent disease it would be good economy to appoint a district medical officer, independent of private practice, with the securities of special qualifications and responsibilities to initiate sanitary measures and reclaim the execution of the Law'

Despite the recommendations of Chadwick's *Report*, Duncan was appointed only part-time, on a salary of £300 per annum, retaining a right to continue with his G.P. duties. This state of affairs was short lived and the following year he was appointed full-time on £750 per annum. It was also crucial that the office was established as independent from the outset.

He took a scientific approach to his work, carrying out research, collecting data and analysing his findings, before producing pamphlets to circulate his reports. In one inquiry looking into the average age of deaths, he revealed that in Wiltshire it was 36.5 years, while in Liverpool the 1841 figure had been reduced to only nineteen. Furthermore, he revealed that the annual death rate in Liverpool was 1 in 28 while in Birmingham it was 1 in thirty-seven. Although the analysis wasn't scientific by modern standards, it was certainly something the local population could understand.

In 1846 as the potato famine struck Ireland, a virulent form of typhus appeared, cutting down large numbers of the population and even hitting moneyed families with their more healthy homes and diets. As Irish workers moved to cities like Liverpool, the 'Irish fever' moved with them and by 1847 the contagion, not all of it connected with immigration, had spread throughout England and Wales, accounting for over thirty thousand deaths. As had happened a decade earlier, typhus occurred simultaneously with a severe influenza epidemic, one which carried off almost thirteen thousand. Towards the end of the 1840s the Irish migration continued unabated and by the end of 1848 another 300,000 refugees swamped the Liverpool population of 120,000. Duncan was quick to monitor the health and effects of this influx, estimating that around 40,000 had contracted either diarrhoea or dysentery, while a further 60,000 had suffered from fever.

His independence in office was essential, and it kept him free from bureaucratic reins, thus enabling him to be a constant thorn in the side of those he viewed as being obstructive to change. A delicate balancing act, as they were also in the positions of authority with the power to effect that change he was so desperate to see. The Select Vestry for example, who ran the Liverpool Workhouse and local Poor Law, were a frequent target, as they were also responsible for the Workhouse infirmary – the local hospital for the poor - and Duncan was constantly pushing them for improvements. Of course, he was asking them to spend money, and this became a cause of great resentment harboured by the Vestry; being told what to do by an MOH not directly responsible to them.

When Duncan was appointed Medical Officer of Health in 1847, he was joined by two further notable appointees, creating a powerful and effective triumvirate tackling the problems of poor housing and sanitation. James Newlands was the new Borough Engineer, and Thomas Fresh, Inspector of Nuisances. Newlands came to the post with very little experience. He was the son of an Edinburgh ropemaker, studied mathematics and philosophy at Edinburgh University, then worked as an apprentice to a local architect. Nevertheless, he soon proved more than capable by engineering the world's earliest integrated sewerage system in Liverpool. He worked closely with Dr Duncan, researching the links between poor sanitation and disease and they called for the clearance of cramped, insanitary slum dwellings to be replaced by spacious and well-ventilated new housing.

Duncan was a propounder of the miasma theory of disease transmission, which held that diseases, such as cholera, were caused by a poisonous form of 'bad air'. Epidemics, therefore, originated in the smells and vapours emanating from rotting organic matter and such diseases were the product of environmental factors such as contaminated water, foul air, and poor hygienic conditions. These infections were not passed between individuals but would affect all those in the locality who were constantly breathing in such mists and vapours, and further, it was identifiable by its foul smell. Such theories began to dominate studies and views on disease by the mid 1800s, and it would not be until the later nineteenth century before germ theory of disease and the work of Snow, Pasteur and Koch accurately revealed that some infectious diseases are caused by micro-organisms, and not miasma. Nevertheless, Duncan was certainly right in what was contributing to such an infectious environment. Even his ideas for whitewashing the courts had an antiseptic effect (not pioneered by Joseph Lister until the 1860s).

Duncan had his enemies of course. There were those in the Council who thought his £750 wage should be used to whitewash the town, while the local press criticised him for failing to acknowledge the diagnoses and miracle cure pills of a local quack and called him a murderer. But there were more pressing matters. Cholera cases were increasing and by the end of August 1849, hundreds of bodies thrown into open pits were now commonplace. Some of the policies, however well meaning, were chaotic, and little thought for example was given to alternative accommodation for the thousands of paupers, especially the newly arrived Irish, who were evicted from the squalid cellars. Many were also illiterate and couldn't read the notices. Duncan and his team continued to carry out their slum clearances, lime washing, inspections of lodging houses, slaughter houses and burial practices throughout the town.

In 1853, under the direction of Duncan, the Health Committee of Liverpool contacted the West Derby Board of Guardians, requesting co-operation in taking precautionary measures to prevent the spread of Asiatic cholera. Local medical officers were to notify the Liverpool Authorities of all cases of diarrhoea and cholera in the area and the relieving officers were to report similar instances and filthy housing conditions known to them. The West Derby Poor Law Union covered an area surrounding Liverpool, from Crosby in the north to Garston in the south, so it was a wise move to try to increase cooperation between the neighbouring authorities. At this time, the disease seemed to be largely confined to Liverpool, but due to the close proximity of Mill Road (the Infirmary for the West Derby Poor Law Union), all necessary steps were being taken to prevent it spreading. Two months later, the Guardians also appointed a Public Vaccinator who would receive 1/6d for every successful case of vaccination. Yet another cholera epidemic broke out in Liverpool in 1854, but the measures had begun to take hold, and deaths were down by 80% on the 1849 outbreak.

Although a corner seemed to have been turned, there was still a long way to go. In 1858 for example, scarlatina killed almost 1,200 children, and measles another 520. Diphtheria and whooping cough were also serious killers among the young, while tuberculosis claimed around 2,000 young and old each year. Nevertheless, death rates were declining. Yet it is astonishing that in sixteen years in office, Duncan never received a pay increase, nor did he have permanent staff. Despite that, he had a passionate concern for the health of the poor of Liverpool and was also well ahead of his time in recognising the power of the media to get across his messages, holding weekly press conferences to keep public health in the headlines and to press for change.

Duncan married twice. Firstly, to Philadelphia Rickarby in 1848, daughter of a Liverpool merchant, but she sadly died in 1850. Three years later he married Catherine MacAndrew, also the daughter of a local merchant, with whom he had a son and daughter. But towards the end of the 1850s, his health began to deteriorate, and while on a family visit to Scotland he died in West Park, Elgin, on 23 May 1863 aged 58 and was buried in the town. He was succeeded in his post by Dr W.S.Trench, who continued the methods which Duncan had pioneered.

It was not until the Royal Sanitary Commission of 1870 and the subsequent Public Health Acts of 1872 and 1875 that it became a statutory responsibility for districts to appoint a Medical Officer of Health, resulting in over 1,000 appointees. Despite the continuing problems of poor housing, conditions did improve from the 1870s, with the construction of new, healthier housing. The Act required local authorities to implement building regulations, or by-laws, which insisted that each house should be self-contained, with its own sanitation and water. This change in the design of housing complemented the public investment in sewers and water supply. In the last quarter of the 19th century, huge numbers of new houses were constructed, with long rows of terraced housing, in grids of streets, easily cleaned and inspected.

Doctor Duncan had been appointed a quarter of a century earlier - if the city had had to wait for legislation, the squalor and mortality rate would not bear thinking about. In his sixteen years in office, his achievements far outlasted his tenure, and without doubt made Liverpool a much better place for its inhabitants.

***

Today, Duncan has not been forgotten in Liverpool. One of the buildings of the Faculty of Medicine at the University of Liverpool is named after him, and the Duncan Society was formed in the city in 1998. Its purpose is to stimulate debate, discussion and understanding on issues and policies which affect the health and quality of life of the people of Merseyside and Cheshire. The Society makes a special contribution through its capacity to bring together community activists, experts of various kinds, professionals, managers and the general public. Members meet every month in the University, and the Society frequently attracts renowned local, national and international figures, who address issues relevant to the health of the region's population. It provides a rare opportunity where a diverse group of people, drawing on their own knowledge and experience, can exchange views and study the challenges and opportunities which face local people, in the spirit of Dr. Duncan, to strive to improve the well-being of the region.

For those in the town centre looking for respite and refreshment, they can take in the ambience and real ales in the public house bearing his name - 'Doctor Duncans' in St John's Square, where various Duncan related paraphernalia and story boards adorn the walls.

Further Reading

Warren. M., Francis, H., ed. 'Recalling the Medical Officer of Health, Writings by Sidney Chave, King Edward's Hospital Fund, London (1987)

Frazer, W. M. (Author), **Ashton, John** (Editor) *Duncan of Liverpool: An Account of the Work of Dr. W.M. Duncan, Medical Officer of Health of Liverpool, 1847-1863* (Facsimile 1997, originally published 1947)

Ashton, John, *The History of Public Health in Liverpool: upwards and onwards, pendulum or helix?*

Burrell, S., and Gill, G.V., The Liverpool Cholera Epidemic of 1832 and Anatomical Dissection - Medical Mistrust and Civil Unrest - *Journal of the History of Medicine and Allied Sciences* (2005) pp.478-498.

On the Net

Mike Royden's Local History Pages
www.roydenhistory.co.uk holds two useful papers:

Royden, Michael W. *The Roots of the New Liverpool Women's Hospital: The early medical care of women and babies in the late 18th/early 19th century* (1999)

Royden, Michael W. *The 19th Century Poor Law in Liverpool and its Hinterland: Towards the Origins of the Workhouse Infirmary* (2000)

Maggi Morris & John Ashton, *The Pool of Life - A Public Health Walk in Liverpool* - www.nwph.net/liverpoolpublichealthwalk

The walk is divided into four quarters; the maritime, the merchant, the institutional and the academic - The walk takes two to three hours in total and is accompanied by a self-guiding map. **Maggi Morris** is Director of Public Health for Central Lancashire and her husband **John Ashton**, was formerly Regional Director of Public Health and Regional

Medical Officer for the North West of England, before becoming Director of Public Health for Cumbria.

JOHN GLEESON WILSON, THE SUPPOSED MURDERER.

4

The Leveson Street Murder of 1849

On the morning of Wednesday 28 March 1849, young Daniel Roebuck was on his way to make a delivery at 20 Leveson Street, a few streets away from his father's earthenware shop at 2 Great George Street, in an area to be found today in the heart of Liverpool's Chinatown. In the mid nineteenth century, this was still an area of densely packed streets with court housing and terraces near to the docks, and populated by hundreds of labourers and migrants. This was also the time of the Irish famine, and thousands had ended up in these cramped conditions in the hope of a better life.

Like many cities in the UK, Liverpool has had its share of appalling murders, but few caused so much outrage and outcry that it would lead to the name of a street being changed to avoid any further link with the dreadful atrocity associated with its name. Just such an atrocity took place in Leveson Street over a century and a half ago, but all trace of its name has long since been removed.

On knocking a few times on the door, the errand boy received no answer, and feeling rather frustrated as the delivery time had been pre-arranged, he looked through the keyhole to see if anyone was about. But what he saw disturbed him, as he was sure he could make out a pair of legs lying across the hall. Unable to get a wide view, and worried that his customer may have taken a fall, he lifted himself up to the parlour window and peered inside. There, lay a scene of unimaginable horror. In a pool of blood were the bodies of a woman and a young child. He jumped back with a start and set off to fetch help, rushing straight into the arms of a policeman as he turned into Great George Street.

Meanwhile, Thomas Hughes, a bricklayer of nearby Back Berry Street, was passing the house moments later, when he saw a young lady at the door who'd also been unable to get in to the house for her music lesson. As she was quite distressed, Thomas offered to help and climbed up on to the railings and looked in the window of the front parlour for her. He too was greeted by the dreadful scene, the woman lying on the floor, her head covered in blood, and the boy with his arms around her waist, his head lying under her. Hearing Thomas' cries, a number of men came over, quickly broke the window and entered the house.

As they moved into the hall they found the mistress of the house, Mrs Hinrichson, lying in the doorway to the front parlour and her legs lying across the hall. She was clearly badly hurt, there was a serious cut on her head, she was still wearing her bonnet and gloves, and there was blood around her on the floor. Stepping over her into the parlour they could see the house servant, Mary Parr, with Mrs Hinrichson's eldest son, Henry George (Harry) aged five, lying alongside her. Tom bent down and asked the boy who could have done such a thing, but he was barely conscious and the words he uttered were unintelligible. But after they went through the cellar and into the back pantry, the scene which greeted them was even more gruesome. There they found the youngest child, John Alfred, aged three, with his throat slit from ear to ear.

More police began to arrive who swiftly sealed off the house and began their investigation. A short while later, surgeon Mr Thomas Slater arrived. A second surgeon, Mr Martin, was already treating Mrs Hinrichson. She was bleeding profusely and was insensible, and Slater went into the front parlour where he found the servant also still bleeding. On examination, he found she had two compound fractures of the skull, while young Harry had an extensive splintered fracture of the skull. A little finger had been cut off, presumably as he tried to shield his head, and was adhered to his frock coat. There were about a dozen cuts to his head and the child was incoherent, but he was living and conscious. A policeman directed Slater to the infant in the pantry. His throat wound was extensive dividing the windpipe and carotid artery, and it was merely the vertebra which kept the child's head from parting from his body. Slater immediately ordered carriages to take the three still living to the nearby Southern Hospital and he ran alongside them all the way.

Despite Slater's valiant efforts, Mrs Hinrichson, viciously battered and stabbed, died shortly afterwards, as did young Harry. To add to the sickening nature of the crime, she was also pregnant with her third child. She gave birth before she died, but the baby was either still-born or died shortly afterwards. Remarkably, Mary Parr regained consciousness. At one point, she was alert enough to make a statement, but afterwards she slipped into a coma and fought for life for 10 days before she died on the morning of Thursday 5 April. Nevertheless, her evidence would prove critical in the capture and conviction of the killer. The Police now had a lead.

Back at the house in an upstairs room, a bowl of blood-stained water was found, along with the likely murder weapons still coated in blood. A heavy fireplace poker, bent out of shape and clotted with blood and hair, had been found next to Mrs Hinrichson. Her bonnet, veil and fur stole were all caked with blood too, which would generate a wave of horror in court when these items were later produced at the murderer's trial. The gold watch, which Mary later confirmed her mistress had always worn outside the house, was missing. Near the kitchen grate, police found the fire shovel and tongs, also badly bent out of shape and covered in blood and hairs. The knife used to kill little Alfred was still in the pantry.

By now, the police had also discovered that the master of the house was Captain John Hinrichson, commander of the ship *Duncan*, a vessel belonging to Messer's James Aiken and Sons of Liverpool, and was at sea on a homeward voyage from Calcutta. He had been away since the summer of 1848 and had only arrived in Calcutta on 25 February. He was not due in his home port until late summer 1849. Born in Grimsby in 1817, Captain Hinrichson met his wife in her hometown of Hull. In the early 1840s, he secured a master's position with Aiken's company and relocated with his wife and young son Harry to Liverpool, where they moved into Sparling Street, off the dock road near the Albert Dock *(my own 4x great grandfather lived a few doors away in the same street)*. In August 1846, their second son, John Alfred, was born. He was baptised at nearby St Marks Church and the family were now living in Hope Place. A couple of years later they moved to a larger house in Leveson Street and took with them their maid servant, Mary Parr aged 28, who had been with them since 1844.

From her hospital bed, Mary Parr told the police that the man who carried out the attacks had originally come to the house on the Tuesday the day before, when he took lodgings at Mrs Hinrichson's for a month. They were regarded as a happy family, and although Ann Hinrichson was receiving a regular income from her husband which she collected from Aiken's while he was away on long passages, she was finding it difficult to manage and had decided to take in boarders. She advertised a room for rent with a card in the window and a man calling himself John Gleeson Wilson, called to apply for the tenancy. He appeared respectable, saying he was a carpenter for the Dock Estate, and on a weekly wage of 2 pounds 10 shillings. He seemed suitably civil and made a favourable impression upon his new landlady, who was only too eager to rent him the back parlour and top front bedroom.

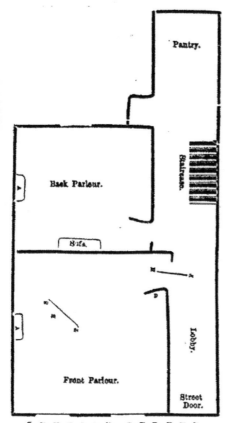

Plan of the murder scene, as printed in the Liverpool Mercury during the trial

The above is a sketch of the ground plan of the first story of the house, which is three steps above the level of the street. Through the window in the front parlour the bodies were first discovered. The servant lay with her head at s and her feet at T. The eldest boy lay in the position marked by the letter B. The feet and legs of Mrs. Hinrichson, it will be recollected, were observed lying in the lobby, and her position is clearly indicated by the letters H and F, the H marking where her head was lying, and the F her feet. Below the head of the unfortunate lady was a large pool of blood, and so copious had been the discharge of the vital fluid, that it oozed through the flooring, stained the ceiling of the kitchen below, and actually trickled down the wall to the very ground, the marks of its progress being still visible. There were two or three indentations in the door of the front parlour, and there is little doubt these were made with the strokes from the poker, whilst the murderous assault was being made upon Mrs. Hinrichson. The back parlour is the apartment which, with a bed-room, was let to the prisoner. The sofa on which the bodies were placed, after their removal from the front parlour, is still in the back room, and is very much stained with blood. A A are the fire-places. In a wash-house or scullery, an apartment down stairs, and immediately beneath the pantry, the body of the youngest child was found lying with the throat cut.

The annexed diagram will illustrate the open and exposed situation in which the house stands where the murder was perpetrated, it being the third house from Great George-street:—

Later, the local press described him as,

'rather striking in appearance, 5ft 7ins tall and rather broad of build, and muscular, his hair brown, short at the back but hanging long and lank over the right side of his face. He was of fair complexion, his face presented several curious characteristics, his ears nearly on a line with his eyes, which were small and had a queer cast, set deeply in the head, cheek bones high, nose rather pointed, cheeks hollow, lips full and pouting, face tapering into a small chin, the tip of which was red, characteristics which cut the face into a mass of sharp angles'.

His behaviour that night in the Hinrichson household was quite normal, and there was nothing out of the ordinary to arouse worry or concern. He was reticent in speaking of himself, although he did disclose that his sister was licensee of the Tranmere Hotel on the Old Chester Road, 'over the water' in the Wirral. 'And when will your luggage arrive?' asked Mrs Hinrichson, during one of the few moments he had been in his room. 'The day after tomorrow', he replied calmly.

The following morning the mistress went out to the market between 10 and 11am leaving the children with the maid servant. Wilson was out early however, and stopped a young lad in the street to ask if he wanted to earn three-halfpence. The boy was Edward McDermott, a labourer of 8 Court, Bannistre Street. Gleeson gave him a letter, pointed out the Hinrichson's house, and told McDermott to let him get back inside, wait five minutes, and then knock at the door announcing he had a letter for Mr Wilson from his (Wilson's) employer. McDermott did as he was told, Mary answered the door and called Gleeson with news that a letter had arrived. He came downstairs and took the letter, which he read with affected gravity. After paying McDermott the balance of his fee, he announced that the letter was letting him know that he would not be needed at the docks that day, and that he was now able to stay in the house. Wilson's ploy had worked.

McDermott later confirmed this encounter to the authorities; 'On Wednesday morning last at about 9.30am, I was coming up the corner of Pitt St when I met Wilson. He asked me would I carry a letter for him and he would give me three-halfpence, I agreed. I am sure he is the same man.'

He remembered his light corduroy trousers and dark shooting coat, together with his features. McDermott was also shown the letter and identified it. Although he could not read he said he remembered 'the shape of the lines'. He said to me, 'Do as I tell you, I want you to watch where I go, just up the street here to number 20, wait five minutes and then knock on the door, ask if Mr Gleeson Wilson lodges here, when the woman says 'Yes', tell her you have a letter from his master. When she gives me the letter I will give you 3d'.

Afterwards, Wilson sat down to read the paper, but was restless and began to pester Mary while she tried to get on with her chores. Later while lying in hospital she told the police,

> 'The children were in the parlour and Wilson drove them out with the newspaper, I was cleaning the grate and he came into the parlour and asked me the price of fire irons, the fender and card tables. He then struck me on the head with the tongs. I don't remember anything more other than the children being in the room and lying there.'

The attack was unprovoked and vicious, Wilson beating her so hard that she sustained a fractured skull, before he turned on young Harry and inflicted similar injuries. Three-year-old Alfred had fled into the rear parlour and into the pantry where he tried to hide, terrified by the screams and commotion, but escape for the poor little youngster was futile. Wilson simply strode towards him, grabbed a white-handled kitchen knife off the table, and cut his throat from ear to ear.

Wilson raced upstairs, tried to clean himself up in the sink, then began to rifle though the drawers. Suddenly there was a knock at the door. Had the mistress returned already? He ran back downstairs, and in a heavy sweat, opened the door slightly ajar. To his relief it was an errand boy, Anthony Carney, a young man of 66 St James Street, nearby. 'I have come from my master, Mr Cox, to deliver potatoes for Mrs Hinrichson - she came into the provision shop this morning,' he told the man at the door. Wilson took the basket, and went inside, but as he was emptying it, the mistress returned, pausing for a moment to tell the errand boy the potatoes were paid for and there was no need to wait. No sooner had Ann Hinrichson stepped inside and closed the door behind her, that Wilson laid into her, beating her senseless with the fireplace poker before she had even taken her gloves or bonnet off. He then ransacked the rest of the house, taking anything small enough he could hide in his coat, before slipping out of the house at midday.

It was at this moment, as Wilson's four victims lay either dead or dying, that the young music pupil and the delivery boy tried in vain to gain access to the house, before passers-by came to their aid, only to be rewarded by the grim discovery.

While the police gathered their evidence and began to reconstruct the horrific events, Wilson was heading out of Liverpool, up Parliament Street towards the Crown Street fields on the ridge above the town. There he headed to a pond in a nearby field known as the 'Figure of Eight Pit' where he waded knee-deep in the water and tried to wash his boots and bloodstained trousers. He threw the letter he'd paid McDermott to bring to the house into the pond, and discarded a blood-stained handkerchief in a ditch nearby. But his strange behaviour had been noticed and would revisit him in court.

His trousers were still in a poor state, so crossing the town along its eastern ridge, he dropped down towards Great Homer Street, where he bought another pair from a pawnbroker. He was able to change in the shop, and on the way out he handed the old pair to a passer-by named Henry Worthington. Henry was later summonsed during the trial and testified that he'd found blood still on them.

Heading back towards town in the early afternoon, Wilson called into a second pawnshop in London Road, where he laid Ann Henrichson's watch down on the counter, part of his plunder that day. But to Tunstall the broker, there was an air of suspicion about Wilson and he refused to deal with him, immediately suspecting the watch to be stolen. As Wilson left, Tunstall beckoned a nearby policeman, suggesting it would be worth following his last customer. He did so for a few minutes, but soon lost him. If he had been up to the job, the bobby would have arrived at the Pier Head Landing Stage, where the strange case took another twist. Wilson stepped onto the ferry and crossed to Birkenhead, then on to Tranmere. But he was not heading to visit his sister. Wilson was on his way to see his wife.

Not only was Wilson married, but he already had lodgings near to the murder scene. Towards the end of 1847, he applied for a tenancy at 34 Sparling Street, at a house kept by a respectable young widow called Margaret Garner, daughter of William Stewart, a well-regarded gentleman living in Tranmere. He gave his name as John Gleeson Wilson. Within months a relationship had developed and Wilson proposed marriage to the young widow which was accepted. They married at St Nicholas, near the Pier Head on 17 December 1848, where he recorded his trade as an 'engineer fitter', telling his wife he was employed on the steam packets. His residence was recorded as Blundell Street, where he may have relocated to once their relationship had begun, to protect the good name of Mrs Garner. Regarding his family, he told his new wife that his father was a foreigner and that he had been brought up by him in London.

It wasn't long into the marriage before he his true character as an overbearing tyrant emerged, and his wife was frequently on the receiving end of a beating. One particular incident aroused her suspicions, especially considering that during their short marriage he was unemployed and didn't appear to have a particular trade. One evening he came home and told her that he had come into a large sum of money, whereupon he took off his old worn coat, ripped it apart and put it on the fire. He then put on a fine coat he had purchased that day (the same coat he was wearing on the day of the murders), but he gave her no explanation of where the money had came from.

Margaret later told how his ill-treatment of her became indescribable, and how he had threatened to murder her. By February, it had become so unbearable that she confessed to her father as to what was going on. He immediately insisted she give up the house in Sparling Street and seek refuge under his protection at home in Tranmere. He also told Wilson never to approach the house, and if he did, Mr Stewart warned him he would have no hesitation in informing the police.

Yet here was Wilson, on the ferry, on the run having committed four murders, intent on seeking out his estranged wife. Not only did they meet, but while begging her forgiveness for all his misdeeds, he sweet-talked himself not just into the house, but into his wife's bed – all unknown to her father. The reconciliation lasted until early the next morning of Thursday, 29 March, when he left to take the ferry from Birkenhead. Yet he stayed on board for three hours, sailing back and forth across the river avoiding detection,

No.	When Married.	Name and Surname.	Age.	Condition.	Rank or Profession.	Residence at the Time of Marriage.	Father's Name and Surname.	Rank or Profession of Father.
53	17th December 1848	John Gleeson Wilson	full	Bachelor	Engineer	Blundell St.	David Gleeson Wilson	Engineer
		Margaret Garner	full	Widow	—	Sparling St.	William Stewart	Publican

18__ Marriage solemnized at St Nicholas Church in the Parish of Liverpool in the County of Lancaster

Married in the Church of St Nicholas according to the Rites and Ceremonies of the Established Church, by ____ or after ____ by me,

This Marriage was solemnized between us,

Marriage entry in the records of St Nicholas, near the Pier Head on 17 December 1848, between John Gleeson Wilson, Engineer, of Blundell Street, and Margaret Garner, a widow, of Sparling Street

75

before the captain told him to pay or get off. On alighting at the Liverpool landing stage, he took a cab to the north end of the dock road, into the heavily populated Irish area either side of Great Howard Street. Porter Street lay between there and the docks, and there he secured new lodgings at number forty-four. Once inside he changed into a fresh shirt and sent his laundry to a washerwoman further along the street, before setting off towards the town to try to sell the watch again.

This time, he tried a pawnshop in Great Howard Street. Wilson demanded £30 but the owner, Miert Samuel, turned him down flat, offering only £8. Wilson skulked out. But in desperation he returned later that afternoon to accept the derisory offer. Samuel was no fool, and seeing he had the upper hand reduced his offer to £6. But despite making the offer, Samuel wasn't truly happy to give him anything at all, as news of the Leveson Street atrocity was circulating the city like wildfire, and this uneasy figure before him looked decidedly suspicious.

Samuel turned to his father, and speaking in Hebrew for a moment, they agreed to tell Wilson that they also had a shop in Dale Street, where they could walk together and Wilson could collect his money. In fact, they had no intention of parting with their money, their plan was to hand him into the Bridewell in Dale Street. It worked. Wilson didn't cotton on until it was too late, and after a struggle he was apprehended. He was quickly searched and out tumbled Mrs Henrichson's watch and purse. Now clearly wrong-footed as events began to overtake him, he gave a flimsy alibi under questioning regarding his whereabouts at the time of the murders. The police were confident they had their man and charged him with the killing of two young boys.

Outside the Bridewell an excited and aggressive crowd soon gathered, and several even tried to get inside. The following morning, the prisoner, heavily shackled, was taken to the

Southern Hospital to see if Mary Parr could identify him. Also in attendance were the magistrates, Mr William Rushton (son of Edward Rushton, one of the founders of the Blind School), the Mayor - local Tory M.P. Mr J Bramley Moore - and Mr Jameson, the magistrate's clerk. The prisoner was brought into the ward and the moment her eyes rested on Wilson she said in a clear distinct voice 'that is the man with the hat on'. Wilson showed no outward signs of emotion. By the time they came out to leave the Southern, the word of his whereabouts had spread through the community like wildfire, and the officials had a difficult time getting him through an angry jostling crowd, by now throwing threatening abuse, intent on meting out their own form of justice.

A pre-trial hearing was held in a packed Liverpool Crown Court before magistrates Rushton and Bramley-Moore, while solicitors Mr Yates and Mr Davenport appeared for the prisoner. Numerous witnesses began to come forward. Detective Marks told the court,

> 'I went yesterday with a plasterer called Michael Kane to a pond in a field at the end of Crown Street, known as the 'Figure of Eight Pit'. In looking along a ditch I found a letter (which he produced). Further on where a man had been sitting I found a handkerchief'.

Michael Kane was duly brought up, who confirmed that he crossed the field on Wednesday and saw a man come up to the pond with his trousers rolled up over his boots. The man had light cord trousers and a dark coat. He waded out into deep water and washed himself, his trousers and boots.

Anthony Carney, the young delivery boy told the court,

> 'My master is Michael Cox, a provision dealer. Mrs Hinrichson came into the shop for a second time about 11am and ordered a peck of potatoes, I was sent with them to the house. I knocked on the door in a hurry, and a young man answered half opening

the door, he was in great perspiration. He took the basket and went inside, as he was emptying the basket Mrs Hinrichson came to the door, I asked were the potatoes paid for and she said, 'Yes'. The prisoner is the man who came to the door'.

The Surgeon, Mr Slater, confirmed that he saw some potatoes that had been emptied on the front parlour floor. Then Tom Finn, a pawnbroker of Great Homer Street, told the court,

'On Tuesday or Wednesday the prisoner came into the shop and bought a pair of trousers, he asked could he change and I took him to a compartment. I wrapped the old cord trousers up and noticed the tops were clean but the bottoms from the knee down were quite dirty. He seemed nervous and agitated. After he left, another customer came in and said that he saw the man give the trousers away.'

He examined the trousers held up as an exhibit and confirmed they were the ones worn by the customer, at which point Wilson cried out 'Have you got my name on them?'

But despite Wilson's futile interjection, the weight of evidence against him continued to pile up and the passer-by, paviour Henry Worthington, to whom Wilson handed the trousers, told the court,

'I was walking along Great Homer Street about 1.05pm and saw the prisoner fitting on a pair of trousers in the shop of the last witness. About 20yds from the shop he asked would I have a pair of trousers, I said yes and took them. I showed them to my mates, the trousers had blood on them and they had been rubbed with dirt.'

He identified the prisoner and the blood spotted trousers presented to the court.

Miert Samuel was the next witness. 'I am a pawnbroker and reside in Great Howard Street', he said.

'I remember the prisoner offering the gold watch for sale. On Thursday morning, they came in, there was another man with him, (not identified). They called me over the way to a public house, I went leaving some customers in the shop. We went into the snug and the prisoner asked me for £30 for the watch. I asked him to call back at the shop when I was not busy. I later called on him in the lodging house in Porter Street, but he was not in, I waited and he came in a car to the door. I looked at the watch and offered £8, he was not willing to take this so I left and asked him to come to the shop if he changed his mind. He came to the shop about 8.30pm that evening, I offered £6 and he accepted. I showed the watch to my father, who thought it might be stolen, I asked the prisoner for a receipt, but he said he could not write. My father spoke to me in Hebrew and said to take him to the police office, and tell him we have another shop in Dale Street. When I got to the police office he tried to get away but I stuck to him close enough, my father suspected he was the murderer.'

Constable Toole of the Bridewell told the court that the prisoner came in with Samuel who put the watch in his hand. He told him he would get a receipt and the prisoner seamed uneasy. He sent for Superintendent Clough who took the prisoner into custody. On searching him he found a purse and 10s-3d. (about 51p). He then went to search his lodgings in Porter Street. The prisoner told Superintendent Clough that he had had the watch for 5 years. But Mrs Hinrichson's mother was in court and she swore on oath that the watch was her daughters.

Superintendent Clough was then called and he revealed his questioning of Wilson in the Bridewell.

'Where were you on Thursday?'

'About the Docks', said Wilson.

'Where you in Cheshire?' [NB. Tranmere in the Wirral was then in Cheshire]

'No'.

'Where were you on Wednesday?'

'At the Clarence Dock'.

'The whole of the day?'

'Yes'.

'Where did you sleep on Wednesday night?'

'At Tranmere'.

'With your father-in-law?'

Wilson looked around earnestly. 'Yes'.

'Did you live at 34 Sparling Street some time ago?'

'Yes'.

'Marry a Miss Stewart?'

'Yes'.

'And you are separated?'

'Yes'.

'Did you engage a car from George's Pier Head?' [a taxi-cab]

'Yes'.

'Did you drive to the top of Porter Street and go into a public house and buy a glass for the driver?'

'Yes I did'.

The Superintendent was then satisfied he had identified the right man and sent for young Mr McDermott who identified him as the man who asked him to knock at the Hinrichson's house. A man who saw him running up Washington Street after the murder also identified him from a line-up. Superintendent Clough told the court that he then charged the prisoner with the murder of the two children in Leveson Street.

Mary Nott, a young woman residing at 4 Lower Harrington Street, was called next. She told the court, 'I worked for Mrs Hinrichson and there was no man in the house, as the captain was away at sea. A man came on Tuesday and took lodgings'. She remembered the prisoner's hat being in the house and identified her mistresses purse. Constable Toole had found the hat when he searched the prisoner's lodgings at Porter Street and produced it in court.

At this point Wilson, finally seeing the cards stacked against him, became extremely angry and gesticulated wildly, before being calmed down by his defence team. But there was still more to come. Constable Tuck then produced two shirts which had been sent to a washerwoman called Jane Wilson in Porter Street. There were clear spots of blood upon the one sent on Thursday on the breast, right arm and skirt. Two witnesses verified the shirts had been sent and belonged to the prisoner.

William Prescot came before the bench and said,

> 'I am a coach driver and work for Mr Hayhurst of Great George Street. I was in Great George Street on Wednesday. Where I stood I could see down Leveson Street and I saw a man coming down Great George Street, he had a dark coat on and his trousers were turned up above his boots, I remarked to another person near me, 'That person is much heated, he has been walking or working hard.' He pulled out a dark handkerchief and wiped his brow'.

Prescot swore that the prisoner was the man he saw and identified the trousers. Thomas Jones, another cab driver, backed up Prescot with a similar testimony.

The court then became very hushed as PC499 Samuel Haigh described what faced him when he entered the murder scene in Leveson Street on Wednesday 12.15pm. He described the position in which he found the bodies, and then produced a poker, much bent, with a massive ornamental head, clotted with blood and hairs, which was found lying next to Mrs Hinrichson. An audible groan filled the court as everyone shuddered at the sight of the gruesome articles. A bonnet, a veil and a victorine [thick scarf] were also lying near her head covered with blood. He produced the woman's cap, saturated with blood. Wilson remained impassive. PC Haigh described the grisly discovery of the infant John in the rear cellar pantry, and the upstairs room where he found a box had been opened and clothes strewn all over the floor. Henry Power, a sergeant in the fire brigade, produced a bent and bloodstained fire shovel, still with hairs upon it, plus a pair of broken tongs also showing traces of blood. PC132 Jeremiah Mangle joined him, and produced the other part of the broken tongs, while PC James Wilson produced a white halted table knife covered with blood found in the pantry.

The evidence against Wilson was overwhelming, and Mr Rushton placed him on remand to await trial. As the prisoner left the dock, a great commotion broke out at the back of the court, while crowds remained outside the session house for hours afterwards discussing the particulars of the affair.

Meanwhile, further investigations continued into the identity and background of Wilson. He spoke with an Irish accent and told the court he was from Tipperary, but his vague responses under questioning deepened the mystery of his origins. But on 28 April 1849, a letter was received from a Mr Dowling in Ireland, which was made public. It revealed that Wilson had been identified by a Mr Featherstone, a magistrate residing in Brurie near Limerick, who had previous dealings with the prisoner. It became clear that Wilson was actually Maurice Gleeson, born in 1823 to a Blacksmith's family in Brurie, noted for their 'idleness and vicious propensities'. In 1847, at the age of twenty-six, he was charged with robbery, but he was never tried, having fled Ireland for London's Limehouse, before he relocated to Plymouth, then Bristol, eventually ending up in Liverpool.

As his notoriety grew, more facts about his background came to light, and his movements shortly before the murder became clearer. Investigations revealed that he had again been in Bristol, this time on 20 March, only eight days before the murder. He arrived in Liverpool on the steamer *Troubadour* on 23 March, and while on board it was said he treated the passengers and crew to drinks, handing over four sovereigns in the process - no doubt ill-gotten gains from his travels. During the voyage, he got on very well with a respectable family who took him ashore at Swansea and gave him dinner. He came back to Liverpool with them, staying with a shipping agent, and contemplated going to America but later changed his mind.

The trial began almost five months later on Wednesday, 22 August 1849, and was a short affair, concluding the following day. John Gleeson Wilson, alias Maurice Gleeson, aged 26, was tried before Mr Justice Patterson in Liverpool Crown Court, and pleaded not guilty to all charges.

There had been an attempt by the authorities to reschedule the proceedings by bringing the date forward at the last minute due to the fever surrounding the trial. Initially, the plan seemed to have worked, as the court was only half full as the proceedings began. To the astonishment of the court officials, the news spread rapidly and the court quickly filled to capacity, and as the day wore on a crowd of two to three thousand had gathered in the street outside.

On the bench alongside his Lordship was William Brown M.P, and the Rev W. Pollock of St Marks (the family church of the Hinrichsons). If there may have been some bias on the bench, the jury was selected almost entirely from out-of-towners;

The Jury:
James F. Devonport, Accountant, Everton, foreman

John Cooper, Builder, Walton-on-the-Hill
Joseph Pearson Dicken, Dentist, Wardleworth
James Byrne, Engineer, Toxteth Park.
George Harriott, Agent, Ashton-in-Makerfield
Obadiah Kirk, Farmer and cotton manufacturer, Ashton-under-Lyne
Thomas Molyneux, Music dealer, Pendleton
John Millars, Marble mason, Salford
William Mercer, Land agent, Newton-in-Makerfield
Arthur Potts, Engine manufacturer, Newton-in-Mackerfield
Thomas Taylor, Merchant, Bootle-cum-Linacre
Richard Tickle, Coal proprietor, Hindley

'Put up the prisoner', said the court clerk Mr Shuttleworth, as a deathly hush spread across the room with all eyes focused on the dock. After a few moments suspense, Wilson stepped up to the bar, seemingly unconcerned with his predicament, appearing in good health and looking none the worse for his imprisonment. The indictment was read and the usual question directed at the prisoner, 'How say you John Gleeson Wilson, are you guilty or not guilty of the crimes?' Wilson, or Gleeson, replied sharply showing great indignation, 'Not guilty'.

And so the trial began, with Mr Sergeant Wilkins, Mr Blair and Mr Paget appearing for the prosecution, Mr Pollock and Mr Brett defending. As in the pre-trial hearing, the witnesses were called and gave their testimony, followed by Mary Parr's sworn testimony which was read to the court. Mr Pollock then addressed the jury on behalf of the prisoner, after which the judge began his summary. The accused leaned forward listening intently, and on hearing the Judge's very strong opinions on his sanity, he began to sigh loudly and became very animated. The jury did not even leave the courtroom to discuss the verdict, so overwhelming was the evidence against him, and took less than five minutes to reach their unanimous decision. The black cap was placed upon Justice

Patterson's head for the inevitable verdict. The public gallery swiftly emptied onto the streets, where they burst out of the doors shouting 'He is condemned!' to great cheers from those gathered outside.

Gleeson was taken below and through the subterranean passage to the adjacent Bridewell, while in the streets above the mobs could be heard cheering. Annoyed and excited by their howls ringing in his ears he exclaimed, 'Damn them, I wish I was amongst them', while he kept protesting his innocence and how he didn't want to die. The following day he requested his original clothes, which was granted, the trousers still bearing the blood stains, which he seemed to be happy with and he even remarked to one of the guards, 'It's a pity I could not wear out such nice clothes'. He then dictated a letter to his father, informing him of the sentence while still protesting his innocence. On receiving a visit from the magistrate Mr Featherstone, Gleeson became tearful and asked about his father and family. He was most anxious to see his twin brother, John (whose name he had used as an alias) but visits from his family were denied him. The local press reported, 'His mother has been dead for many years but he speaks of her in a most kind and affectionate manner. She seems to have been a hard-working woman who struggled hard to curb the propensity of her husband and shield her children from the ruin of his drunkenness and evil habits'. Any doubts of Gleeson's true identity were now dispelled.

The hanging was set for noon on 15 September 1849, and such was the animosity universally felt for the prisoner, that the execution was starting to develop into a major event. Interest was so great, that local railway companies even laid on special trains from the industrial towns in Lancashire and Yorkshire, while as early as the morning of the day before the execution, wily cart owners drew up against the wall of Kirkdale Gaol adjacent to the scaffolding, offering space on their makeshift viewing platforms to willing punters. Mr Gibbs, the governor of the gaol immediately ordered them away and police were called to erect barricades. Although below the scaffold, a small space was fenced off for the press, friends, and those who gave evidence at the trial. The police presence remained through the night as a considerable crowd had begun to gather, determined to stay until morning.

Wilson pictured in his Kirkdale cell which appeared in the pages of the Liverpool Journal newspaper while he was awaiting execution

One group of Liverpool businessmen even hired a steamer to give their workers a treat on the Mersey. The programme included a visit to the Mersey lightship, returning at 11.00am, and stopping at a point near Bootle where they could witness the execution, following which they journeyed up river to Eastham for lunch.

As the hour approached, Gleeson continued to protest his innocence and one Catholic priest was taken in by him and began to express sympathy, so much so that several of his colleagues, to satisfy any doubt, were allowed into Gleeson's cell to make their own enquiries. The first Catholic priest to visit Gleeson was grossly insulted by him, and others came away quite distressed by Gleeson's vindictive character and any lack of remorse, plus his continued refusal to make his peace with God. In fact, the prison officers were more damning, believing him to be vain and flattered by the notoriety which he had acquired and was looking forward to a final twisted moment of glory. Through the days leading to the execution, he began to refuse food, turning a deaf ear to the guards, then just as suddenly as he had decided on his hunger strike, he demanded his rations, not only for that day, but all food in arrears.

The morning of 15 September was a bright sunny day, and there was a festival atmosphere with over 100,000 people gathered in Kirkdale on the suburban edge of Liverpool to the north of the town. Every vantage point was taken, and for miles around there was a seething black mass of people. Every street leading to the gaol was crowded, mothers leading children by the hand, fathers accompanying daughters, husbands and wives, brothers and sisters. Excitement was higher than on a national cup day at Aintree. The focus of their attention was described in great detail in the Liverpool Journal,

> 'The scaffold at Kirkdale was a simple construction. Two strong beams about four yards apart projected from holes in the wall. From uprights above these crossed the fatal beam, and around this was an iron chain and link which hung down from the reception of a hook, to which was attached the rope. Suspended from below the projecting beams was a kind of framework or box with folding lids, the outside being covered with a black cloth. On top of this was placed the culprit, the greater part of his body being exposed when he first stepped below the drop. About breast high was passed round the scaffold an iron rod. When the bolt was withdrawn, the top of the box or framework fell inwards and the criminal became suspended. The entrance to the scaffold was through two iron folding doors in the wall. The scaffold was erected at the north-west angle of the gaol, the angle was at no great extent, and as the fatal erection extended only a few feet from the wall, spectators to obtain a view had to take up positions in the fields outside the end of the road which led on either side to the entrance of the gaol.'

The stumbling form of Gleeson, still in his white shirt, was escorted out, flanked by two priests in black robes. He was still protesting his innocence, but his words were now drowned by the rage of the crowd. Chief executioner William Calcraft was unwell, and had been replaced by seventy-year-old George Howard of York, who proved himself completely incompetent, although his shortcomings not doubt provided more entertainment for the baying onlookers. Wilson was quickly pushed against the scaffold, the noose and hood slipped over his head, and the trap door bolt swiftly released. However, the drop had been incorrectly measured and was too short, while the white hood placed over his head barely reached his eyebrows. Wilson's face was now exposed to the throng and instead of the drop breaking his neck he slowly strangled to death. The horrified Howard hastily pulled the cap down over Wilson's face, but not before Wilson looked straight at him, terror clearly evident in his bulging eyes as his face began turning purple. In full view of the gathered mass below he struggled and writhed for fifteen minutes. Many must have felt they had got their money's-worth and it was a just end to a vile murderer, but it was too much for some who fainted on the spot.

*Kirkdale Gaol where John Gleeson Wilson was incarcerated
and the scene of numerous executions*

On the Sunday immediately prior to the execution, the *Duncan* docked in Liverpool at 2am. On board was Captain Hinrichson.

His family would not have to face the awful task of telling him the dreadful news. When his vessel had put in to St Helena some months earlier for water and supplies, a company agent had stepped aboard to tell the Captain that he had sad news, 'Well' said the Captain, 'these are my mates I have no secrets tell me before them'. The agent, however, insisted and beckoned him to his own cabin where he broke the news privately. The Captain stared straight ahead at first, but then staggered and fell in a fit to the floor. Mary Parr's son was also on the *Duncan*, and he too was given his own sad news to bear.

The journey home was tortuous. In Liverpool, friends boarded the vessel, and on seeing them he wrung his hands and cried, 'My wife, where is my wife?' and pleaded with them to take him to where he could see where she and his children were laid to rest. 'Is there not one left?' he asked. 'Where is my Ann, my little Harry and my Alfred?' He was urged to come home, but he cried, 'I have no home'. Only after much persuasion did he leave the vessel, where his friends took him to Upper Pitt Street, where he was taken in by his mother-in-law, Mrs Harrison. On reaching the house, the distraught sea-captain threw himself into her arms still crying, 'Where is my wife?' He was so disturbed that a surgeon from 100 Mill Street was summoned to attend to him, and after he was rested it was decided that Captain Hinrichson would return to Hull to stay with relatives. He was talked out of seeing the murderer before his execution.

Regarding the final resting place of the Captain's family, they were interred in St James Cemetery, (now St James' Gardens below the Anglican Cathedral). On the Saturday evening of 7 April 1849, the remains of the maid Mary Parr, who had died two days earlier, were placed in the same grave as Mrs Hinrichson and her children, while the burial service was read by the Reverend M. Green, Curate of St Marks, their family church.

An Account of the Murder of Mrs. Henrichson at Liverpool,

together with her two little Boys, and an Infant she gave birth to before she died of her wounds, and also of Ann Parr her Servant, who gave witness before she expired in the hospital against a Lodger by the Name of MORRIS, perpetrated in Mar. 1849 and Prisoner, whose Name is not exactly known, remains to be tried summer assizes.

Correct LIKENESS, of the MURDERER.

Of all the crimes that guilty man,
  Hath wrought since murd'rous Cain,
No monster hath or ever can,
  Create more lasting pain.

Than him at Liverpool of late,
  Who a whole family slay'd,
A mother and three children state,
  Besides the servant maid.

A Captain Hinrichson, abroad,
  Bound from Calcutta, home,
Some months ago left his abode,
  To plough the ocean's foam.

In order to maintain his wife,
  And two young children, dear,
Who tender lov'd them as his life,
  For them did persevere.

And she as saving as her sire,
  Let lodgings now and then,
The last, a fiend of darkness dire,
  Turn'd out the worst of men.

From good appearance, first he took,
  A bed-room and a parlour,
Nor did they take him by his look,
  A villain or a broiler.

One day he struck the boy a blow,
  The servant's heart bewild'ring,
Told him her mistress wont allow,
  Strangers to beat her children.

With that the ruffian was enrag'd,
  With a poker knock'd her down,
Striking her when she was engag'd,
  Cleaning the grate 'tis found.

He next attack'd the eldest child,
  Which likewise lifeless lay,
Then murder'd the little infant mild,
  That backward ran away.

He cut its throat from ear to ear,
  The others seeming dead,
When Mrs. Hinrichson did appear,
  The poker beat on her head.

The lady had to market been,
  And when the food was brought,
He took the several baskets in,
  'Midst murd'rous scenes he wrought.

When the unconsc'ous lady came,
  He finished his work,
And took the gold watch with the same,
  And left the house—to lurk.

The police came—a horrid deed,
  These mangled victims shew'd,
Three of them were not wholly dead,
  But were with blood imbrued.

The murd'rer at a clothier's shop,
  Was into custody given,
And will perhaps be on the drop,
  Whilst they inhabit heaven.

They took him to the hospital,
  Where those poor suff'rers lay,
Ann Parr, the servant knew him well,
  Swore what she had to say.

Her agonizing mistress gave,
  Birth to a little boy,
And soon was fitted for the grave,
  With Ann he did destroy.

Now he's committed to his cell,
  Till summer's next assizes,
In Kirkdale Gaol, in durance dwell,
  And wait till law chastises.

And next the funeral moves on,
  The mother and two boys,
With mourners fifty thousand strong,
  Over departed joys.

And in the cemetery plac'd,
  Near Huskisson's monument,
Where the poor mother wept and pac'd,
  And loudly did lament.

Together with her sorrowing friends,
  The place was filled with tears,
The minister a mound ascends,
  Exhorts with feeling prayers.

And show'd by nature prone to wrong,
  How Cain his brother slew,
That grace, alone, would tempers strong,
  By sovereign power subdue.

Reminded all that stood above,
  Their awful early tomb,
They soon as well might victims prove
  Be called to their last home.

When they would have to stand before,
  The Judge of earth and heaven,
That they should make election sure,
  And have their sins forgiven.

WILSON
Printer,
Bideford.

There were several broadsides published during the time of the case. This one printed in Devon appeared before the trial.

THE LIVERPOOL TRAGEDIES

Come all you feeling Christians and listen unto me,
The like was not recorded in British history,
It's of three dreadful murders committed, I am told,
By one John Gleeson Wilson, for the sake of cursed gold.

On Wednesday the 28th, consternation did prevail,
In Leveson Street in Liverpool, where thousands did bewail,
The fate of this poor family, who we're left to deplore,
Snatched from a father's fond embraces, who ne'er will see them
more.

This monster in human shape did go there to dwell,
And that he went for plunder to all it is known full well,
And when this callous villain saw their defenceless state,
He did resolve them all to kill and rob them of the plate.

His bloody work he did commence all in the open day,
By striking at the children while their mother was away,
The servant girl did interfere, said, "should not do so,"
Then with a poker in his hand he gave her a severe blow.

Numberless times he did her strike till she could no longer stand,
The blood did flow profusely from her wounds, and did him brand,
Then the eldest boy of five years old, in supplication said,
"Oh master, spare our precious lives, don't serve us like the maid."

This darling child of five years old he brutally did kill,
Regardless of its tender cries, its precious blood did spill,
The youngest child to the kitchen ran, to shun the awful knife,
This villain followed after and took its precious life.

The surgeon thus describes the scene presented to his view,
A more appalling case than this he says he never knew,
Four human beings on the floor all weltering in their gore,
The sight was sickening to behold on entering the door.

The mother's wounds three inches deep upon her head and face,
And pools of blood as thick as mud, from all of them could trace,
None could identify the boy, his head was like a jelly;
This tragedy is worse by far than Greenacre or Kelly.

To the hospital in this sad state they quickly were conveyed,
The mother with her infant dear, and faithful servant maid,
Thousands did besiege the gates, their fate for to enquire,
But in three days from incise wounds, both of them did expire.

'Twill cause the captain many a pang to know their awful doom,
His loving wife and children sent to an untimely tomb,
'Twill make his hair turn grey with grief, no skill their lives could
save,
And he did go, borne down with woe, in sorrow to the grave.

But now he's taken for this deed, bound down in irons strong,
In Kirkdale Jail he now does lie, till his trial it comes on,
May God above receive the souls of those whom he has slain,
And may they all in heavenly bliss for ever with him reign.

– **J. Harkness, Printer, Preston**

Criminal records register of those indicted at the Assizes sessions. The entry for John Gleeson Wilson is highlighted above.

Later, Captain Hinrichson returned from Hull and resumed his maritime career. He captained further vessels and also became dock master at Toxteth, Huskisson and Queens Docks. In the year following the murders, the former home of the Hinrichsons in Leveson Street was converted into a beer-house, and many a morbid curiosity was satisfied by some who were keen to take a drink there. The front room parlour (where the maid and young Harry were murdered) was converted to a bar and tap-room, and the local press reported,

> 'We presume every party indulging in a glass of four-penny is entitled to have pointed out to him the precise spot on which the murders took place, the spots of blood etc, whilst the privilege of descending to where the villain consummated his butchery by cutting the youngest child's throat, is limited to those who luxuriate in the higher priced and more palatable description of malt liquor. However this may be, the proprietor is likely for some time to reap a good harvest'.

It may have been a profitable experience for the licencee, but for the local residents the atrocity had become a blight on their lives. Landlords and property owners were also finding their property greatly reduced, and following a local petition, a Meeting of the Health Committee in December 1850 agreed that the name Leveson Street should be changed to its original name of Grenville Street South, which remains its name to this day, giving no hint of the dreadful events of March 1849.

Further Reading

Liverpool Journal 31 March 1849, 28 April 1849, 1 September 1849, 15 September 1849 and 28 December 1850

Burke, Edmund (ed.), *The Annual Register, or a Review of the Year in History and Politics 1849,* Volume 91, p424-429 (1850)

An Account of the Murder of Mrs Henrichson at Liverpool (Wilson, Bideford, Devon. 1849)

Youd, John, 'Verses on the Trial and Sentence of John Gleeson Wilson', printed in the *Liverpool Journal*, 31 March 1849

On the Net

Old Mersey Times www.old-merseytimes.co.uk/levesonstmurder.html

Theirs is yon house that holds the parish-poor,
Whose walls of mud scarce bear the broken door;
There, where the putrid vapours, flagging, play,
And the dull wheel hums doleful through the day;
There, children dwell who know no parents' care;
Parents, who know no children's love, dwell there!
Heart-broken matrons on their joyless bed,
Forsaken wives, and mothers never wed;
Dejected widows with unheeded tears,
And crippled age with more than childhood fears;
The lame, the blind, and, far the happiest they!
The moping idiot and the madman gay.
Here too the sick their final doom receive
Here brought, amid the scenes of grief, to grieve,

– ***The Village***, George Crabbe 1773

5

The Poor Law and the Workhouse in Liverpool

By the time Crabbe wrote his mournful verses about the rural workhouse, Liverpool was no longer a village, and in marked contrast the powers that be had opened a large, fearsome looking institution on the top of Brownlow Hill overlooking the expanding town. Where the village workhouse may still have retained some sense of looking after its own, Liverpool Workhouse would swiftly earn a reputation as a place that only the truly desperate would wish to enter. This was not the first workhouse in Liverpool. In fact, its origins were to be found in the foundation of Poor Law legislation over a century earlier.

The seeds of the Poor Law are in the Elizabethan desire to remove vagrants and beggars from the streets and to introduce a legislative framework to deal with the growing problem of the poor. In 1601, during the reign of Elizabeth I, an Act of Relief of the Poor was passed which was to be the basis of Poor Law administration for the next two centuries. It divided the poor receiving relief into three categories:

(i) the able-bodied who were to have work provided for them.

(ii) the rogues, vagabonds, and beggars, who were to be whipped or otherwise punished for their unwillingness to work.

(iii) the 'impotent' poor (the old, the sick and the handicapped), who were to be relieved in almshouses.

By the provisions of the Act, each parish was made responsible for its poor. It would appoint its own Overseers of the Poor (usually the church wardens and a couple of large landowners) who would collect the poor rate. The money would then be spent in four main ways:

(i) 'for setting to work the children of all such whose parents shall not be thought able to maintain them.'

(ii) 'for setting to work all such persons married or unmarried, having no means to maintain them, and who use no ordinary or daily trade of life to get their living by' (that is, the able-bodied pauper).

(iii) 'for providing a convenient stock of flax, hemp, wood, thread, iron, and other ware, and stuff to set the poor on work'.

(iv) 'for the necessary relief of the lame, impotent, old, blind and such other among them being poor and not able to work'.

The Act also made it legal 'to erect, build and set up convenient houses or dwellings for the said impotent poor and also place inmates or more families than one in one cottage or house' - the initial authority for the erection of workhouses. A number of parishes took up this option realising there was a considerable saving to be made compared with supporting paupers within their own homes or as vagrants.

Further Acts were passed over the next two centuries to extend the administration or to prevent abuse of the system. However, there was a disparity between the size of parishes in the north of the country compared with those in the south, which was ignored in the initial implementation of the 1601 Act. Childwall, for example, comprised 9 townships, each of which were of similar size to parishes in the south. This anomaly was largely addressed by the settlement Act of 1662, which made each township responsible for its own poor, especially if they had resettled elsewhere. Parishes were permitted to send paupers back to their own parish to receive relief if they became a burden. (This stayed in place until 1945). In Liverpool, following the devastation of the Civil War (1648), displaced 'yong Children and Beggars wch…are found Wandring and begging contrarie to Lawe…' shall be 'shipt for the Barbadoes or otherwise to be put apprentices if ye belong to this Towne'. The New World was now receiving the poor of Liverpool - this was the earliest known reference to emigrants from the town. Numbers steadily increased as paupers were transported over the next century, many of whom were apprenticed for four to eleven years on plantations.

Liverpool was already acting independently of the parish of Walton-on-the-Hill (of which Liverpool was a part) in administering its own poor relief. In 1656 it was *ordered that hereafter this towne shall keep and maintaine their own poore, and that the poor of all other places shalbe kept out from begging here'.* To further reduce expenditure, a Beadle was appointed to keep out the beggars, with a bonus of 6d for every rogue whipped.

A second key development in poor law legislation was Knatchbull's General Workhouse Act of 1723, which enabled single parishes to erect a workhouse if they wished, so that they could enforce labour on the able-bodied poor in return for relief. This 'workhouse test' would enable parishes to refuse relief to those paupers who would not enter them. Nationally, the building of workhouses increased considerably under this Act, and by the end of the century their number had increased to almost 2,000, most holding between 20 to 50 inmates. In Liverpool, a small workhouse was used in Pool Lane, off South Castle Street from

1723, but as the system became more complicated and expensive, a building was erected on a plot of land behind the Bluecoat Hospital on the corner of College Lane and Hanover Street in 1732. The poor rate was reduced by a third, especially now that the poor were suffering the workhouse test and there was strict application of the law; for example, there would be no relief for the outdoor poor, unless a written order was given by the mayor or a Justice of the Peace.

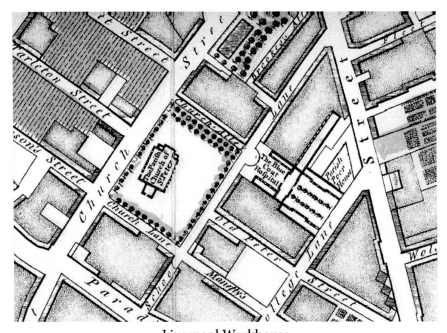

Liverpool Workhouse
An extract from Eyes Map of Liverpool 1765 which
shows the workhouse centre right

In the surrounding parishes and townships, if a workhouse existed it was usually a small cottage rented for the purpose. Records in many cases appear to no longer exist and although certain references have been found, the existence of the building itself is often still dubious. In West Derby however, we can be more certain;

the parish workhouse known as the Old Poor House, is known to have stood since 1731 on the northern side of Low Hill, near to the present site of the Coach and Horses, and was in use until the late 1830s. Other rural workhouses were known at Halewood (1723-1837), Huyton (1732), Prescot (1732-50), Speke (1742-76), and Woolton (1834-37). Others may have existed, probably for a short period, at; Allerton (1776), Childwall (1776), Ditton (1776), Hale (1776), Cronton (1770-89), and Wavertree (1776) (where a local parishioner was paid to marry a woman and take her off the poor relief!).

Halewood was a typical example where local townships largely dealt with their own poor. Records show that overseers spent money on outdoor relief, mainly distributed to the sick and unemployed on a short-term basis, and more permanently on orphans and the elderly. Paupers were boarded out for a year at a time in the community, while others received money for board, clothes, shoes, coal and services of a doctor. A copy of the new Act was purchased for 7d in 1722, following which a cottage was rented from Earl of Derby at 6d per year. Most of the overseer's time and expense was spent dealing with the problem of policing the 'settlement' issue. Inevitably, much of what is written about this period reveals the grim face of the poor law administration. Attitudes in the local townships were probably more informal and more sympathetic than those of the hard-pressed overseers of the Liverpool Vestry constantly battling against the huge demand placed upon them. As Janet Hollinshead observed in her study of eighteenth century Halewood,

'When the Overseers of the Poor could provide Hannah Hitchmough, an elderly lady, with not only her board and clothes, but also with tobacco to smoke, and when they also gathered flowers for a pauper, Samuel Stevenson's funeral, it does suggest that they knew the people concerned and that they cared'.

The West Derby Union Workhouse
The West Derby Union Workhouse, Low Hill in 1821, by William Herdman. The workhouse is the detached building to the right.

In Liverpool, it was inevitable that given the expanding size of the town and poor, the impracticalities of the 1723 law would be revealed. Consequently, following an unacceptably high level in the poor rate, outdoor relief was reintroduced as the workhouse could not cope with the numbers. In 1771 the new purpose built workhouse was opened on the outskirts of the town, high up on Brownlow Hill. Despite several alterations and additions to the building, it soon became inadequate at coping with the rapidly expanding pauper population and the poor health suffered by so many of the inmates. Six houses were added to the south-east wing in early 1777 and by November that same year a further six houses had been added to the opposite south-west wing. A new public dispensary followed in 1780, and a further four houses were opened as a small hospital block for casual paupers in 1786. A lunatic asylum, funded by public subscription was added the following year. The House of Correction was also constructed in 1780s, next to the quarry on the eastern side of the workhouse. Its purpose was to cater for those able-bodied pauper's who were, in the opinion of the authorities, reluctant to work, and the aim was to 'correct' such attitudes.

In 'Recollections of Old Liverpool' by James Stonehouse (a local man in his nineties looking back over his life's experiences), he recalled a visit to the House of Correction in the late 18th century,

'It was, in Mr. Howard's time, a most miserably managed place. In 1790 it was a vile hole of iniquity. There was a whipping-post, for instance, in the yard, at which females were weekly in the receipt of punishment. There was also 'a cuckstool,' or ducking tub, where refractory prisoners were brought to their senses, and in which persons on their first admission into the gaol were ducked, if they refused or could not pay 'a garnish.' This barbarous mode of punishment was common in Lancashire, and Cheshire.

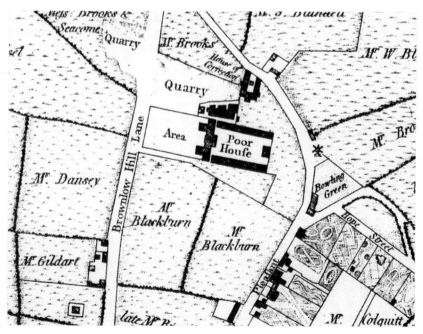

Extract from the Eyes map of Liverpool 1785 showing the new Liverpool Workhouse

The Liverpool Workhouse opened in 1771

This prison was in the course of the following years much improved, as it was found by Mr. Neild very clean and orderly through the exertions of Mrs. Widdows, the keeper. Mrs. Widdow's salary was £63 per annum. She had resolutely put down the cuckstool, and the whipping-post was becoming in a complete state of desuetude [inactivity]. A pump in the men's yard was used as a place of occasional punishment for the stubborn and refractory. The prisoners were without any instruction, secular or religious. No chaplain attended. The allowance to each prisoner was a two-penny loaf, two pounds of potatoes, and salt daily. I believe, from all I could learn, that the Liverpool prisons, bad as they undoubtedly were at the close of the last and the beginning of the present century, were in better condition than others elsewhere'.

A more formal insight in the workings of Liverpool Workhouse comes from Eden's 1797 survey of the state of the poor in England:

The parish contains 2,102 acres and in 1773 the population was 34,407; in 1790, 55,732, of whom 6,780 lived in cellars and 1,220 in the workhouse. The Poor are partly maintained in the

Workhouse, and partly relieved at home. The house is well situated on a rising ground in a detached situation, and is in many respects constructed upon an eligible plan. The old people in particular are provided with lodging in a most judicious manner. Each apartment consists of three small rooms, in which are the fire-place and 4 beds, and is inhabited by 8 or 10 persons. These habitations are furnished with beds, chairs, and other little articles of domestic use that the inmates may possess, who being thus detached from the rest of the Poor, may consider themselves as comfortably lodged as in a secluded cottage, and thus enjoy, even in a Workhouse, in some degree, the comfort of a private fireside. The most infirm live on the ground floor; others are distributed through the upper storeys. They all dine together in a large room, which occasionally serves as a chapel. The children are mostly employed in picking cotton, but are too crowded, 70 or 80 working in a small room. About 50 girls are bound apprentices in sprigging muslin. The house receives from 1s. to 2s. 6d. a week for each. A few old men are employed in boat building. Tailor's and other trades are carried on in the house. The number of persons in the house has varied from about 900 to a little less than 1,200 from 1782 to 1794. From a comparison of the house expenses in 1790 to 1794 it is clear that the annual expense of a pauper in the Liverpool Workhouse does not exceed £7, which may be considered moderate when compared with the heavy charges in other parts of England. Weekly bill of fare: Breakfast, every day—Oatmeal, hasty pudding, known as burgo, and milk. Dinner—Monday, Friday—Milk pottage and bread; Tuesday, Thursday, Saturday—Lobscouse, i.e. beef cut into small pieces and boiled with potatoes; Wednesday, Sunday—Broth, beef and bread. Supper—Monday, Tuesday, Saturday—Milk pottage and bread; Wednesday, Sunday— Broth, beef and bread; Thursday, Friday—Milk and bread. The bread is household bread. According to the table of expenses, 142½lbs. of ale and beer at 1d. per lb. are consumed every day, and about 434 gallons of sweet milk (at 8 lbs. to the gallon) every week. About 2,700 out pensioners are also relieved, at a weekly expense of £56 9s. The committee refuse relief to such poor as keep dogs.

In 1801 it became necessary to erect a Fever Hospital to the south of the main building (it was bigger than all the other Liverpool Hospitals put together) and a smallpox ward was added in 1823.

In Liverpool, where the committee of overseers had evolved into the 'Liverpool Select Vestry' in 1821, a more rigorous implementation of the Poor Law followed to combat the heavy operating cost. Abuses in relief were investigated; the labour test became more stringent; able-bodied men were put to work building roads, cultivating land, and breaking stones; while pauper inmates whitewashed cellar dwellings in the town. Meanwhile, the facilities were made even grimmer in case the punters fancied an extension to their sabbatical. Not surprisingly there was a steep drop in expenditure.

Generally, management of the Poor Law across the country was inefficient and high costs of indoor relief had led to Gilbert's Act in 1782, which provided rigid guidelines on how parishes could combine into 'unions'. The Act gave instructions on how to manage a workhouse and together with a recommended set of rules, the aim was produce standardisation as far as possible. Now the unemployed able-bodied poor would be provided first with outdoor relief and then with employment, while indoor relief in poorhouses was confined to the care of the old, sick, infirm and their dependent children.

The later years of the century saw an economic depression, where during times of extreme hardship, emergency measures were taken by parishes rather than the raising of wages by employers. The Speenhamland system introduced after 1795 was largely applied in the southern agrarian areas, where wages were brought up to subsistence level by the issue of a weekly dole. Farmers took advantage of this and lowered wages paid to their labourers, knowing that parishes would take the burden of the difference. The economic problems this caused over the following decades, attitudes to the pauper, and the demands for a right to a standardised system of relief, pressured the Government into setting up a Royal Commission in 1832 to investigate the Poor Law.

When the Commissioners concentrated their inquiry on the extra costs paid out by overseers, the replies from the parish officials in the West Derby Hundred were either unhelpful or curt. Walton, Much Woolton and West Derby, for example, paid no extra money to able-bodied men in their parishes, Toxteth Park and Everton gave little detail in their replies, while Liverpool, Ormskirk and Prescot were more forthcoming, suggesting that demands increased during the winter and relief was largely unnecessary in the vicinity of an expanding prosperous port like Liverpool. The overall conclusion of the Commission was that most of the poor were aged, infirm or widows. In the rural villages further away from the town, handloom weavers were the only major group who required relief while still in full employment, but they were quite literally a dying breed as the shift towards factory production was expanding.

The New Poor Law

Following the conclusions of the Commission, the government introduced a Bill which contained most of its recommendations, and while there was great opposition to the proposals from many quarters, there was too much disunity for it to be effective. Royal Assent was granted on 14 August 1834 and the Poor Law Amendment Act was placed on the Statute Book.

The new Act minimised the provision of outdoor relief and made confinement in a workhouse the central element of the new system. To qualify for relief, it was not sufficient for the able-bodied to be poor, they actually had to be destitute. The measure of this was their willingness to enter the workhouse, and it was originally planned that this was to be the only provision for relief. Only the truly deserving - in the opinion of the government - would be those 'desiring' to reside in such a repellent institution. To help them in their decision, the surroundings were made as unpleasant as possible as an obvious deterrent to those seeking relief.

Consequently, married couples were separated, and children taken from their parents. Overall, inmates were segregated into seven groups according to age and sex; - aged or infirm men or women; able-bodied men or women over 16; boys or girls aged 7-15; and children under seven. Each group was assigned its own day rooms, sleeping rooms and exercise yards. They could see each other, but not speak during communal meals or at chapel, and could only meet at infrequent intervals at the discretion of the guardians.

By the terms of the Act, a central administrative body was created - the Poor Law Commission, which in turn ordered that parishes were to be grouped together into poor law unions, to provide the finance to build the workhouses. Each union was to be run by professional officers under the jurisdiction of an elected Board of Guardians.

In Liverpool, opposition to the changes was vehement, the Vestry believing they were already operating in the spirit of the Law. Indeed, when Gilbert Henderson was sent to investigate Liverpool on behalf of the Commissioners, he was most impressed with what he saw. For example, he witnessed the thorough investigation each poor relief applicant was subjected to by members of the Vestry. In one morning, he saw 250 cases dealt with, most of whom were refused relief. His report to the Commissioners was a favourable one - his only complaint was that the Thursday 'liberty hours' were being scandalously abused by the paupers. The poor rate was especially looked upon in favourable light by the investigator - the national average in 1832/3 it was 9s 9d, in Liverpool in was under 4s per head.

Gilbert Henderson reported:

When visited in September 1832, Liverpool Workhouse contained 1,715 inmates, and can accommodate in winter, 1,750. The present governor has had the management about twenty-eight years: on his appointment in 1804, there were 800 inmates; no separation of the sexes, only five weaving-looms, and no other employment for the paupers beyond the necessary business of the house. The doorkeepers were paupers, who frequently took bribes for admission, and the house was altogether in a most disorderly state. The governor procured a paid doorkeeper, separated the sexes as completely as the nature of the building would permit, except in cases of married people, who had small apartments allotted to them; he also exacted from each person able to work, a reasonable portion of labour daily, for which purpose dry picking of oakum was introduced: this is a tedious and irksome process of manual labour, by which junk, old shipping-ropes cut into pieces a few inches long, is untwisted, the yarns separated and reduced to shreds by the hand and fingers, and by rubbing against the apron worn by the picker: there is nothing unwholesome or straining in this employment, but it is tiresome, and various attempts were made to evade it: one mode tried was by boiling the junk in water, after which it is easily pulled into shreds, but the ropes lose their efficacy to resist water, and consequently the oakum is unfit for caulking, its destined use. The introduction of labour thinned the house very much: it was sometimes difficult to procure a sufficient supply of junk, which was generally obtained from Plymouth; when the supply was known to be scanty, paupers flocked in; but the sight of a load of junk before the door would deter them for a length of time.

The children, nine years of age, are taught to weave, and their time is divided between school and the looms; under this system they thrive better, and the instruction they get in weaving promotes their being apprenticed. The choice of the children is complied with as far as possible in apprenticing them; some are bound to tradesmen, tailors, shoemakers, etc., some go to sea, but the largest proportion, until recently, went to cotton factories, where most of them were bound to persons of respectability; on leaving the workhouse, they are told to send information if they are not well treated. It is easy to ascertain how those fare who were apprenticed in Liverpool, and the others are visited by some of the overseers usually every year, but at all events once in the course of two years. The apprenticing and visitation of the children is occasionally adverted to in the Reports of the select vestry. Instances not unfrequently occur of individuals who have served their time with credit, calling at the workhouse or at the select vestry, and stating that they are able to earn a comfortable subsistence.

The inmates of the workhouse were formerly allowed to go out every Thursday afternoon; this permission led to many irregularities, the paupers frequently returning drunk, and begging or otherwise misconducting themselves in the streets to the scandal of the establishment. They also used to go out on Sundays to church, but a chapel has been built within the workhouse and a regulation was adopted in 1831, which restricted the liberty of leaving the house to the first Thursday afternoon in every month, except in the case of paupers upwards of sixty years of age, who are still permitted to go out every Thursday. The Catholics go out to chapel at eight every Sunday morning, and return at ten. Thus, one condition of entering this workhouse is submission to constant confinement, except for a few hours every month.

The rooms are well ventilated, floors kept clean, and sprinkled daily with chloride of lime, and the walls frequently whitewashed. Although the cholera has been so prevalent in Liverpool, only nine cases occurred up to 6 Sept 1832, in this establishment; four of these proved fatal, one being the case of a pauper who, before his admission, had been employed as a bearer of the litter in which cholera patients were carried to the hospital. The governor lays great stress on classification generally, and on a complete separation of the sexes; there are lock-wards for males and for females in this establishment, and the governor thinks them essential to prevent the most depraved inmates corrupting or annoying decent and orderly paupers: in the small houses, in which two or three married couples live together, those of congenial habits and character are placed together.

When the workhouse was visited, some of the boys and girls were busy weaving, but the greater part of them were in a spacious school-room under the chapel; their general appearance was satisfactory: the oakum-shop was almost filled by men seated on benches and picking oakum. The hours of work are from six in the morning to six in the evening in summer, and from eight until four in winter, allowing half an hour for breakfast, and one hour for dinner; persons eighty years of age and upwards are exempted from any labour, but from all under that age and in health, a task is required in proportion to their ability and strength; those who, from age or infirmity, have a limited task, are allowed to choose their own time for performing it, and used formerly to pick the oakum in their own rooms; but owing to the risk of fire, this practice has been discontinued, and all this work must now be done in the shop.

A full measure of employment is exacted from the able-bodied, the object being to discourage laziness, and, as the governor expressed it, to "work them out." The consequence is, that not more than twenty of the inmates were able-bodied men. The aged people appeared the most cheerful inmates; the avowed principle of management is to make them and the young most comfortable. The women were all employed, chiefly in sewing, attending to the young children, acting as nurses, and performing household offices.

A general appearance of order and discipline prevails throughout the establishment. The governor, who is a steady systematic man, stated that 1000 or 1800 paupers were as easily managed as 500. He has two salaried clerks, a schoolmaster, and two weavers acting as overlookers, who receive salaries; and the governor's wife has two paid female assistants; the rest of the establishment is conducted by paupers selected from the inmates.

A fever hospital, a detached building, for 140 patients, is supported by the parish, within the walls, and forms part of the workhouse establishment; the diet, wine, etc. for the patients, materially increase the general expenditure; female paupers act as nurses, and having some privileges in consequence, are usually desirous to be so employed.

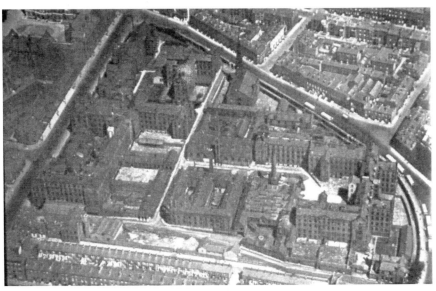

Liverpool Workhouse, Brownlow Hill
By the early 20th century the building of 1771 had expanded considerably to cater for the needs of city

Despite opposition to the New Poor Law in Liverpool, the changes finally took place in March 1841 when the Liverpool Poor Law Union was established. The Select Vestry were duly replaced by a Board of Guardians, who planned in early 1842 to reconstruct the Brownlow Hill workhouse at a cost of £52,000 to house 1,800 inmates - a figure that would soon prove to totally inadequate. However, opposition was so vigorous that an Act was passed in June the following year to exempt Liverpool from the New Poor Law Act, and the Select Vestry were given legal authority to assume the role of the Board of Guardians.

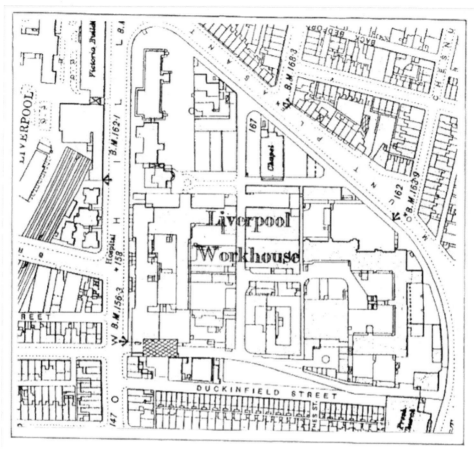

The full 'estate' shown in a map of 1905

In the surrounding rural areas and now part of suburban Liverpool, twenty-three parishes, stretching from Ince Blundell in the north, to Garston in the south, combined to form the West Derby Union, one of the largest in the country. Formed in 1837, it was to be run by a Board of Guardians, the members of which were elected representatives from each parish. That same year the Poor Law Commissioners despatched their first order to the West Derby Union instructing them that under the terms of the new Act the united parishes should, 'contribute and be assessed to a common fund for purchasing, building, hiring or providing, altering or enlarging any workhouse or other place for the reception and relief of the poor of such Parishes.'

The Guardians immediately declared that the old parish poor houses, now under their jurisdiction, were totally inadequate to cater for the demands of the new legislation. A search was begun to find a site suitable for the erection of a new workhouse, large enough to provide accommodation for the poor of the entire West Derby Union.

Before the end of the decade, the Board had succeeded in purchasing land from Thomas Shaw, lying either side of Mill Lane in Kensington among the local sandstone quarries and brick-fields. By 1841, the workhouse was complete and the transfer of inmates from the Old Poor House on Low Hill took place during the summer of that year. This was the first occupation of the Mill Road Institution, although it soon suffered a setback when the building caught fire in March 1843, damaging a considerable quantity of clothing and bedding.

No sooner had the occupants moved out of the Old Poor House, than the Liverpool Select Vestry applied in March 1842 to rent the building to alleviate the overcrowding at Brownlow Hill. The rent was payable quarterly at a rate of £80 per year, which seems to have been misappropriated by Mr Dolling, the Overseer of West Derby. A considerable sum considering he probably earned around the same figure each year.

The new Mill Road Workhouse of the West Derby Union was barely complete before it was realised that it was already too small. The Guardians soon pressed the new Poor Law Board for permission to extend the site. Their calls however, went unheeded until the Poor Law Board permitted a makeshift measure which entailed the erection of a new chapel and school (on the site later occupied by the Nurses' Home), thereby providing room for additional dormitories in the main block, which formerly housed such facilities. Further alterations were carried out after additional space was created following the Guardians' resolution to send all sick patients to the fever hospital in Netherfield Road. Such fated patients were occupying precious workhouse accommodation.

It was intended that the 'fever sheds' and 'any other spare rooms' were to be used as workshops, 'in which competent persons would be employed in the instruction of the boys in some useful trade or occupation'. The men were not to be left idle either, the Guardians added, 'further, that a quantity of land be taken in the neighbourhood for spade husbandry to employ adult and able-bodied paupers'.

Problems caused by the lack of suitable accommodation for the sick came to a head in 1852, when it was decided to build a new hospital fronting West Derby Road (on a site now lying between Home Street and Hygeia Street). It would be known as West Derby Union Workhouse Hospital. No illustrations or views of Mill Road Workhouse (or the Hospital) appear to exist, and nothing survives regarding personal accounts. However, in the early 1860s, the Reverend John Jones, a congregational minister from Kirkdale, who was convinced that 99% of pauperism was due to the temptation of alcohol, set out on a mission to prove his case. In search of evidence, he inevitably toured the three workhouses of the locality; Liverpool (Brownlow Hill), Toxteth (now Sefton General) and West Derby (Mill Road). At last we have a first-hand account of what lay within;

> 'We come first of all to the West Derby Union Workhouse. As we pass in through the gate, a building of moderate proportions stands before us. We have seen structures having a far more imposing aspect; but still how unlike it is to the "Parish Poor House" which the poet has revealed to us'.

After comparing what he saw with the image conjured up by the poet Crabbe's description of the pitiful rural poor house, he moved inside and again noted the contrast:

'How different the scene around it is! Here we have commodious and amply lit apartments, made cheerful by blazing fires, while the floor, and tile walls, and the furniture, in point of cleanliness, must please the most fastidious, and be found to meet the requirements of the most stringent of sanitary officers.

And here, too, are the men and women with their uniform attire, some of them more or less decrepit, forming themselves into a circle around the fire; others more active, standing or moving about; and others darning stockings or sewing a garment.

But here is another class - these are bedridden most of them will probably rise up no more. How feeble does this one look, how wan the other; how distressing the cough of a third; they feel they have come to the workhouse to die, but they seem resigned to their fate and thankful for the care and attention bestowed upon them. But for such a provision they know it would fare badly with them, huddled up as they would be in some corner of a dark cellar on a heap of straw; but here they repose on a comfortable couch, attended to by the nurse, cared for by the doctor ministered by the chaplain, and often cheered by the kind look and word of the governor: Yes, they may well indeed feel thankful that their last days shall pass away under such circumstances, although a pauper's burial and a pauper's grave await them...'

A not too distressing account, compared to contemporary descriptions of the horrors witnessed at the notorious Brownlow Hill workhouse, and far removed from Dickensian imagery. (Especially those scenes described in Oliver Twist and his requests for more gruel).

In Brownlow Hill, scores of sick persons in every stage of nearly every known illness (a large proportion of them incurable or very old and entirely helpless) were nursed, if it could be called nursing, by able-bodied pauper women selected from the adult wards of the Workhouse. Seldom of reliable or compassionate character, it is unlikely that any of the 'nurses' had received formal training. In 1865, Agnes Jones, a Nightingale nurse who tried to improve the nursing at Liverpool Workhouse wrote:

'I am almost distracted between sickness and anxiety and drunkenness. I have one head nurse in great danger. These ex-pauper women whom we are training were paid their wages on Friday, and the next day five came in tips... How little I can do!'

At Mill Road, similar problems were encountered. Several times nurses were dismissed for drunkenness or fighting on the ward. In September 1863 for example, Elizabeth Hamilton, a nurse on the fever ward was finding the horrors of her job too much. The ward was already over capacity and patients were being turned away and sent to the Netherfield Road fever hospital. Temptation proved her undoing and she sought solace in the entire supply of wines and spirits which had been ordered for the patients under her care. Not surprisingly, she was found in an extreme state of drunkenness while on duty, whereupon she was given a month's notice to leave her £18 a year job.

Within three years of her arrival in Liverpool, Agnes Jones had worked herself to death, dying from typhoid contracted from the victims under her care. Nevertheless, her work was carried on, and Liverpool Select Vestry resolved to adopt her reforms in the Brownlow Hill workhouse.

Florence Nightingale said of her:

'In less than three years she reduced one of the most disorderly populations in the world to something like Christian discipline.

She converted the Liverpool Select Vestry to the conviction, as well as the humanity; of nursing the pauper sick by trained nurses, the first instance of its kind in England.'

The squalid conditions of a typical Liverpool court

Three Unions

It was clear that the West Derby Union was far too large to manage efficiently, therefore Toxteth Park Union was formed on 13 May 1857 to lift the increasing burden being placed upon the Mill Road Workhouse. A new workhouse for Toxteth was erected in Smithdown Road which could take 600 paupers, plus a further 100 in its new Infirmary (later Sefton General Hospital). To further alleviate the cramped conditions at Mill Road, the Guardians placed an advertisement in the local press in May 1862, indicating their desire to secure land of not less than 20 acres, on which they intended to erect a new workhouse. It had been reported that:

'...the present workhouse has long been inadequate to the requirements of a rapidly increasing Union... the Guardians have for years been patching and adding to a building which was originally never contemplated to afford accommodation for a Union containing 156,000 inhabitants and provide accommodation for a rapidly increasing number of casual wayfarers which exceeded 4,000 during the last six months.'

Within a couple of months, 37 acres belonging to the Earl of Sefton situated at Walton-on-the-Hill, had been purchased at a cost of just over £11,000. The Guardians had already sold the West Derby Union Hospital on West Derby Road for the same figure and intended to raise a similar sum to cover the costs of the new building by the sale of Mill Road.

The first stone of Walton Workhouse was laid on 29 March 1864, by Thomas Haigh, Chairman of the West Derby Union Board of Guardians. The work on the new building (later to become known as Walton Hospital) was expected to take four years.

During October and November of 1867, Mr Crane, an Officer from the Poor Law Board, visited the local workhouses of Liverpool, Toxteth and West Derby, in order to report on their condition. His report on Mill Road Workhouse described the workings shortly before their transfer to Walton,

'...the workhouse is wholly, insufficient for the wants of the Union. By the removal of the schools and by other means, it has been of the most part converted into a hospital and infirmary. Nevertheless, it is not large enough even for the sick and infirm poor. No detached infirmary seems to have been erected, nor is there any detached fever hospital. Contagious and infectious cases are placed in separate wards in the main building. At present, there are 427 cases on the medical list. There is no resident medical officer, but 2 medical officers constantly attend. There are 15 resident nurses with salaries varying from £15-30 per year with rations etc. for each. Four of these act as cost night nurses. The Guardians provide all drugs at about £400 a year. They have also appointed a dispenser who is in attendance during the whole of each day. The fever wards especially are too full. Great attention is evidently bestowed on ventilation, which is effectively kept up as far as possible: and the utmost cleanliness prevails throughout the establishment. It is only by such precautions that so large a number of cases have hitherto been congregated with safety in so limited a space.'

And, regarding Walton,

'I visited the new workhouse which is in an advanced state. It is highly desirable that the new hospitals there should be completed with as little delay as possible, so that the sick may be removed from the old workhouse and placed under the care of a medical officer who should reside in the new workhouse and devote his whole time to the duties of his office'.

Walton Workhouse was formally opened on 15 April 1868, at a final cost including the land purchase, of £65,000. It had accommodation for 1,000 'inmates' and was almost full by the opening day. The former Mill Road inmates enjoyed a 'good dinner and a half pint of ale each (oranges for the youngsters), and tobacco and snuff for the aged'. During the afternoon, guests toured the building to the accompaniment of various airs played by the juvenile band of the workhouse. Later that night, dignitaries dined at the Adelphi Hotel where the Chairman of the Guardians praised the Union with an oratory of self-glorification, concluding:

'No doubt in many of the metropolitan workhouses the poor were harshly and unfairly treated, but in the provinces workhouses were as a rule, fairly and charitably conducted.'

As we have seen in both Brownlow Hill and Mill Road, even before Walton opened it was realised that space would soon be short. Consequently, Mill Road Workhouse, originally due to be sold to help fund the new Walton institution, was reprieved. While the new workhouse was under construction, a programme of alteration was put into operation to turn Mill Road into a workhouse hospital for the sick poor to help prevent the anticipated strain on the hospital wards at Walton. After the transfer of inmates in 1868, the conversion plan was stepped up on the now vacated building.

The period of transition was difficult. Wards had to be opened at Mill Road earlier than expected when smallpox became rife at Walton in 1870. The Board of Guardians issued a directive in January 1871 ordering the Medical Officer to vaccinate all children in the Mill Road workhouse, '...*as soon as practicable after admission or birth, and do give to the Master certificates stating the cause why any particular child cannot be vaccinated*'.

The following week, the Guardians took a step further in an attempt to control the spread of infection, when a special sub-committee entitled 'the Smallpox and Infectious Diseases Committee' was formed, which was given full powers to 'act as they may deem most advisable in the present emergency.' (The emergency being described as an epidemic of smallpox and relapsing fever). Meanwhile, the board found time to send a petition to Parliament objecting to the Bill presently in the Commons, which called for the prevention of the removal of poor persons to Ireland. The ramifications for workhouses would be considerable should such legislation be placed on the Statute Book. Greatly affected would be the Liverpool workhouses, which had witnessed a massive influx of Irish since the 1840s, the majority of whom were now consigned to poverty.

Boards of Guardians had the power to send paupers back to the parish from which they came, unless that parish paid for their upkeep in the workhouse of their new abode. Not a penny would be spent on those who did not qualify for relief within that Union. Nor were the Guardians averse to sending paupers abroad to the colonies. Canada was their usual choice. In April 1884, the Board decided that '*the several poor persons… being desirous of emigrating to Canada, the necessary steps to be immediately taken to effect the emigration and that a sum not exceeding £14 .3.0d be expended for each person upon the common fund of the Union…*' The oldest of these poor persons was sixteen, and the youngest, a girl aged four and a boy just two. It begs the question how children aged two and four, without parents, could 'desire' to sail on a crowded boat halfway across the world into the unknown. This was not an isolated incident; several transportations were underwritten by the West Derby Board before the end of the century, in an effort to alleviate the 'burden' they placed on the Union.

One man in particular, however, was concerned about transportation. Harris P. Cleaver, Clerk to the West Derby Guardians and a man noted for his devotion to his work (his father had been the Clerk before him, from 1847 until his death in 1880), had deep reservations regarding the transportation of such young children. Fearing for their treatment, he travelled to Canada at his own expense to investigate their situation.

So distressed was he at what he observed regarding the condition under which many of the children were living, that upon his return he persuaded the Guardians to discontinue this policy and to find an alternative to keeping the children in the workhouse. A short while later, funding was made available, and in the late 1880s the Cottage Homes were opened in Fazakerley to house school children. Liverpool Select Vestry followed suit and shortly afterwards a similar scheme was carried out to erect Olive Mount Children's Homes. The West Derby Union widened their facilities for children when a Children's Convalescent Home was opened in Heswall later to be renamed the Cleaver Sanatorium.

The spectre of incurable disease lay over the workhouse for a greater part of half a century following the opening of Mill Road. Due to widespread squalor, poverty, and poor sanitary conditions, smallpox, cholera and typhoid claimed thousands of victims. Even for those illnesses that could be treated, medicines were in short supply and cases would be referred to professional vaccinators, who had to provide their own drugs. Even the post of Medical Officer was hardly a position of autonomy. The final word on many decisions frequently lay with the Guardians - while action would rarely be determined until the following board meeting. Consider the ludicrous situation caused by this procedure when such lay people (none of whom had a medical qualification between them), were required to give authorisation to the M.O. to 'amputate the foot of a woman named Smith, an inmate of Mill Road Workhouse'.

Nevertheless, the latter years of the nineteenth century were a period of great medical progress, and together with new attitudes within the nursing profession, foundations were being laid to take care for the sick and poor into the twentieth century. Many new institutions, taking advantage of modern developments and techniques, were being opened in Liverpool - such as the Royal Southern (rebuilt in 1872), the Hospital for Women in Shaw Street (1883), the Homeopathic (1884), and the new Royal Infirmary (1890). Workhouse Infirmaries, however, were clearly not at the forefront of such developments, yet change was undoubtedly necessary.

Despite the fact that Mill Road had been reprieved and altered to take on a new roll in the early 1870s, it was becoming increasingly obvious that the building was inadequate, outdated, and above all, unhealthy. There was no alternative. It would have to be condemned. The old building had, in the past, been adapted where possible, but it was generally agreed that they had gone as far as they could along that road and a completely new purpose built establishment was necessary to provide modern hospital facilities.

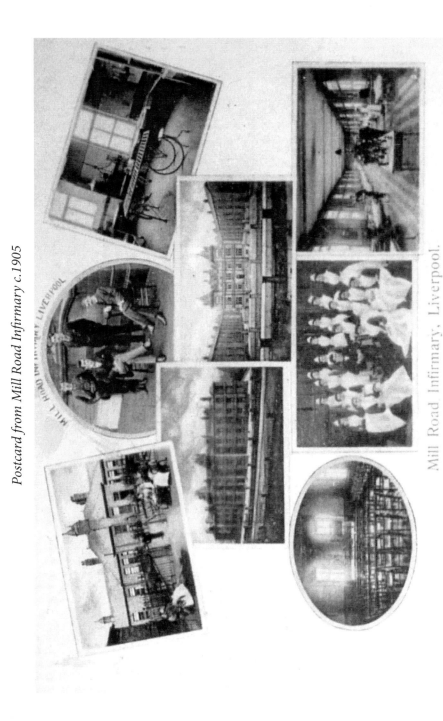

Postcard from Mill Road Infirmary c.1905

124

The old building was pulled down in its entirety, leaving only the detached Lower Hospital for 'imbeciles' (built in the 1850s) at the rear of the main block close to Atwell Street. The sick patients, meanwhile, were transferred to the Test House in Belmont Road, the vagrant workhouse of the West Derby Union (later known as Newsham General Hospital). The foundation stone for the new building was formally laid on 18 March 1891.

As work continued into the mid-1890s, Mr Jenner-Fust, the Local Government Board Inspector, told the West Derby Guardians at their weekly meeting in March 1893, that *the Mill Road Infirmary when quite completed would be one of the best specimens of a workhouse infirmary in the country'*. 'Workhouse' was the crucial word. The new venture, although a modern building, was still not up to the standard of the voluntary hospitals, and it would be another 50 years before it came anywhere near losing the 'poor relation' tag among its regional counterparts.

Poverty in England throughout the Victorian period was largely equated with immorality, irreligion and intemperance. Furthermore, there was little chance of overturning a poor law which was outdated and based on a profound misconception of the causes of poverty at its introduction. It was ironic that when another local civil servant, Mr Holding commented,

> '...party politics are coming more and more to the one thing - to the idea of social reform - we are getting nearer and nearer every year to the idea that the young and the old who cannot work and cannot keep themselves have a right to be kept by the community...',

he was merely outlining the provision of the Old Poor Law, which had been so ruthlessly cast aside over fifty years earlier.

The initial care of the destitute fell largely on the shoulders of the parish doctor, who worked for a meagre salary in impossible conditions. They could admit serious cases to the Poor Law hospitals but it was less easy to admit patients to the better equipped voluntary hospitals. Even as late as 1909, the stigma and fear attached to the workhouse infirmary showed no sign of abatement;

> '...the parish doctor is always available. But the poor do not like the parish doctor and they will adopt any device rather than summon him. They dread what they know to be too often the burden of his message: 'You must go into the Workhouse Hospital'. Of course, we know it is very silly of them to dread the workhouse hospital but that does not alter the fact that they do dread it and that they dread the parish doctor...'

The respectable poor preferred to endure almost any degree of neglect or misery at home rather than be sent to the workhouse.

Dissatisfaction with the Poor Law and disagreement over its objectives again led to the setting up of a Royal Commission in 1905. It concentrated on the relevance of the old Act within a modern urban industrial society, how far charity was funding areas originally covered by the Act, and to what extent new welfare agencies were undermining the provisions of the Poor Law.

The Commission found it impossible to find common ground as a united body, issuing conflicting Majority and Minority Reports in 1909. Both were ignored by the Liberal government, but the Local Government Board responded to them by tightening up its administration, especially regarding indoor relief, while Asquith prophesied, *'You will find that Boards of Guardians will die hard'*. Meanwhile, 'Lloyd George's Ambulance Wagon', that vast programme of social reform which might eventually make the Poor Law unnecessary, gained momentum, but the opportunity to finally bury the 1834 Act was squandered. Over the next three decades the Poor Law was gradually dismantled. Already in 1908, the Children's Act had given local authorities new powers to keep under privileged children out of the workhouse. On New Year's Day 1909, old-age pensions were introduced; in the same year labour exchanges were set up to help anyone without work find a job, and in 1911 the National Health Insurance Act was passed which provided state benefit for sickness and maternity. The term 'workhouse' was dropped in 1913 in favour of 'Poor Law Institution' and indoor relief was increasingly confined to the 'helpless poor'; children, old people and the sick.

In the West Derby Union, in an attempt to improve administration and financing of what was now three unions operating in the same city, the West Derby Union was enlarged by its amalgamation with the Select Vestry of Liverpool and the Township of Toxteth Park. This merger formally commenced on 1 April 1922 by the terms of the Liverpool Corporation Act passed the previous year. The new authority would operate under the retained name of the West Derby Union. Chamberlain's Local Government Act of 1929 was the death knell for the Poor Law. Unions and their Boards of Guardians were finally swept aside and responsibility for the destitute passed to the new Public Assistance Committees within County and Borough Councils. So began a difficult period of transition in the face of Local Government cuts and stringent economies in Liverpool, where demonstrations and riots against the tough measures occurred as early as 1931. After 1929, municipal hospitals, which had previously been run by Poor Law Unions, combined with voluntary hospitals to provide hospital care through the 1930s and into the war years.

With the election of the Labour Government in 1945, came the introduction of the Welfare State, based on the recommendations of the 1942 Beveridge Report. Social care would be from 'the cradle to the grave' and with its sweeping reforms and the formation of the NHS on 5 July 1948, the Poor Law was well and truly consigned to history.

Further Reading

Oxley, G. W., 'The Permanent Poor in South West Lancashire under the Old Poor Law' in *Liverpool and Merseyside* **ed. Harris, J.R.,** p16-49, Frank Cass, London (1969)

Royden, M. W. *The People's Hospital - A History of Mill Road* (1993) Liverpool

Midwinter, E. C. 'Liverpool and the New Poor Law' in *Old Liverpool,* Devon, David & Charles (1971)

King, C. D., The Liverpool Brownlow Hill Institution, in *'The Poor Law and After: workhouse hospitals and public welfare',* Journal of the *Liverpool Medical History Society* (1999)

On the Net

Higginbothom, Peter, www.workhouses.org

6

Lewis's of Liverpool

The Story of an Iconic Store

When the receivers were called in to the owners of Lewis's of Liverpool in early 2010, it marked the beginning of the end in the slow demise of the iconic and much loved department store. But it wasn't the first time in recent years that Lewis's had hit trouble, as the company went into administration in 1991, only to suffer the indignity of being taken over by its century old rivals Owen Owen. The business limped on through a variety of re-launches and attempts at modernisation, but after 154 years of trading, Lewis's closed its doors for the final time on 29 May 2010. Since then, the building has been gutted and is now an integral part of a new development project, the Central Village, which also incorporates the adjacent site of Central Station, turning the area into seven-acre complex comprising retail, leisure, and residential facilities. A far cry from the vision of founder David Lewis, but one he may well have embraced to take the store into a new century with a modern outlook.

Lewis's Department Store was established as far back as 1856, when David Lewis founded his small clothing shop in 44 Ranelagh Street, and by his death in 1885 it had become the largest department store in Liverpool. David Levy, as he was originally known, was born in London in 1823, the son of Wolfe Levy, an immigrant Jewish merchant from Germany. At fifteen, David moved to Liverpool in 1839, sent by his father to take up an apprenticeship with the tailoring firm of Benjamin Hyam & Company, and within 18 months he was manager of the Liverpool branch. He Anglicised his name from Levy to Lewis, and shortly after he was trusted with opening new branches in Scotland and Ireland, while supervising existing branches. His home was in heart of Chinatown in 55 Kent Street, and by 1851 it had evolved into a large lodging house, where he had given accommodation to several of his staff of 'draper's assistants'. Five years later in 1856, at the age of thirty-two, he had decided to strike out on his own and took premises in 44 Ranelagh Street, Liverpool, where he opened his Gent's Tailoring Shop, selling men's and boy's clothing, most of which were made in his own workshop. This first shop was quite small at only 24 feet long with a single entrance onto the main street, and with his slogan 'Lewis's are the Friends of the People' he set out to forge a good relationship with his customers, mainly the working class, for whom he was producing top quality ready-made goods.

Later that same year, now with good prospects ahead of him, he travelled to Dover where he was to be married. His new wife was Bertha Cohen, the daughter of Reverend Raphael Isaac Cohen. Bertha and her sister Theresa were born in Hamburg and came to England shortly afterwards, but while still infants their mother died, and the sisters were sent back to Hamburg for schooling and to be cared for by family, returning to their father when their education was complete. Her marriage to David Lewis took place on 6 September 1856, at Sussex House, the Jewish boarding school and part-time synagogue founded by her father in Dover, who also performed the ceremony.

130

David Lewis

They returned to Liverpool, where David continued work in Ranelagh Street, while he and his wife moved into a large town-house at 16 Upper Canning Street, in a leafy Georgian Terrace on the plateau above the town, an expanding salubrious area populated by the merchant and professional classes. (Only a short section of the street remains, the rest of it now under the Liverpool Women's Hospital, but the rest of this Georgian suburban landscape remains very well preserved – in fact, Liverpool has more Georgian town housing still existing anywhere in England, outside of London). In 1861 the in-laws had come to stay – Bertha's parents and her sister were visiting from Dover during Easter, while also living in the house was David's nephew, Benjamin Levy. Bertha's family were frequent visitors, but it was during a stay in 1865 that her father died. He was buried in the Liverpool Jewish Cemetery in Deane Road.

As a businessman, David Lewis established strong ethics from the outset - he refused to haggle; he would fix a low price and stick to it; he did not give credit; he was always willing to exchange unsatisfactory goods; he never borrowed money; and he always fed his profits back into the business. This may have proved a hindrance in maintaining large stocks, but it did prevent insolvency. In 1859, he began a new venture in the fashionable Bold Street, where he opened new premises – by 1864 they had earned a reputation for selling all the latest women's fashions from London and Paris. In the meantime, while these new ventures were doing so well, he was gradually buying up the adjacent buildings either side of the original Ranelagh Street premises, thereby extending trade into a much larger store with several departments, which included women's shoes by 1874 and tobacco by 1879. A rooftop clock tower was added, which became a notable local landmark.

View of Lewis's good house of business in Ranelagh Street, Liverpool, where the public are provided with the very best articles, all at fair princes - Illustrated London News, February 1883

After a trip to Paris in 1877, where Betha's sister was now living with her new husband, David returned home full of ideas and inspiration after taking in the shops and fashions of the city. He quickly set to work on his latest venture, a new store called 'Bon Marché', located a few yards down from Lewis's in Basnett Street (where it runs into Church Street). This was a separate store with a different outlook and clientele, specialising in women's fashion and

Lewis's Bon Marché store

novelty items, and also contained space for exhibitions. Inside the shop, there was even a model of the Strasbourg Cathedral clock to add to the style. He also opened one of the world's first 'Christmas grottoes' there in 1879, which he called '*Christmas Fairyland*'. This was Lewis's first real adventure in trying to give punters a whole new shopping experience.

As success grew, he began to look further afield and invested in new stores in Manchester, Birmingham and Sheffield. The Manchester shop opened in Market Street in 1877, purpose built with six departments, later extended to cater in fresh groceries. Later, they specialised in velveteen, and trade was so successful that a mail order section was introduced. By 1885 the building had grown to seven floors with a full-scale ballroom on the fifth floor, which was also used for exhibitions. The huge store in Birmingham was opened in 1885 on Corporation Street, initially specialising in women's fashion. It was not all success however, Lewis's opened a fourth store in Sheffield in 1884 but due to a local recession it proved unprofitable and closed in 1888.

His contacts in the Liverpool shipping community brought added benefits – he was able to buy direct, cutting out the middle men, thereby making many luxury goods affordable for the working classes. It has been suggested that Lewis was even responsible for tea becoming the national drink, as his 2 shilling tea was cheaper than all other chains, and flew off the shelves.

While his competitors were often slow or reluctant to spend money on advertising, Lewis had no such qualms, and by the 1880s as much as 10% of gross profits were being pumped into both in his Liverpool and Manchester stores to cover publicity. In 1869 he began publication of handy memorandum books costing a halfpenny, with cover advertising and inserts, and in 1882, keen on improving the education of the labouring classes, he launched his *'Penny Readings'*, with extracts from contemporary writers such as Dickens, making books cheaply available to the masses.

Another stroke of genius involved the most unlikely of ventures. The *SS Great Eastern,* Brunel's giant iron sailing steam ship – by far the largest ship ever built at the time of her 1858 launch - was a frequent visitor to the Mersey, but towards the end of her working life she was laid up in Milford Haven, South Wales.

On 28 October 1885, the ship was put up for auction. Louis S. Cohen, Lewis's Managing Director, made a private offer of £20,000 for the ship, but this was rejected by the owners, and the auction went ahead. Cohen was out-bid by an offer of £26,200 paid by Edward de Mattos of London Traders Ltd, who intended sending the vessel to Gibraltar as a coal hulk. Cohen still sensed an opportunity, and offered to charter the ship for a year, on condition that it was made available for the 'Liverpool Exhibition of Navigation, Travelling, Commerce and Manufactures' to be held in 1886. This was accepted and he then arranged for a party of 200 to travel on board from Milford Haven to Liverpool to arrive in time for the exhibition.

However, what might have started out as a wonderful idea for a cruise along the coast to Liverpool with friends and business associates aboard, soon deteriorated into a nightmare. It had taken four days to make her ready to sail, not least the removal of 300 tons of marine growth from the hull. The paddle engines failed continuously, and much time was spent patching leaks. The first attempt to sail her out of port failed, and it was put off until the following day when she made it out at a sluggish five knots. No sooner was she out at sea, that her engines failed again and holes were found in the steam pipes. Passengers even arranged for telegrams to be taken ashore to let friends and relatives know they were still alive. The fire alarm sounding the next day when rotten wood fell onto the boilers seemed to confirm they were on a journey to hell. Thankfully, the fire was quickly extinguished, and after a journey around the north-west coast of Wales, the ship sailed up the Mersey on 1 May 1886 to be greeted by a quarter of a million people lining the banksides to watch the arrival of the famous vessel.

Meanwhile, painters and sign writers had been busy throughout the trip, and by the time she graced the river, there were a number of advertisements adorning the ship's sides. On the port side towards Birkenhead the spectators were faced with:

LADIES SHOULD VISIT LEWIS'S BON MARCHE
CHURCH STREET

while on the starboard side towards the stern facing Liverpool was:

LEWIS'S ARE THE FRIENDS OF THE PEOPLE

and towards the bows:

RANELAGH STREET LEWIS'S BON MARCHE
LIVERPOOL BASNETT STREET,
MANCHESTER, SHEFFIELD, BIRMINGHAM

and finally on the paddle box:

THE BON MARCHE LIVERPOOL

with Lewis's name in 30 feet high letters.

She proceeded to her mooring at New Ferry (until recently there was pub opposite the mooring called the *Great Eastern* with memorabilia recovered when she was broken up) where they now had six days to convert her for Lewis's grand scheme. The company converted the ship into a floating entertainment palace. The former cable laying tanks were converted into 'Music Halls', a bar was installed in the Grand Saloon and a dining room in the Ladies saloon. To provide entertainment for the expected crowds, stalls and sideshows were spread around the ship, while a group of trapeze artists performed their act between the Tuesday and Wednesday masts. A souvenir booklet was available on board, and for the price of 1d, punters could have a screen print of pictures of 'Lewis's Great Establishments', plus the *Great Eastern* printed on their own handkerchiefs - yet another clever advertising ploy. The whole venture was a roaring success and in the first month alone 50,000 people paid 1 shilling (5p) to go aboard, while another 20,000 visited over the four days of the Whitsun Bank Holiday. They operated it for the duration of the Exhibition and in total half a million visitors were welcomed to enjoy the on-board amusements. Very few companies and owners made money out of this mammoth vessel, but Lewis's had applied their golden touch here too.

Within a couple of years, the Great Eastern had gone, but after being towed to the Clyde and back searching for a shipyard to take her, she returned to be beached at Rock Ferry and was broken up by 1889. Her top mast survives; it was later purchased by Liverpool Football Club to use as a flag pole and still stands at the Kop End in Anfield.

*Great Eastern anchored in the Mersey at New Ferry during her use
in advertising Lewis's Department Store 1886...*

*...and a special screen printed handkerchief to mark
the occasion, available on board*

But the purpose of her charter by Lewis's was to be a part of the 'Liverpool International Exhibition of Navigation, Travelling Commerce and Manufacturers' in 1886. This was the first international exhibition in Britain outside London, and after nine months' preparation it was opened by Queen Victoria on 11 May 1886. David Lewis, along with some of his rivals in local retail, such as G. H. Lee and Owen Owen, was one of the guarantors, while other major contributions came from White Star Line owner Thomas Ismay and the Earl of Derby.

The site was on 35 acres of land purchased from the Edge Lane Hall estate, just east of Wavertree Park and the Botanic Gardens in Edge Hill. The centrepiece was an iron and glass pavilion with a 100' high dome, purchased from Antwerp where it had served as their International Exhibition Hall. Access to the site was provided by a new road - Exhibition Road - built between Wavertree Road and Edge Lane. (The Littlewoods building was later built along part of its course). The London and North West Railway even built a new branch line from Edge Hill with a temporary station (also called Exhibition Road) adjoining the grounds for the benefit of visitors, and it was here too that the Queen arrived. After she was met by the band of the Grenadier Guards playing *Rule Britannia*, she noted that they and her guard of honour had been standing for several hours in the relentless rain, and she promptly decreed that overcoats be added to their uniform.

The array of these exhibits was quite astonishing. Local ship owners and merchants of Liverpool built a 50' high pavilion containing dozens of examples of their typical imports. There was all manner of maritime exhibits, including telegraphy, torpedo boats, marine tricycles, lifesaving equipment, and numerous maritime inventions. There was even a full-size replica of the Eddystone lighthouse, 170' high, and at night its beam could be seen 40 miles away. There were commercial and science exhibitions and a large section given over to air travel where a cigar shaped 'captive balloon' ascended to 250 feet every hour on the hour, driven by a *'Dr. Woellfort, aeronaut'*. There were daily events and parades, concerts, marching bands, light shows, and parades of animals from a local city zoo, and Japanese rickshaws transported visitors round the 35 acre site. The exhibition closed on 8th November. The pavilion was dismantled in 1900 and the site is now part of Liverpool Innovation Park.

Liverpool International Exhibition, 1886

But tragically, David Lewis did not see the spectacle of the *Great Eastern*, nor the Exhibition on which he had spent so much time and investment. He had passed away at home five months previously, on 4 December 1885, after a long illness and was interred in the Liverpool Jewish Cemetery in Deane Road. He left an estate valued at just over £125,000. He and Bertha did not have children, but members of both sides of the family had been involved in the business for some years, and Bertha's nephew Louis Samuel Cohen, succeeded David as head of the family business. He was born in Sydney, Australia in 1846 and had married David Lewis's neice May Levy, who had also been born in New South Wales in Maitland, after David's brother Benjamin had emigrated there.

During David Lewis's life his advantageous position enabled him to make bequests to numerous charitable causes and he had gained a reputation as a philanthropist. He headed the local subscription list for the persecuted Jews of Russia, and gave large sums in support of the Liverpool synagogue. After his death, the residue of his estate was left to his brother in Sydney, Australia, Lewis Wolfe Levy, but after Lewis's death the estate was split equally between his nephew, Benjamin Wolfe Levy, of Maitland, New South Wales, and B. W. Levy's brother-in-law, Mr. George Judah Cohen. The inheritance was put into trust for charitable purposes in Liverpool and Manchester, in accordance with the expressed wishes of David Lewis. As one of the executors, Benjamin Wolfe Levy founded the David Lewis Trust in 1893 and two committees were set up for both Liverpool and Manchester. Shortly afterwards, a concerned group of people in Manchester applied for funding to provide a facility for people with epilepsy. The Manchester Committee decided to support this venture and purchased land in Alderley Edge. The David Lewis Centre for Epileptics was opened in 1904 on the site and still operates very successfully today, providing exceptional education and support to individuals with epilepsy, autism and complex learning disabilities.

In Liverpool, the committee began to look at the predicament of the Northern Hospital. By the 1880s it was in such poor condition that the only alternative was for it be demolished and a new hospital erected. With the financial support of the David Lewis Trust, a new hospital was planned and the foundation stone was laid on 19th October 1896. The building was opened on 13th

March 1902 as the David Lewis Northern Hospital, and occupied a site bounded on one side by Great Howard Street and on the other by Leeds Street. (The hospital finally closed its doors in 1978 prior to the opening of the new Royal Liverpool Hospital).

The Liverpool executors then founded the David Lewis Hotel and Club Association in 1906, on the corner of Great George Street and Upper Parliament Street, initially as a place for seafarers, but it also served as neighbourhood centre for the Liverpool docklands. It had sports facilities and recreation rooms, and the 'David Lewis Theatre' - which could hold a thousand people - was added to the main building. The theatre staged concerts for the local community and later doubled up as a cinema after gaining its licence in 1914. After serving the community for several decades it was finally demolished in 1980 and the site redeveloped.

The Great Fire at Lewis's - 1.30am 24 December 1886
The view is towards Ranelagh Street and Fairclough Street corner

After the death of her husband, Bertha continued to live in their Princes Park home until 1890, when she moved to the south of France to be near her sister Theresa, who had become her closest companion. In 1896, she moved to Boulogne-sur-Mer, where she died, just a few weeks before she was due to lay the foundation stone of the new David Lewis Northern Hospital in Liverpool. Bertha was brought home and laid to rest alongside her husband in the Liverpool Jewish Cemetery.

As if in a final act of the demise of the founding father, the Liverpool Lewis's store caught fire in 1886 and was gutted by the blaze. But as a testament to the strength of the family and the company, recovery was swift, and Lewis Cohen began to preside over a period of consolidation. As a teenager, he had arrived in London from his home in Australia to be educated before his expected entry into the family business. He attended Edmonton House, followed by University College, after which he moved to Liverpool in 1864. In 1869 he returned to London to marry May, bringing her back to Liverpool where they set up their antipodean home-from-home in 62 Sefton Terrace, Princes Road, with Louis' cousin Burnett Cohen, and his brother-in-Law David Levy, all of whom were from New South Wales. Louis and May soon moved into a large family home in 30 Alexandra Drive in Aigburth, before moving to a large mansion known as the *Priory,* which overlooked the Mersey in leafy St Michael's-in-the-Hamlet. Next door neighbours were the well-known Melly family, the birthplace of writer and jazz singer George Melly. Louis entered local politics in 1895, becoming a member of Liverpool City Council for Breckfield Ward, Everton, and within only five years he was Lord Mayor.

Under his direction the Ranelagh Street store was completely redeveloped, although due to the war it was carried out piecemeal between 1910-23. It was built to a design by Gerald de Courcy Fraser, but Louis would not see the store fully finished, passing

The refurbished Lewis's store following the fire of 1886

*Postcard of the store showing the rebuilt corner of
Ranelagh Street and Renshaw Street*

away at the *Priory* on 7 September 1922. Control passed to his sons Harold and Rex Cohen, who took the company public in 1924. Consequently, expansion was rapid, and new stores were once again opened; in Glasgow (1929), Leeds (1932), Hanley in Stoke-on-Trent (1934) and Leicester (1936). Lewis's were generally among the largest department stores in their respective localities, with a very broad range of goods on sale, even selling concert tickets and installing food halls. A further diversity came in 1928, with the opening of a banking department in each store. It was incorporated as a subsidiary limited company in 1934 and was owned by Martins Bank from 1958 to 1967 when it was bought by Lloyds Bank. It continued to operate into the 1980s.

My own grandmother worked both in the Liverpool bank and the restaurant for many years, and as the twilight of her life approached and senility took hold, our family finally realised she would need round the clock care after a couple of phone calls were received from the police. On both occasions they had picked her up on a deserted Toxteth street in the early hours (ostensibly walking to work at Lewis's), and then another call was received from staff when she had turned up to work in the restaurant. But she had retired many years earlier – such was the draw of the place where she loved working on the subconscious of her deteriorating mind.

Into the Second World War the city suffered particularly badly, being the most heavily bombed outside of the capital. The May Blitz was the worst of it and the most destructive of all nights was on Saturday 3 May 1941, during a relentless week of bombing. Throughout the night, wave after wave of bombers throbbed overhead, pouring thousands of tons of high explosives and incendiaries on to the city.

At precisely fourteen minutes past midnight, Lewis's was hit by a high explosive bomb. As well as the structural damage, it also took out the sprinkler system, and was followed by further direct hits

Lewis's Store c.1904

Lewis's redeveloped 1910-1923 to Gerald de Courcy Fraser's design

consisting of oil bombs and three more high explosives. The whole west end of the store was now ablaze, and several firewatchers who had been on the roof were killed. The administration block at the east end on Renshaw Street was cut off from the fires by the stairs and the lift, and with the wind blowing away to the west it survived intact, and was later incorporated into the rebuild. The other end of the building in Ranelagh Street was a different story. The contents of the furniture floor were reduced to six inches of ash, and as the intense fires raged through to Blackler's department store across the road, the mains water supply failed, and firemen had to use the large steel dams in front of the Adelphi Hotel, topped up throughout with water from its swimming pool.

The gutted building following the Blitz

Three fifths of the store were gutted, and the basement was flooded to a depth of several feet. The wall facing Central Station was deemed unsafe after debris collapsed on the refreshment rooms, which resulted in the closure of the station. To the credit of all at Lewis's, the store reopened a few days later in the remaining Renshaw Street section. Most of the surrounding area was also badly damaged, including Blackler's, where there was nothing left of the interior. The destruction of so many familiar and well-loved buildings touched most Liverpudlians. If they had not suffered a family bereavement, there were few who did not lose something here.

One of the victims that night was forty-six-year-old Andrew Lund, from Cromarty Road, Old Swan, who was on duty fire-watching at Lewis's. Such was the level of destruction his body was never found. His daughter, Lilian Langford, recalled,

> 'The saddest thing about it is that he had changed his fire-watching shift as a favour, with a young man, from the Friday night to the fateful Saturday night. This changeover was arranged between themselves, so therefore it was really unofficial. This made the situation extremely difficult regarding obtaining a death certificate. As my mother was unfit to do anything, I had the very unpleasant task of having to visit temporary mortuaries to try to identify bodies, articles, clothing, etc, that might have been related to my father. Then I had to go to court, to explain the situation, so that my mother could obtain a death certificate. This was so she could get 10 shillings a week widow's pension. My father served in the First World War and came home disabled. Then he was killed in the Blitz, by a stroke of fate because he shouldn't really have been at Lewis's that night. It's just so terrible.'

The rebuilding of the devastated city centre took years to complete. There were still many levelled sites well into the 1960s and 70s, and as a port in decline, redevelopment was often slow. Lewis's opened a temporary store, while a newly commissioned building, again designed by Gerald de Courcy Fraser in 1947, was in construction on the old site (part of his earlier façade at the east end of the building in Renshaw Street was retained and incorporated into the new building, which was built to a similar height). By 1951, the new Lewis's building was ready to open and must have given local people such a boost to see it rise once more - and in spectacular fashion. It was elegant in a stripped-down classist style, again with a Portland stone façade, with an interior containing marble clad hallways, fluted columns a two-storey colonnade with Doric-style half columns at the corner entrance. The building was over half a million square feet inside, and had 4 passenger lifts, complete with lift attendants (who were usually war veterans with a disability resulting from service). With added foresight, there was an underground link to the adjacent Central Station, catching shoppers as soon as the escalators brought them to the surface, while the group also bought out the fashionable and popular Reece's Restaurants next to the station.

The new building provided an impressive spectacle to shoppers descending Mount Pleasant or Brownlow Hill. It would be the first sight of the shopping quarter to greet them, and gave firm reassurance that the city was rising out of the ashes. Construction continued on the store, and in 1953 the fabled fifth floor opened, with its swish hair salon and restaurants which oozed quality with their crisp white linen and silver service. The decor was in a contemporary Festival of Britain style, which included a huge tiled mural of such significant design that it was later to be grade II listed. The whole floor was glamorous with the intention of bring colour back to the lives of people used to the drabness of post war rationing and bomb sites.

But the most famous part of the building was yet to be completed, and this was timed to coincide with the centenary anniversary of Lewis's. Outside, on the flattened corner façade was the statue *Liverpool Resurgent*, installed between 1954-6 by sculptor Sir Jacob Epstein. This statue has become a famous landmark, a nude male figure leaning out purposefully from the prow of a ship, symbolising the renewed vigour of the city and its people, rising from the horrors of war. To locals he affectionately became known as '*Dicky Lewis*'.

The resurgent post war building, but before the installation of the Epstein statue in 1954

For such a building to become iconic in the eyes of Liverpudlians, it had to have something more about it than just a department store. But being a department store, the flag ship of the company, and one of such high reputation, went some way to placing it above all others - and then there was its role in popular culture. Getting the bus into 'town', this was usually the first main stop for those alighting – friends would meet outside Lewis's - it was convenient, and everyone knew where it was. Then after the installation of Epstein's statue, the main steps below were usually crowded with those who had agreed to meet under *Dicky Lewis*. To be 'stood up' underneath the statue was a rite of passage for many hopeful young lovers. It was an easy way not to hand out your phone number to a persistent suitor – *'Oh ay lar, goway will yer, warrayerlike? – al see yuz underneath Dicky Lewis on Satdee'*. Or as Peter McGovern sang in the 1962 anthemic song '*In My Liverpool Home*'

> *'We speak with an accent exceedingly rare,*
> *Meet under a statue exceedingly bare...'*

And then, of course, when she didn't turn up, you would be *'standing there like one of Lewis's'*. A regular comparison to the shop window mannequins – a comment also frequently used towards the dozy or idle. [Can I just add that I'm not speaking here from personal experience? Honest.]

Lewis's even has its ties to the Beatles. A young Paul McCartney worked as a temp in the store before his other job started to pay better wages, and on 17 October 1961 the Beatles' very first fan club performance was held at the David Lewis Theatre. This was in the days before Ringo, with Pete Best on drums, and just after the release of *My Bonnie,* which prompted Brian Epstein to go and see them in Cavern a few days later on the 8 November. A year later they actually played in Lewis's store itself, at a staff party held on the top floor in the 'Lewis's 527 Club' on 28 November 1962 ('No Admission after 10pm, no pass-outs, light refreshments only'). The date was hemmed in between the London recording sessions for *Please Please Me,* which were quite literally on the days either side of the Lewis's staff party, and even earlier that same evening they had time to play a session at the Cavern. Coincidentally, at the time of writing, a rare original ticket for the party came up for auction in 2013, especially rare as they were usually torn in two on entry. It was sold at the annual Liverpool Beatles Auction (organised by The Beatles Shop on Mathew Street) held fittingly at the Paul McCartney Auditorium in the Liverpool Institute for the Performing Arts on Saturday 24 August 2013, with an estimate of £2500 - £3000. The original cost was 3/6d (17½p).

LEWIS'S '527' CLUB

DANCE

Wednesday, November 28th, 1962
in the Staff Restaurant—6th Floor

Dancing 8 p.m. to 11.30 p.m.

music by the

'Dee Valley' Jazz Band and Pam

with a session by

'The Beatles'

3/6

ENTRANCE: CROPPER ST. DOOR   No passouts   No admission after 10 p.m.   Light Refreshments

In 1951, the board had decided to purchase the famous London store of Selfridges, similar in many ways to Lewis's, but by 1965 they were taken over by Sir Charles Clore's Sears chain, who were moving into the ownership of department stores after taking over shoe retail chains such as Dolcis, Manfield and Saxone. This saw the launch of the *Miss Selfridge* label and the introduction of young fashion departments across all the Lewis's stores. But by the 1970s, competition was becoming fiercer and Lewis's could no longer compete on the same scale they had enjoyed previously. Concession brands were introduced, and department sizes were cut to bring the stores more in line with others. This new look Lewis's was re-launched with new stores opening in Bolton, Newcastle, and Lakeside in Thurrock, while those which were not doing so well were sold off, such as the Bristol store which went to John Lewis.

By the 1990s however, fashions had changed and Lewis's were struggling, finally going into administration in 1991. Several stores in the chain were bought by their long-time rivals Owen Owen, (with David Lewis no doubt rolling in his grave) although they continued to operate under the Lewis's brand name for several years. However, by the late 1990s, they began to sell off branches which were no longer viable to other operators, such as Debenhams and Alders. Sears plc was acquired by Philip Green in 1999, who made further changes, such as reviving toy sales under the label 'Kids HQ'. The Leicester branch was bought out by management and traded under 'Lewis's of Leicester', before eventually closing down. Birmingham had closed and Manchester too in 2001, leaving Liverpool as the last remaining store still trading under the Lewis's name. On 28 February 2007, the Liverpool store, facing 'cashflow difficulties', went into liquidation and a few weeks later on 23 March it was sold as a going concern (along with Owen Owen) to Vergo Retail Ltd, enabling the store to continue to trade as Lewis's. (Vergo Retail was actually incorporated and controlled by David Thompson, the Managing Director of Owen Owen Ltd). Unfortunately, the troubled retailers were not helped by the *'Big Dig'* project going on in the city. This was a collection of various civil engineering projects in Liverpool to regenerate the city, and was part of the ten-year plan for the city's 2008 European Capital of Culture status. The city may have gained the new Liverpool One shopping centre, but it also had a damaging effect in other areas, as implementation of the scheme was protracted, severely hampering the ability of the city to perform as a commercial centre. It helped send Owen Owen into administration, and cut off Lewis's from customers for months on end.

However in 2010, Vergo Retail also went into administration, and the rights to the Lewis's name were bought by Lewis's Home Retail Ltd, a company formed in 2009. In February 2010 the dreaded announcement came - the store had reached the end of the line.

And so, after 154 years of trading, Lewis's closed its doors for the final time on 29 May 2010.

It had been hoped that Lewis's Department Store would be an integral part of the new Liverpool Central Village Development, with Lewis's taking up about 100,000sq ft of revamped space within the building. However, the extensive construction work could not take place while the store was still operating. With no other site available to use as a temporary home to continue trading, Lewis's was wound up and the development went ahead without them.

The closure was marked by an exhibition dedicated to Lewis's fifth floor held at Liverpool's National Conservation Centre from 26 February to 31 August 2010, while interviews with the staff and photographs were placed on the project's website. The fifth floor of the Liverpool store was once a bustling mecca, embellished with the latest modern designs. But once it closed in the late 1980s, it remained in an eerily deserted time-warp, still furnished with its original fixtures. Local artist and photographer Stephen King was commissioned to capture Lewis's fifth floor and the people that worked there. As well as the thousands of interior photographs, he also photographed thirty-eight former staff members, who were also asked about their time at Lewis's. The interviews were conducted by Claire Hamilton and filmed by Jackie Passmore, and used to accompany the images in the book *Lewis's Fifth Floor: A Department Story*, in partnership with Liverpool University Press. The exhibition also included an atmospheric film by Jackie using audio from the interviews she filmed and footage created using a Super 8 camera. By the time the exhibition closed, over 40,000 visitors had come through its doors.

After the closure in 2010, some of the former staff recalled their times at Lewis's.

Doreen Roberts (née Gibbs) saying,

'My father Harry Gibbs was the senior manager in charge of the restaurants on the fifth floor, the cafeteria, and the food hall in Lewis's from 1954 until the 1970s. My mother and my sisters regularly had lunch or high tea in the Red Rose restaurant. It really was a luxurious experience with silver service the norm. Quite the place to go in Liverpool. My father brought his experience from working on Cunard cruise liners in the 1930s, which I believe set the standards that were so in evidence in the restaurants.'

Harry also had a film clip of the Beatles playing at that 527 club party, but now long misplaced. If that film should ever turn up again...

Mary Spreadbury mentioned one famous visitor...

'Well, Liberace came in with his brother... very, very charming man really, really lovely man, and his brother George was his manager. At the top of the Red Rose room where the balcony is, well the curtains used to close across there, and we'd lay off and have the private functions there, or if it was anyone special, and that's where he was. Him and George actually went in the kitchens afterwards and thanked everybody, he went in with his brother and said 'thank you very much for a lovely day'.

Tina Jackson, described how it wasn't just about the shopping,

'We've had some great times on the fifth floor... even if it wasn't actually eating in the restaurants or having parties. When I first started there, the Mersey room used to have a 5 till 7 club and they were for the juniors. We never used to work late on a Thursday so you used to go up and have records playing and it used to be like a club, and we used to have a dance but that was only for your 15 to say, 18 year olds… we used to get subsidised with meal tickets because we weren't on as much money as the people over 21, so that was a nice time for us'.

Derek Antrobus described special arrangements for certain shoppers,

'There was no typical day in Lewis's. Every day was different. Sometimes it was hilarious because if there was a celebrity like Ken Dodd, or anybody that was a celebrity on at the theatre, such as the Empire, and they wanted to come and do some shopping, rather than do it during the day they would open the shop just for an hour just for those people, and then they would come round. You never got any refusals to work, especially when Ken Dodd came, because they used to love him coming round because it was an entertainment in itself, they never asked for overtime'.

In reality, Lewis had been in a slow decline for some years, but its closure still came as a shock to most, and there seemed to be an air of collective guilt that we had somehow let the old place down. Maybe if we all promised to go in more often, everything would be ok. But of course, habits had changed, fashions had changed, and well, we just took her for granted. And now, with the plans for the multi-million pounds Central Village Development going ahead, the Ranelagh Street building was integral, but Lewis's as a store was no longer a key player, and her lease was not renewed. With nowhere to go, the only alternative was closure.

While Lewis's is not be part of the development, the building certainly is, although only after some major surgery. When complete, the store will have altered beyond recognition, and to the consternation of many, a new archway has sliced clean through the centre of the old store's facade, opening out below the famous statue - but for the developers it signals a gateway into a new era. It will provide a spacious access to the seven-acre site that backs onto Lewis's, which for years has been little more than a disused goods depot for Central Station, after it had long ago moved underground. While high streets are witnessing shop closures at a rate of knots, this development is a renaissance zone, with a parade of restaurants and cafes, hotels, a six-screen cinema, office space, apartments, and two-tier shopping streets overlooking central water features. March 2013 saw the first part of the revamped Lewis's building opened as an Adagio 'Aparthotel' - the first UK venture by the European hotel chain.

When it was rebuilt just after the war, this five floor, 500,000 square foot institution was the world's largest department store. Richard Peel, from the developers Merepark, speaking to *It's Liverpool* magazine said, 'They don't make buildings like this any more', 'It's like we're refitting the Titanic', said colleague Neal Hunter. 'The scale is immense. And the build quality is incredible… just look at these girders – those rivets look like they went in yesterday,' he said, as he pointed to the bright red mass of struts and supports. They knew it was a sensitive project and had tried to be sympathetic to the building's heritage. The developers have restored all the original windows, kept the iconic brass handrails on the stairs, the food-themed tiles in the cafe, and much more, while preserving some of the iconic features so loved by its former clientele. But in one last cry of protest, the old building was refusing to go quietly, and was soon causing the developers headaches running 15% over budget.

'We're not another Liverpool One', declared Richard Peel. 'Our offer is more leisure and entertainment, and we're very much a decompression zone, where the city can come to unwind, spend their free time, meet friends and enjoy themselves.'

Those days when single shops were cathedral like edifices, where families arrived for a day out – mother having her hair done in the salon, dad and the children lost in the toy department before meeting up in the restaurant for lunch - may be long gone, but not too far removed from Richard Peel's vision.

Former Lewis's employee Edwina Swaden described her visits on alternate Saturdays, summing up what the store was about on both sides of the counter,

'Lewis's plays a huge part of my growing up, my mother took me to Lewis's every Saturday when Everton were playing away. My parents had a pub in Kirkdale, so we could be in town very quickly, my mother always dressed the part and my sister and I were never allowed to go to town in our casual clothes. First stop would be Lewis's biscuit counter, where there was every conceivable biscuit set out in their big square tins, baby ginger nuts were my favourite. Next floor the hat department, mother was a hat lover. Third floor, a very quick look around the toy department, which always had the best grotto at Christmas. Bypass the fourth floor, unless you needed furniture, then the best floor in the store.... the cafeteria, self-service on a Saturday, steak pie chips and peas and a glass of orange juice for me, plaice and chips for mother and sister, if we had time and the money, apple pie and the best custard you've ever tasted! How could you not love Lewis's 5th floor. Years later as a teenager I worked in Lewis's, I worked as a Players cigarette girl, then I used to model, doing all the shows in the various stores in Manchester, Birmingham, Leicester, Blackpool and of course Liverpool. Some of my happiest memories are modelling in the restaurants The Red Rose and Mersey Room, the staff and regular customers were such wonderful characters. I did make a couple of visits to the posh restaurants as a paying customer, but only on my birthdays. Happy Days!'

And so, the story of Lewis's moves into yet another phase. Fire, the horrors of the Blitz, economic downturns, and takeovers, have all failed to see it off, and what would David Lewis think of it all? He was all for progress, but surely would have fought tooth and nail to ensure his business would be part of such an exciting new development. In this nation of shopkeepers, David Lewis stood high above others, and together with those who followed him in the company, turned his tailoring business into a Liverpool icon.

They were happy days indeed.

Further Reading

Briggs, Asa *The Friends of the People: the centenary history of Lewis's* (1956)
King, Stephen, *Lewis's Fifth Floor: A Department Story* (2010)
Cook, ALM, *The David Lewis Story 1823-1885* (1960)

An early view of the railway at the turn of the century, looking north along St George's Dock Gates and New Quay (official street names usually referred to as part of the 'dock road') with access to the Pier Head to the left, St Nicholas and the original Tower Buildings to the right.

7

The Docker's Umbrella

Liverpool's Overhead Railway

'The time will come when Merseysiders must rue the day when they permitted the City Fathers to throttle the lifeblood of this unique undertaking and in addition to scrap the last vestige of their remarkably efficient tramway system.'

– H. Maxwell Roston
(General Manager, Liverpool Overhead Railway)

In early 2008, a listener to the BBC Radio 4's *Making History* programme wrote in, lamenting about how much of Liverpool's fine architecture had been destroyed, not necessarily by the Blitz, but in the decades afterwards. And not just the buildings, what about an entire railway? A railway that ran from the Dingle in the south of the city to Seaforth in the north, passing the full seven miles of docks fronting the Mersey, had completely disappeared. In contrast to plaudits regularly handed out for admirable preservation on such notable landmarks as the Albert Dock, what intrigued the *Making History* team was that so little of the railway seemed to have survived the 50 years since its passing, and how colour photos revealed the way it had dramatically altered the city's dockside. So, to find out more, the producers despatched reporter

Dylan Winter to Liverpool to discover what had happened to the 'Ovee'.

Dylan arrived by train at Lime Street and I met him across the road outside the Liverpool Walker Art Gallery. We had arranged to go by car along sections of the route of the railway while discussing its history and demise. We headed down towards the Pier Head, then left down the Dock Road towards the Dingle, following the railway's southern course. Dylan was an ebullient, likeable fellow, a veteran filmmaker and journalist, now in his fifties, and a keen sailor currently engaged in an epic voyage around Britain in a 50-year-old Mirror Offshore triple keelboat. As a keen dinghy sailor myself, our conversation wandered into the common realms of sail until we pulled over at the Herculaneum Dock and walked up the ramp that once linked a bridge from Horsfall Road across the Cheshire Lines railway adjacent to the Dock Road. Here we had an elevated view of where the former overhead stations of Brunswick, Toxteth and Herculaneum once stood along the opposite side of the road.

Dylan, microphone in hand, fiddled with a few settings on the recorder and he immediately transformed into presenter mode as we strolled up the cobbled ramp to view the surroundings.

> 'I've come along the Mersey to almost one end of this incredible railway, and the amazing thing is, that something that was so significant for Liverpool, and also so significant from an engineering point of view – let's just remember that it was the world's first overhead electric railway, beat Chicago, beat New York - that the infrastructure of this massive engineering venture has pretty much disappeared'.

And so began an interesting few hours delving into the past history of the railway, which also took me into areas where I had not been before. Although it was a beautiful late summer afternoon, the breeze coming across the Mersey was strong, and was a constant interference on the recording. Eventually, we took what refuge we could by sitting huddled, side by side on the kerbside, with our backs to wall at the top of the ramp, shielding the mic from the wind. We were a strange looking pair to anyone passing, especially with the microphone held between us. To compound our frustration, right on cue as we began recording, the police helicopter suddenly appeared above. Maybe they had spotted us and wondered what we were up to. And so we waited for what seemed like half an hour, but in reality was about five minutes, as the noisy bird hovered above, no doubt monitoring peak hour flow of traffic out of the city. Then we were left with just the breeze again and we started our journey through the history of the railway.

There had been ideas for a high-level railway along Liverpool's docklands as early as 1853, but they were thwarted at the time by dock engineer Jesse Hartley, who believed they would compromise his dock expansion plans and make them too costly. Then in 1877, the powerful local ship owner Alfred Holt suggested an overhead tramway based on the recently opened New York Elevated Railroad. This idea was based on a single-track system with passing loops, but it was thought this design would be inadequate to cope with projected passenger numbers. Instead, the plan accepted five years later, was for a full double track line running from the most northerly docks at Seaforth, along the dock road past the Pier Head, and onto the most southerly dock at Herculaneum. The tracks would run over the top of the existing dock traffic railway, with the total projected length of the line being just over six miles. It was estimated that the system would need the revenue from eight million journeys per year just to break even (the eventual cost of the whole undertaking being a staggering £3,466,000, or £331 million by today's standards).

But there seemed to be an insurmountable problem facing the Mersey Docks & Harbour Board (MDHB) to build it, as permission had been denied them by the government. Worried that the MDHB was a non-profit organisation, the government feared it would not be able to manage the railway commercially. A new venture, The Liverpool Overhead Railway Company, was formed by local investors in 1888, who agreed that the land for the Railway was to be leased from the MDHB, but the Railway Company had the powers for compulsory purchase. In reality, the MDHB had found itself a convenient way to pick up cheap land. Construction work commenced in October 1889, following the commission of leading design engineers, Sir Douglas Fox and James Henry Greathead, with J.W. Willans of Manchester as the building contractor. By January 1893, the works were finished and a running trial and inspection took place on 13th of that month.

The Liverpool Overhead Railway was officially opened on 4th February 1893, by Robert Gascoyne-Cecil (the 3rd Marquess of Salisbury, former Prime Minister and the then Conservative Leader of the Opposition). No doubt this was with some trepidation - the last time a railway was opened on Merseyside by a Prime Minister (the pioneering Liverpool to Manchester Railway in 1830) the Mayor of Liverpool, William Huskisson, was knocked down and killed by Stephenson's Rocket. But all went smoothly, and the following month it was opened to the public with services commencing on 6 March. It was the first electrically powered overhead railway in the world and the first to be protected by electric automatic signals. The track bed was made of rolled steel sheets to stop any unwanted debris falling upon unsuspecting passers-by below, and it also provided a welcome shelter from the rain, which earned its famous nickname 'The Dockers Umbrella'. The targeted eight million passenger journeys were reached as soon as 1897 when the system moved into profit.

The railway originally ran from Alexandra Dock in the north to Herculaneum Dock in the south, a distance of six miles, with eleven stations along its standard gauge track. Although it was built to ease congestion along the docks, the railway was also marketed as a tourist attraction, as it provided amazing views of the dock system, the shipping and transatlantic liners on the River Mersey. But this was a railway primarily for the industrial working class. By far the most regular users were those employed as dockers or the related ancillary industries nearby, and consequently there were few luxuries. The stations were fairly basic with simple wooden waiting rooms, the majority being two elevated platforms accessed by separate staircases from the ticket office positioned at ground level.

The journey commenced at Alexandra Dock, where up to 4,000 tons of cargo a day was passing through Liverpool's largest berth at the north end of the dock complex. Hundreds of stevedores worked here and it was one of the busiest stations on the line. Running south, the next stop was Brocklebank Dock, passing the unusual pumping station built in the style of a Bavarian castle at Langton Graving Docks. At its peak, Langton would have its own station between 1896-1906. On to Canada Dock, the centre for the timber trade, which can still be glimpsed in the brief early film clips shot by the Lumière Brothers from a moving carriage (discussed later). Around 700 yards south was Sandon Dock station, serving the nearby graving docks which was closed in 1896 when Huskisson Dock and Nelson Dock stations were opened on either side. Between Nelson and Clarence Dock stations was a switchback section, where the line descended to ground level to pass under a high-level coal railway before rising again giving the brief feeling of a rollercoaster. Over a double-decker swing bridge, which also carried steam locomotives at Stanley Dock, where hundreds of people worked in the huge warehouses, and on to Princes Dock, one of the busiest on the Mersey, where passengers would have alighted to board the huge liners bound for America, such as the Mauretania and Lusitania.

A short distance on was the Pier Head station, one of the closest stops to the town centre which also served the large number of shipping offices in the city, and consequently one of the busiest sections of the railway. South of the Pier Head, the stations were situated closer together. James Street was next, giving close access to the underground James Street Station across the road, where Wirral trains arrived from under the Mersey. Facing the Albert Dock, and where the Liverpool One complex is today, was the Custom House station at Canning Dock, then it was on to the south docks of Wapping, Brunswick and Toxteth Docks, where thousands of men were working on the vessels each day. The railway's original southern terminus was at the major fuel centre of Herculaneum Dock, where there were also several graving docks.

On 30 April 1894, the line was extended northwards to Seaforth Sands and southwards to the Dingle on 21 December 1896, mainly to attract suburban traffic outside the peak working hours where business had started to drop off. The Dingle was the line's only underground station and was located within the suburban housing of Park Road. However, for the track to reach the Dingle, a 200 ft. lattice girder bridge had to be built from the Herculaneum section to the raised tunnel entrance, which ran half a mile through the sandstone rock to the terminus. Finally, on 2 July 1905, a northward extension was connected to the Lancashire and Yorkshire Railway's North Mersey Branch at Seaforth and Litherland to enable quick access to Southport.

As a major port during the war, Liverpool became the most bombed city outside London, and the Docks - a significant target during the Blitz - suffered extensive damage during the raids. Consequently, the Overhead Railway suffered badly due to its close proximity. At Canada Dock the line took a direct hit, where the public were greeted the following morning by a bomb crater, lying where two complete spans of the railway had been the previous day. There was a similar scene of devastation on the railway at the front of James Street Station, and elsewhere staff of the Liverpool Overhead Railway Company were twice bombed out of their offices. The following month, raids caused a warehouse at

Wapping Dock to collapse on the line, while tracks at Brunswick were buckled by the heat from burning railway wagons. The ship *Malakand*, containing 1,000 tons of high explosive, was hit by a bomb in Huskisson Dock during the May Blitz of 1941 and the huge explosion damaged several sections of the nearby railway track. Therefore, because of the destruction it became impossible to ride the whole length of the railway, consequently a shuttle service provided buses running between the damaged sections, enabling passengers to complete their train journeys in full.

At a time when steel and raw metals were in desperate need for the war effort, the Overhead was vital to keep the port operational, so that every effort was made to organise swift repairs after the air raid damage. By November 1941, the railway was restored to full working order and had reopened. It was such an integral part of the port infrastructure, that by 1945 it was carrying 14 million passengers, almost double the figure for 1939.

The Overhead Railway in 1907
The Pier Head redevelopment shows the completed Port of Liverpool Building, but the Cunard and Liver Buildings are yet to be constructed

Blitz damage on the James Street section, May 1941

The Overhead Railway shortly before closure in 1955

James Street

Facing Water Street

Following the war, as the railway was a local undertaking, it was not nationalised in 1948 with the rest of the British railway system. Some modernisation did take place, and although it was still heavily used by passengers, especially dock workers, structural surveys revealed that expensive repairs, estimated at £2 million, would be needed to ensure the line's long term survival. The Liverpool Overhead Railway Company could not afford such costs and went into voluntary liquidation. Despite considerable objections, the line was closed on the evening of 30 December 1956. The final trains each left either end of the line, marking the closure with a loud bang as they passed each other. Both trains were full to capacity with well-wishers and employees of the company. Demolition was swift and began in September 1957. By late 1958 the entire structure had been removed, leaving very little trace of the railway, save for a small number of upright columns found in the walls at Wapping, and the Dingle tunnel.

Although the line closed to much vociferous protest, most argue it was inevitable. Despite the war repairs and money spent on it in peacetime, the original design of tracks laid on cast-iron cylinders had resulted in so much corrosion that replacement would prove prohibitive. Revenues were dwindling due to the shrinking dock traffic; car ownership was increasing, and much of the labourers housing along its route was being cleared. Town planners seemed too inspired by the modern concrete cities of America, and this rusty old thoroughfare was yesterday's model.

After Dylan Winter and I had taken in the Herculaneum area, I looked up and pointed out the tunnel portal set into the sandstone cliff overlooking the ground level Cheshire line entering the new Brunswick station. This was the site of the elevated gantry that once linked the tunnel to the southern end of the Overhead Railway. We decided to go to old terminus of the tunnel, a journey we would now have to take by road as the tunnel was inaccessible and blocked at its entrance.

In the Dingle, at the bottom of Park Road set among rows of terraced streets, the former station terminus can still be accessed via a concealed entrance at the end of an alley (the original ground level station building being long gone and replaced by a nondescript brick building). The gates were open and we entered the upper ramp, where the tiled walls with their LOR motifs clearly revealed its former use. Cheekily unannounced, and switching on the recorder, we moved down to stand on the access bridge. Constructed to replace the original passenger bridge, this now allowed cars access to down below, where an engineering garage was now *in situ*. 'This is quite bizarre', declared Dylan into the mic, 'It's an Overhead Railway but we're going underground!' At the bottom, we met Nigel Willis-Brown, who agreed with Dylan – 'the underground terminus of the Overhead Railway – sounds like something dreamt up after a bad night out' he said. Nigel is the proud co-owner of this historic underground station/garage. 'We've been fixing cars in here for at least the last 25 years'. 'It's not a bad place to work actually' said Dylan, a champion of the great outdoors. 'It's alright, but your face goes like grass under a plank after a while, as you don't see the sun or the real light of day', came the laconic reply. 'Can you walk down the tunnel with us a little bit Nigel?' Friendly and affable, but no doubt put out by our uninvited intrusion and with one eye on the clock, 'If you insist' he said, 'although I'm really trying to put a gearbox back in a Capri actually'. (Dylan later made a tongue in cheek apology when the piece went on air: 'and if you're that person still waiting for your Capri to have its gearbox fixed, then everyone at *Making History* is really sorry for the inconvenienced caused').

It felt quite eerie. In December 1901 Dingle station was the scene of the Overhead's worst disaster when an electrical fire on board an incoming train got out of control. The train came to a standstill in the tunnel, 80 yards short of the platform, owing to the failure of its rear motor. The driver's attempts to reset the tripped circuit breaker caused an arc which resulted in the coach's woodwork catching fire. Fanned by the strong tunnel draught blowing from the portal, within minutes smoke and flames had quickly engulfed the train and terminus killing six people. There was so much devastation that the station was closed for more than a year.

I kept these thoughts to myself as we carried on walking down the tunnel while Nigel described the former appearance of what lay before us. 'The tunnel is 605 yards long cut beneath housing through solid red sandstone and the widened section here, this is where the station was, there was a platform in the middle and the track either side, and this is where the Overhead Railway ended.' Single buffers were still set in the wall at the track end, where two sidings were added beyond the station, accommodated within a further 41-yard section of tunnel, giving the structure an overall length of 809 yards.

While we were walking back towards the entrance, Nigel let on about another piece of hidden history, now owned by the local museum. 'In a Liverpool warehouse they've got one of the old

Overhead Railway motor coaches and they are going to restore it and make it absolutely the way it was'. 'Where's that?' asked Dylan. 'Well it's at a hush-hush location', continued Nigel. 'We actually do the work for some of the museum's vehicles, so we know what's happening there'. 'So if I ask the right questions to the right people I'd get in?' said Dylan. 'Yes, you would, yes', said Nigel, looking a little apprehensive as though he had given away the secret location of some hidden treasure. He needn't have worried. In fact, Dylan didn't let on that we had already visited the warehouse that morning, and he had just recorded a perfect link which he later edited in to preview the conclusion to the piece.

Security was tight at the secret Museum warehouse in Bootle, as hundreds of artefacts were in protected storage, anticipating the opening of the Museum of Liverpool in 2010 where they were to be put on display. Sharon Brown, curator of land transport, invited us inside. This time our credentials had been double checked and the appointment made well before our visit. 'It just looks like any other warehouse I have to say, but, when the door opens, well, that is astonishing' declared Dylan into the microphone. 'There in the workshop in front of me, along with a railway engine and a railway traction engine was this beautiful carriage. Tongue and groove timber, all immaculately restored, stained dark brown, glowing under the lights, windows all round that gave the passengers a perfect view of the Mersey and the dockyards', he gushed. He asked Sharon how the carriage survived. 'It was preserved by British Railways for many years and it was presented to the Museum in 1961', said Sharon. 'It was put on display in the transport gallery which opened in 1970 and was a really popular exhibit'.

'People were allowed to go on it and there were film shows for children'. Dylan interjected, 'But that's only a few years after the railway had closed, so it must have been really fresh in people's memory?' 'Absolutely, and to be honest, even though it's fifty odd years later, it's still fresh in people's memories, the enthusiasm for the coach and for the railway itself is amazing really', replied Sharon.

The preserved carriage, the centre piece of the Liverpool Overhead Railway exhibition at the Museum of Liverpool on the Pier Head

Dingle Station today; taken from the access bridge

After the railway closed, the rolling stock were moved to sidings to await their fate. Each train consisted of three coaches, a motor coach at each end, and an un-powered trailer coach between them. The carriage that was undergoing restoration in the Bootle warehouse is the only example of a motor coach to survive and is now on exhibition in the new Museum of Liverpool Overhead Railway Gallery at the Pier Head. It was one of a batch built between 1892-1899 and it served on the railway until it closed in 1956. It is one the original motor coaches which has electric motors mounted beneath the floor, a driving cab at one end and third class accommodation with wooden seats. In July 2010, its new home was ready and it was transported on a lorry trailer travelling some distance from Bootle to the Pier Head down the dock road along its former route. Visitors to the Museum can now climb aboard the carriage, which is fixed at the exact height of the original railway at 4.8m (16 feet) above the ground. The displays also explore why the railway was eventually pulled down in the late 1950s and the legacy it has left behind.

Only one other example of rolling stock is still in existence, today housed at the Electric Railway Museum (formerly the Coventry Railway Centre) just outside Baginton, near Coventry Airport. This is First Class Trailer Car No.7, an example of the LORs modernised fleet dating from 1947, which comprised of new aluminium bodies on the original 1890s under frame, complete with air operated sliding doors. Given its chequered life after the railway closure, it is astonishing that it still survives. It was first used as an office by a coal merchant, and then by a firm of car breakers. During this period, it lost its bogies and almost all of its interior fittings, before finally being sold to the Southport Railway Centre where it was housed in their shed, mounted on a pair of accommodation bogies.

Unfortunately, the centre closed in 1998 and most of the stock was relocated to Preston, but Car No.7 was regarded as surplus to requirements and was now in need of a new home. The Suburban Electric Railway Association acted quickly to acquire the coach and it was moved to Coventry in August of 1998. Full restoration is intended once funding has been acquired and it is planned that she will sit alongside the Museum's carriages from the Wirral Line to provide 'fine examples of the tradition and triumph of Merseyside's suburban electric railways'.

Two film projects are also worthy of mention. A short film can be viewed on the Museum of Liverpool website and came about through a partnership between the Museum and the University of Liverpool. It imaginatively recreates what it was like to sit on the Liverpool Overhead Railway in its heyday in the late 1890s. Dr Richard Koeck has combined original film footage from the Lumière Brothers, with a series of digital animations to retrace the full journey of the Liverpool Overhead Railway along the waterfront. Dr Koeck is a senior lecturer in the School of Architecture and director of the Centre of Architecture and the Visual Arts at the University of Liverpool. His interest in the Liverpool Overhead Railway stems from working on the research project *City in Film: Liverpool's Urban Landscape and the Moving Image*. He used an historical Ordnance Survey map as a point of reference, and the animations create precise geographical references between the locations where the films were shot and those seen on the maps. The Lumière footage was shot from the Liverpool Overhead Railway in 1897, and is thought to be the first motion pictures shot in Liverpool. The remarkable films capture an exceptional moment in space and time of Liverpool as the 'gateway to the Empire'. Visitors to the Liverpool Overhead Railway gallery can explore the film and the maps in a touch screen interactive, as well as viewing the digital animations on a scale model of the route of the Overhead Railway.

The second is a project by professional film maker Steven Wheeler, although this is a labour of love which he has to fit in around his regular work when time allows. Entitled *'Gone but Not Forgotten - Memories of the Liverpool Overhead Railway'* - this is the working title for a documentary film currently in production and intended to be made available on DVD. Clever animated sequences from a computer-generated re-construction of the Overhead as it was during the 1950s are utilised, although the emphasis on the documentary is actually on people's memories. Interviews include dockers who travelled on it, employees who worked on it, and Mike McCartney, brother of Paul, recounting their childhood trips from the perspective of excited youngsters. Regular updates, film clips and photographs can be viewed on Steven's website and Facebook pages.

The railway can also be seen in the final scenes of the film *The Clouded Yellow* (1951), featuring Jean Simmons, where her character travels by the Overhead Railway to one of the docks. British film-maker Terence Davies also shows extensive archive footage of the railway in his *'Of Time and the City'*, a 'cinematic autobiographical poem' made to celebrate Liverpool's 2008 year as Capital of Culture.

There may be scant remains of the railway, but what is left certainly caused upheaval in the summer of 2012. Workers at Roscoe Engineering, based in the disused Dingle railway tunnel where Dylan and I had paid a visit, called the emergency services when part of the roof of the tunnel collapsed around 11.30am on 24 July. No one was injured, but the five members of staff were evacuated safely from the tunnel, while up above, Police cordoned off Park Road and nearby side streets amid fears that the tunnel collapse could cause homes to shift. The collapse involved an area of the roof measuring around 20 metres wide by 10 metres and around three metres thick. More than 100 homes near the business were evacuated as a precaution, but following an assessment by a structural engineer, people were later allowed back into their homes.

Half a century has passed, and the city of Liverpool has moved into a new phase. Many feel the Overhead Railway would have been perfect for tourism and to serve the vibrant life that has returned to the former dock sites, with more development proposed to the north. It seems even more frustrating when viewing the elevated sections of the modern Docklands Light Railway in London, plus proposals to build an elevated electric Monorail in Cardiff. Even to hear former London mayor Boris Johnson when he talked of the possibilities of building a raised cycle network to link the capital's mainline rail stations, like the High Line in New York. The congestion that the Liverpool Overhead Railway was built to relieve has returned, such a tragedy it is no longer there to alleviate it.

The Liverpool Overhead Railway, the 'Ovee', 'The Dockers' Umbrella', the world's first electric elevated railway - now a distant memory, much loved and much missed. Opened in 1893, stopped in its tracks in 1956, and apart from the lovingly restored carriage in a fitting museum display, little else to show it was ever there. Soon there will be few left who travelled on it or remember what it looked like. I am proud to say I went on it just before it closed. I might have been 6 months old and remember nothing about it, but to me it doesn't matter. I was there.

Further Reading

Gahan, John W., *Seventeen Stations to Dingle: Liverpool Overhead Railway Remembered;* Countyvise (1982)
Bolger, Paul, *Docker's Umbrella: History of Liverpool Overhead Railway;* The Bluecoat Press (1992)
Jarvis, Adrian, *Portrait of the Liverpool Overhead Railway* (1996)
Trinity Mirror Group *The Liverpool Overhead Railway: A Celebration of the Dockers' Umbrella a Transport First* (84 page magazine souvenir 2011)

On the Net

Suburban Electric Railway Association (Car No.7)
www.emus.co.uk/lor.htm

Museum of Liverpool www.liverpoolmuseums.org.uk

Steven Wheeler film documentary www.liverpooloverheadrailway.com

Subterranea Britannica
www.subbrit.org.uk/sbsites/sites/l/liverpool_overhead_railway/index1.shtml

Thomas Parker 'The Liverpool Overhead Railway'
www.localhistory.scit.wlv.ac.uk/genealogy/Parker/OverheadRail way.htm

Andy Gaskell 'The Liverpool Overhead Railway'
www.mersey.pwp.blueyonder.co.uk/lor/lor.htm

8

Ruth Harwood Bowker

Titanic Survivor

'Control your Irish passions, Thomas. Your uncle here tells me you proposed 64 lifeboats and he had to pull your arm to get you down to 32. Now, I will remind you just as I reminded him, these are my ships. And, according to our contract, I have final say on the design. I'll not have so many little boats, as you call them, cluttering up my decks and putting fear into my passengers.'

– J. Bruce Ismay, Director of the White Star Line

'The press is calling these ships unsinkable and Ismay's leadin' the chorus. It's just not true.'

- Thomas Andrews, Managing Director of Harland and Wolff Shipyards

When the largest and most luxurious vessel in the world, the *Olympic*, visited Liverpool on 31 May 1911, one young woman was so taken with the ship that she decided her future was no longer with a Liverpool confectioner where she was working, but with the White Star Line on this sumptuous vessel. Not only did she live her dream, but she was also later transferred to the sister ship, the even larger *Titanic*, due to sail from Southampton on her maiden voyage on 10 April 1912. This was Ruth Harwood Bowker, and this is her forgotten story.

In 1881, the Bowker family were living in the High Street in Ware, Hertfordshire, a few miles north of London. The father, Edward Harwood Bowker, a medical practitioner, was born in Chesterfield, and had met his wife Annie Sowersby in Doncaster, where they married in 1876. She was born in Pickering, the daughter of a Yorkshire corn miller. Soon after, they moved to Ware, where Dr. Bowker took up a new practice. Three children arrived in quick succession, Geoffrey in 1880, Janet in 1881, and Cuthbert in 1882, all with the middle name Harwood.

Within a few years, an opportunity came for Dr Bowker to move his young family back up north, nearer to his roots and those of his wife, and by 1891 they had relocated to Leeds. A new practice had been found in the suburb of Wortley at 18 Wallace Street. Yet at the time of the census in April 1891, Young Janet, now aged 10, was not at home. In fact, she was staying with her Aunt Mary (Pallister, née Sowersby), her mother's older sister, in Doncaster, where the family had a farm. The Pallisters had come to visit Ware in April 1881 and were recorded in the Bowker home ten years earlier. Whether Janet had moved there permanently or it was just a short visit is unknown, but she was the only member of the Bowker family staying there.

But there was still no sign of Ruth. Later records show that she was undoubtedly a member of this family, but so far there was nothing on the census, no birth recorded on the public register and no church record of a baptism.

By the turn of the century however, the family had completely broken up. The children, now in their late teens and early twenties, had all left home to make their way in the world independently.

The eldest, Geoffrey, had begun work as a bank clerk in Sheffield, and was lodging with a young colleague, at the home of a local shopkeeper in the suburb of Ecclesall. Cuthbert had qualified as an electrician, or electrical engineer, an occupation which would bring some security in an expanding market. He had taken lodgings on his own in a terraced house in Stoke. Janet meanwhile, had travelled much further, taking the daring step to leave the family home in the north, and to relocate herself in Margate on the north cast coast of Kent, where she found a position as a bookkeeper in the Royal York Hotel, an impressive Victorian establishment in a prominent spot on the promenade. (Today the hotel still dominates the sea front, although it is now converted into private residential flats).

Yet still no sign of Ruth. But this must be the right family. Ruth was known to be born in Ware and had the middle name Harwood. More devastating for the family was the separation of Dr. Bowker and his wife Annie. In 1901 Edward Bowker, now 50, had moved out of the family home and was living as a lodger back in his home town of Chesterfield. He was staying at 18 Knifesmith Gate, in the centre of town, in the home of Mary Roper, a 64 year old widow and temperance housekeeper, and her daughter, 22 year old Jenny. However, there was no record of the whereabouts of his wife Annie, nor the family home. The Wallace Street house in Wortley was no longer occupied and was the only house in that street not even recorded on the 1901 census, although a gap seems to have been left by the enumerator as though he was going to return to it later. Was the house uninhabited? Or had Annie gone away? She does not seem to be with any of her family either. And what of Ruth?

By 1906, Cuthbert seems to have made the decision to try his luck in Canada. A new Minister of the Interior, Frank Oliver, had been appointed in Canada who favoured a strong immigration policy, especially those from Britain, and declared that Canada had to reinforce its British heritage if it was to become one of the world's great civilizations, while at the same time his new Act denied access to numerous categories of 'undesirable aliens'. British emigrants signed up in their droves. Cuthbert, a qualified tradesman was an ideal candidate, and in 1906 he boarded the *Empress of Britain* at the Pier Head in Liverpool bound for Montreal, on what appears to have been a one-way ticket.

Sometime after Cuthbert had left for North America, Geoffrey moved to the north west, taking up residence in a cottage in Little Sutton in South Wirral. His mother Annie moved in with him, with no other means to support herself and still separated from her husband. Ruth Harwood Bowker also appeared for the first time on a census record; at the family home of forty-four-year-old Henry Williams, at 15 Pembroke Road, Bootle, Liverpool, a large town house. Henry was a confectioner, who specialised in making sweets and chocolates, while his wife Edith was a pastry cook. This was their own business and the household was also home to four more workers, all girls in their mid-twenties, which included a domestic servant and Ruth, who was employed as a 'Lady Help'. Mrs Williams had recently had a new baby and it was no doubt that the mistress needed to return to her work as quickly as possible, hence the engagement of Ruth. The other two residents were pastry cooks, one employed in the bakehouse, the other as the shop assistant. But where had Ruth been and why would she move here? It is most likely that she wanted to be near to her brother Geoffrey, but especially her mother now that her marriage had ended.

There was however, no sign of Janet.

Geoffrey was still a bank clerk, and Little Sutton was a small rural village on the high road between Birkenhead and Chester, not far from Ellesmere Port. He was living in 'The Cottage' in Station Road, only a few yards from the bank. In the 1911 census, his

(Above) **1891 Census**

Janet H Bowker, aged 10, recorded at the home of her Aunt Mary (Pallister, née Sowersby), her mother's older sister, in Doncaster, where the family had a farm

(Below) 1911 - Ruth Harwood Bowker appeared for the first time on a census record; at the family home of forty-four year old Henry Williams, a confectioner of 15 Pembroke Road, Bootle, Liverpool

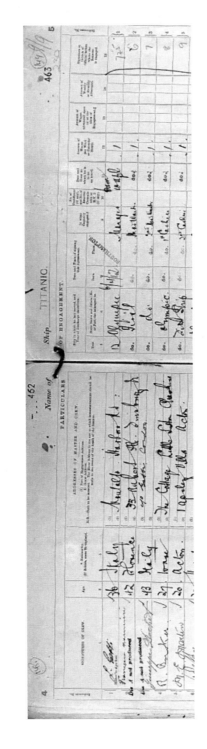

Crew register for the Titanic, shows 'R.Bowker aged 27, born in Ware, of The Cottage, Little Sutton, Cheshire, formerly of the Olympic and engaged as 1st Cashier from 10 April'

mother Annie declared that she had had three children and all were still living, a standard question asked by the enumerators. But, if that was the case, there was no fourth child - Ruth must also be Janet – they were the same person! Why she changed her name is unclear. Her birth name was Janet Harwood Bowker and this is consistent in the records until the census of 1911. Could it have had something to do with her father, did she want a fresh start away from her roots? All very unclear. Within months, Ruth was away again, this time returning to her career in catering bookkeeping where she had already gained experience in the hotel business.

But while she was still in Bootle, there was excitement and a great air of expectancy in and around the port of Liverpool at the news that the *Olympic* was to visit the city. It had been a few years since The White Star Line - founded and based in Liverpool - had ordered three vessels from the yard of Harland and Wolff. These were to be the greatest liners the world had yet seen, both in size and luxury, where no expense would be spared. By the early 1900s, the White Star Line had been facing a growing challenge from its main competition, Cunard Line, and their head offices being only a few yards apart on the Liverpool waterfront, and the fact that the main protagonists knew each other very well personally, only increased the rivalry. In 1907, the White Star Chairman, J. Bruce Ismay, and the American financier J. Pierpont Morgan, who now controlled the White Star Line's parent corporation, the International Mercantile Marine Co., began discussing plans to increase the fleet. Cunard had just launched the *Lusitania* and *Mauretania* – the fastest passenger ships then in service – and Ismay proposed to commission a new class of liners that would be bigger than anything that had gone before as well as being the pinnacle of comfort and luxury.

Construction of the *Olympic* began three months before *Titanic* and her keel was laid in December 1908. She was launched on 20

October 1910, and after her sea trials left Belfast for Liverpool, her port of registration, on 31 May 1911, where she spent a day open to the public. This was timed to coincide with the launch of the *Titanic* to gain maximum publicity. The White Star Line operation had only just moved to Southampton to cope with the larger vessels and Liverpool still regarded them as their own. There was great excitement in the town, and Ruth Bowker was undoubtedly affected by it. A short time later, she joined the *Olympic* as cashier in the restaurant – this was the largest and most luxurious vessel afloat and it's likely she regarded it as the job of a lifetime.

The *RMS Olympic* was now the lead ship of the White Star Line's trio of Olympic-class liners, and at 882 ft 6in she was the largest British built vessel afloat, and but for the short time *Titanic* and the *Britannic* were at sea, she would remain so, until the launch of the *Queen Mary* in 1934. She remained in service for 24 years, from 1911 to 1935, including service as a troopship during World War I, which gained her the nickname *'Old Reliable'*.

Her maiden voyage commenced on 14 June 1911 from Southampton, calling at Cherbourg and Queenstown, reaching New York on 21 June, and she was captained by Edward Smith who would also captain the *Titanic* the following year. Designer Thomas Andrews was also on board and he too would sail on the *Titanic*.

On 6 April 1912, Ruth Harwood Bowker signed on as the new chief cashier of the á la carte restaurant on the newly launched *Titanic*, due to sail for New York on her maiden voyage on Wednesday 10 April. Her address was recorded as her brother's home, The Cottage, Station Road, Little Sutton. (Meanwhile, her father Edward, whose health was failing, had been taken in by his sisters Agnes and Janet Bowker, both Private School Mistresses, at 34 Fairfield Road, Chesterfield).

On the *Titanic*, the á la carte restaurant was a little part of Paris located within this magnificent ship. It was an attempt by the White Star Line to bring an added touch of class to the dining experience. There was even a trio of violin, cello and piano that played exclusively in the Reception Room on the way in to the á la carte restaurant and the Cafe Parisien. It was located between the third and fourth funnel on B-Deck, and was grandly decorated with French walnut panelling, gilt and elegant carvings. The à la carte restaurant and Cafe Parisien were patronised only by the wealthiest passengers, as those travelling first-class had their meals included in the price of their tickets in the first-class dining saloon. But to dine in the à la carte restaurant and Cafe Parisien, they had to pay the bill as per the menu, effectively paying twice for their meal. Only the richest passengers could afford such indulgence. The reason for this is that the á la carte restaurant was not operated by White Star as they had invited Luigi Gatti, a famous London restaurateur, to run it. Most of the restaurant staff were employed and paid by Gatti rather than by White Star. The à la carte restaurant was open all day long for lunches, dinners, and parties, unlike the other restaurants on board, which only opened at meal times. It is likely, therefore, that Ruth was required to work demanding shifts.

On 14 April, wealthy Pennsylvanians George and Eleanor Widener, hosted a dinner party in the á la carte restaurant dedicated to Captain Smith, since this was his last voyage. Ruth was still working, busy cashing up the evenings takings, when the ship hit the iceberg. She later described how she had felt a slight shock, and then a curious grating noise. Initially, she carried on working, as like many others on board that night, she didn't think the noise she had heard was that serious. But there was soon a knock at the door and she was told to go up on deck. When she got there, she noticed that the engines were stopped and blowing off steam. Being unable to learn anything definite, she went below to her cabin. On the way, she met Mr Andrews, the designer of the ship. He told her to get her lifebelt and go on deck. Ruth asked him as to whether anything serious had happened, Mr Andrews replied, 'Oh yes - she is going down'.

Ruth wasn't the only one he spoke to in this manner - a number of people remembered Andrews being all over the deck, helping people get ready, which is also recorded in Walter Lord's book 'A Night to Remember' (1955). But a similar scene was featured in James Cameron's film *Titanic* (1998) when the fictional character Rose has an almost identical exchange with Andrews. Ruth described her encounter only days afterwards without the influence of later reportage.

Together with her junior colleague, 2nd cashier Miss Mabel Martin, she grabbed her coat and went up to the boat deck where they were already making preparations to launch the boats on the port side. Boats 7 and 5 had already been lowered on the starboard side, just as the first boat on port was being filled. This was No.6, being overseen by Charles Lightoller, with Captain Smith alongside him, while Ruth and Margaret kept back waiting to be told what to do next.

As the boats were swung out, Lightoller took the Captain to a corner of the boat deck and cupping his hands over his mouth and the Captain's ear, yelled at the top of his voice, *'Hadn't we better get the women and children into the boats sir?'* He nodded in reply, and the order 'women and children first' was barked out above the noise of escaping steam. Lightoller's plan was to get the women and children standing by into the boats, lower them, and when safely on the water, then fill them up from the gangway doors on the lower decks. He was worried about lowering the boats eighty feet fully laden. But this was never carried out.

Lightoller began to fill the boat with the numerous first-class women passengers waiting patiently when suddenly the deafening din from the escaping steam which they had endured for the last half hour suddenly stopped and there was a death like silence to accompany the initial exodus. Miss Bowker was told to get into a boat on the port side by Captain Smith himself. Although Ruth and Mabel Martin made it clear they were crew members they were still ordered in. She was still reluctant to do so, until dragged in by one of the sailors.

Quartermaster Robert Hitchens was put in charge of the boat. He was at the wheel of the *Titanic* from 10pm that night, and at 11.40pm was ordered to steer 'hard astarboard' to avoid the iceberg, although by then it was too late. At 00.23 he was relieved from his post and he raced up to the boat deck under orders to help with the boats. He was instructed by Lightoller to get into boat No.6 and to take the helm and to head for the distant light. He later told the US Inquiry that there were 44 on board; himself, 38 women, 1 seaman, 2 male passengers, an Italian boy, and a first-class passenger - a Major Arthur Godfrey Peuchen. This was wildly incorrect, being overestimated by around twenty. Lightoller estimated there were 35 occupants aboard when it was lowered. Major Arthur Peuchen later testified that 24 occupants had been aboard; himself, 20 women, 1 quartermaster (Hitchens), 1 sailor (Fleet), and 1 stowaway. Lookout Fredrick Fleet testified that 30 were aboard. (Both the British Inquiry and Gracie estimated the survivors from Lifeboat No.6 to be 28. It is now thought there were 25; 19 women passengers, 2 women crew, 2 male crew, 1 male passenger, 1 male stowaway).

While Lifeboat No.6 was descending, Hitchens called up that he would not be able to handle the boat without more seamen. Lightoller, having only two crewmen to help him, neither of which he could spare, called out desperately for anyone with sailing experience. Canadian businessman, Major Arthur Peuchen, who had been helping load the lifeboat, volunteered. 'Are you a seaman?' Lightoller asked. 'I am a yachtsman of the

Royal Canadian Yacht Club and I can handle a boat,' replied the Major. Lightoller responded that if Peuchen were enough of a sailor to climb out on the davit and lower himself down the rope, then he could get into the boat. Captain Smith interjected, feeling it was too risky, and suggested he go below, break a window and climb in from there. Peuchen, thinking that wouldn't be feasible, called below instructing the crewmen to throw him the end of a loose rope that was hanging from the davit arm. To swing out precariously, and drop 60 feet in heavy clothes and a bouyancy aid, was no mean feat for a 53-year-old. (It was at this moment that Major Peuchen's wallet fell out of his pocket and landed in the sea. Amazingly, it was recovered from the wreck site in 1987).

The other crew member was Fred Fleet – he was a 24-year-old seaman from Liverpool and was the lookout, the first person to have spotted the iceberg from the crow's nest. He would be an important witness in both the US and UK inquiries. All the female passengers in No.6 were travelling first-class and included Helen Churchill Candee, a celebrated American author, journalist, feminist and interior designer. But the passenger to become possibly the most well-known was Margaret 'Molly' Brown, the Denver millionairess and socialite, later to be daubed with the moniker 'unsinkable'. Initially, she was reluctant to get aboard, and it took one of the crew to physically drop her into the boat as it was being lowered, although it was swinging alarmingly against the side of the ship as it completed its descent. Once on the water, Hitchens began to undo the pulleys, shouting to Peuchen 'Get down and put that plug in'. (The plug was for a hole that allowed water to drain from the lifeboat when stored on deck). The Major fumbled around on his knees in the dark without success and called for Hitchens to swop places. Hichens replied furiously, 'Hurry! This boat is going to founder!' but he meant the Titanic, not the lifeboat. He was an experienced mariner and mindful of the suction power of the ship, which had been witnessed when she was leaving Southampton having dragged the neighbouring vessel *New York* from her moorings as she departed, and Hitchens was terrified of being taken down as she sank.

Once the lifeboat had been made ready, the quartermaster ordered Peuchen to sit and row beside Fleet. A nervous and shivering Hichens stood at the tiller of the lifeboat, urged them to row away quickly from the liner, predicting the dire consequences for them all unless they got a move on. Ruth also took to one of the oars to help.

After a few minutes of rowing, Peuchen suggested that Hichens let one of the women take the helm so Hichens could take a turn at the oars. He gave this idea short shift and retorted, 'I am in charge of this boat! It's your job to keep quiet and row!' As they moved away from the ship, a stowaway crawled out from under the bow, believed to be a young Italian. (It is now thought that he was a twenty-two-year-old third-class Syrian emigrant named Faheem Leeni, later known as Philip Zenni. According to Helen Candee, he was originally ordered in by Captain Smith after the Captain had been told that they had no seamen in the boat, and she thought he was injured while getting in. Ruth described him later as a *'young boy'*). He had a broken arm or wrist, and was unable to handle the oars and the poor man was on the receiving end of Hitchen's abuse - this was an example of the conduct that would gain him notoriety.

As Boat No.6 began to make some headway, they heard Captain Smith's voice through a megaphone summon them to return for more passengers. Smith and Lightoller were both well aware they hadn't been able to fill the boat once she was on the water, and was still nowhere near her capacity of sixty-five. But Hichens chose to ignore the orders of the Captain, declaring 'It's our lives now, not theirs'. Many of the women protested, especially as many had left loved ones behind, while a French woman sitting near Helen Candee was constantly calling out for her son.

On her return to the UK, Ruth described the scene to her brother, which she couldn't help but observe as she helped to row the boat away. Viewed from this level, with all her countless lights blazing, Ruth described the *Titanic* as a spectacle of fairy-like beauty. It seemed to her an insult to human intelligence and human handicraft that such a gigantic craft should ever sink. But at length it was obvious that her bow was dropping slowly. Ruth looked on as tier by tier the lights went out, and then suddenly there was a series of explosions. The ship broke in two, and there was an astounding rattling noise, as though the machinery had broken loose. Finally, she sank quietly. The ensuing cries, she quietly told Geoffrey, still rang in her ears, and she would never forget that sound as long as she lived.

Helen Candee also described the scene as the stricken vessel slowly slipped beneath the surface. The momentary silence was swiftly filled with the dreadful calls and cries that she called a 'a heavy moan as of one being, from whom final agony forces a single sound.' Slowly, the moaning grew weaker until it finally died away into the deathly stillness of the icy Atlantic night.

Several of the survivors in Boat No.6 constantly urged Hichens to turn back and rescue some of those in the water, and time and again Hitchens refused, telling the passengers, 'There's no use going back, 'cause there's only a lot of stiffs there.' Hichens later testified at the US Inquiry that he had never used the words 'stiffs' and that he had other words to describe bodies. Furthermore, he argued that he had been given direct orders by Lightoller and the Captain to row to where a light could be seen (a steamer they thought) on the port bow, drop off the passengers and return. Jack B. Thayer, a survivor, later said, 'The partly filled lifeboat standing by, about 100 yards away never came back. Why on earth they never came back is a mystery. How could any human being fail to heed those cries?'

The survivors also accused Hitchens of frequently reminding them that the lifeboat was going to drift for days without food or water, hundreds of miles from land, no protection from the cold, and would be totally helpless if a storm came up. If they didn't drown they would starve to death, and being without a compass, he didn't even know which direction they were going. Peuchen seemed reluctant to cross the unpredictable Hitchens, for which he was later criticised by Molly Brown in the pages of the American press.

A short while later, Boat No.16 came alongside No.6 and they lashed both boats together. Hitchens sat down to rest. The exhausted women, unimpressed by his lack of contribution on the oars, appealed for another seaman to come over from Boat No.16, and a stoker climbed over to help with the rowing. After 15 minutes, it was suggested they loosen the lashings so they could begin to row once more, and that the injured stowaway could take the helm to allowing the resting Hitchens to row. He again refused and protested that he was in command and they were going to stay put. Some of the women now began to taunt him to shame him into rowing, to which he replied with further expletives. The stoker told him 'Don't you know you're talking to a lady?' to which he replied, 'I know who I am speaking to and I am commanding this boat'. By now patience had run out, and Molly Brown told the others to row just to keep warm, but after further ranting by Hichens in a desperate move to keep control of the lifeboat, Molly Brown threatened to throw him overboard. As tempers settled down, Ruth and the others began to row once more.

As dawn broke, the RMS Carpathia steamed into view and slowed to a halt at 4am, precisely at Titanic's last known position. The crew looked out and could see nothing, but suddenly a green flare blazed from 300 yards' distance ahead. In the dim morning light, they could make out the outline of a lifeboat, and Captain

Rostron started up his engines, manoeuvring his vessel to pick up the survivors on the port side, but an iceberg came into view dead ahead and he had to swing the other way to avoid it. The sea was now growing choppy as a fresh breeze was picking up. No.2 was quickly tied alongside and the first of the survivors began to climb the swinging rope ladder.

Meanwhile, according to later reports, Hitchens informed his charges that the *Carpathia* was not there to rescue them, but to pick up the bodies of the dead. Hichens denied these accounts by the passengers and crew in Lifeboat No.6. He defended his initial actions saying he had been concerned about the suction from the *Titanic* and later by the fact that being a mile away from the wreck, with no compass and in complete darkness, they had no way of returning to the stricken vessel. Those on deck could now make out in the half-light the other lifeboats on all sides spread over a four-mile area, although it was still hard to distinguish them from the dozens of small icebergs that littered sea, among which there were also a few 200 foot monsters. Several of the boats were strung together in a line, while those closer tried to out-row each other while shouting out their cries of relief. Four miles away, Lightoller was maintaining a balancing act with twenty others on an upturned lifeboat, wondering if they could last much longer. In the daylight, he was able to attract the nearest lifeboat and all were transferred over safely. Over the next few hours, the *Carpathia* picked up all the survivors, with Boat No.12 being the last at 8.30am. A few minutes earlier at just after 8am, No.6 finally arrived after rowing the last few hundred yards. As she came alongside, a heavy sea was now running and three or four unsuccessful attempts were made to get close. Each time they were dashed against the keel and bounced off like a rubber ball. Their frightening experiences were not yet over. A rope was sent down, which was spliced into four at the end to secure the boat, then the Jacob's ladder thrown down to them. Those observing the final rescue described how they were hoisted up, to where a dozen of the crew and officers and doctors were waiting. They were caught and handled as tenderly as though they were children.

Such was the experience of all those in Lifeboat No.6, that it is often featured more prominently in many of the films and documentaries that have been made about the disaster. The 'unsinkable Molly Brown' is ubiquitous and her nickname has become part of the memory. Ruth described how her boat was one of the last to be picked up, but before the *Carpathia* arrived the sea and wind had got up so that the lifeboat threatened to capsize. Their bulky lifejackets probably saved them from pneumonia. She told her brother that once on the *Carpathia*, they were treated with every possible kindness, though the discomfort on such a small ship was naturally considerable. It was indeed a ship of mourning, adding that terrible stories were told by some of the survivors who had remained on *Titanic* to the last.

Ruth Harwood Bowker was a witness to the whole harrowing experience, and as a survivor of the disaster was later recorded on the official Titanic Discharge Register, which revealed that White Star Line paid her off with £1 14s 4d (£1·72p), while 2nd cashier Mabel Martin received 17s 2d. Their wages and engagement ended the moment the vessel went down.

On display at Merseyside Maritime Museum's *Titanic, Lusitania* and the *Forgotten Empress* gallery are souvenirs of *Carpathia's* rescue. They include a life-jacket worn by a Titanic survivor and two thole pins (rowlocks) from Lifeboat No.9, all obtained by 19-year-old *Carpathia* crew member Ernest St Clair of Liverpool. A nameplate from Titanic's Lifeboat No.4 was removed by the *Carpathia's* carpenter and given to her young quartermaster J J (Benjamin) Kirkpatrick of Wallasey. Two brass White Star flag emblems from a *Titanic* lifeboat were unscrewed by another seaman and mounted on wooden plaques.

Extract from the Titanic Discharge Register – her entry reads 'Miss R Bowker aged 27, born in Ware, formerly on the Olympic, joined on 10/4/12, discharged on 15/4/12, wages due £1/14/4, character very good'. The number of her discharge book (looks like a passport) was entered above her signature. The book owned by her colleague Mabel Martin, who was alongside her in the lifeboat, has survived and was sold at auction in 2016 for £3250. Inside it states - date and place of discharge/ 15.4.1912/ Lat 41° 15"n/ Long 50° 14'w', 'Description of voyage/ Vessel lost', 'Signature of Master/ White Star Line s/s Co/ per J. A. Shepherd'.

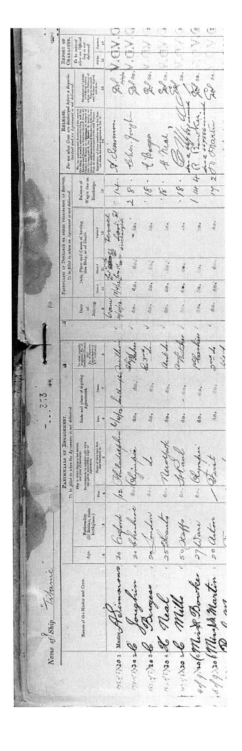

The *Carpathia* arrived in New York on 18 April, and although she was a Cunard vessel she headed straight to the White Star Line berth, but this was to unload the lifeboats, before she returned to her home berth. As the vessel had entered New York harbour, Ruth described how frantic efforts to obtain news were made by the American journalists, many of whom had chartered tugs, from which questions were bawled at the *Carpathia* through megaphones, such as 'Did John Jacob Astor die like a hero?'

On arrival, the crew and staff were ordered to stay in New York, to await the US Senate Inquiry into the sinking. With great haste, the Inquiry opened the following day at the Waldorf Astoria Hotel, but was soon moved to Washington DC, lasting 18 days overall until 25 May. In addition to Bruce Ismay, 4 officers and 34 crew were detained as potential witnesses. Meanwhile, the 172 crew members not involved in the Inquiry, were berthed on the Red Star Line vessel *Lapland* in New York, which was allowed to depart for the UK on Saturday 20 April. Ruth was on board and described the return journey as 'a delightful passage which greatly benefited shattered nerves and exhausted bodies'. Back home her brother and mother waited anxiously for news, as stories spread around Little Sutton village that she had perished in the disaster. Then on 18 April, (although it wasn't reported in the *Chester Chronicle* until Ruth was leaving for the UK on 20 April), just one word gave the family the news they had hoped for;

> *Our Little Sutton correspondent, writing on Thursday, says:*
> We are glad to say that the fears concerning Miss Bowker, of The Cottage, who was supposed to have gone down in the ill-fated Titanic, have been dispelled by a cable received this afternoon from that young lady on board the Carpathia stating "Safe." Brief as the message is, it has brought comfort to many in the village.

When they arrived at Plymouth on Monday 29 April, they were ushered into a Third Class dockside waiting area. Their ordeal was still not over, as they were now required to make sworn witness statements to British officials about their experience of the disaster. In addition, they also had to appear before the Receiver of Wrecks, before they were finally released. The poor crew had to spend the night in the waiting room, and although basic facilities had been provided including blankets, they must have thought this nightmare would never end. Female staff, including Ruth, were put up at a nearby hotel. The following afternoon, all business concluded, they were finally released. There would be brief respite for some of the crew, as the British Board of Trade Inquiry commenced in London on 2 May and lasted 36 days until 26 July. Ruth was summonsed to attend from 11 May, but there is no record of her being called or giving evidence. She was paid £9 expenses for her attendance, which confirms her presence, plus her brother Geoffrey gave a lecture on her experiences on 15 May to an local audience in Little Sutton schoolhouse, with the proceeds (£5.10s) going to the Liverpool Titanic Benefit Fund, and it was remarked that her non-attendance was due to her being away at the London Inquiry at the time.

If life wasn't traumatic enough for Ruth, she now had to deal with the news that her father Edward had passed away in Chesterfield aged sixty. How close she was to her father by mid-1912 remains unknown.

Her time with the White Star Line may well have ended with her experience with the *Titanic*, and as war approached both sister ships, the *Olympic* and *Britannic*, were pressed into war service, the former as a troop ship and the latter as a hospital ship. Many of the surviving crew did sign on with White Star Line again. But one particular crew member must have believed she was jinxed. Stewardess and nurse Violet Jessop, was on board the *Olympic* on 20 September 1911 when the ship collided with the *HMS Hawke*, suffering serious damage, but was able to limp into Southampton. Violet transferred to the *Titanic* and survived the ordeal after getting into Lifeboat No.16. She then signed on for the *Britannic* and was on board serving in the British Red Cross when the vessel hit a mine in the Adriatic and sank on 21 November 1916 with the loss of thirty lives. As the vessel was sinking, she leapt into the water but was sucked under and struck her head on the ship's keel before surfacing and being rescued by a lifeboat.

What Ruth was doing during the war years still remains a mystery, but she was now living in 2 Hans Road, Brompton Road in London. Today this building faces the corner entrance to Harrods in Knightsbridge, and it may have been a small hotel where Ruth may have found employment, rather than staying as a resident. It's not until 1922 that we have sight of her again when she is listed as a passenger on the P & O vessel *China* bound for Marseilles on 1 December. It is likely that she was travelling as a companion to Mrs Esther Roche, a 50-year-old widow, of 28 Bloomsbury St., London WC1 who was recorded immediately above her on the passenger list. The vessel was bound for the Far East and they were the only two passengers to disembark at Marseilles, both travelling first-class. It could also be argued that Ruth may not have been in a position to travel first-class on her own, she had already been employed in Liverpool as a 'Lady Help', so it is certainly feasible that she was a paid companion.

During the rest of the 1920s we lose trace of her again, until by 1929 that is, when she had returned to the catering trade, and was living in at the Curzon Hotel, in King Charles Road, Surbiton. By the following year, she had moved to live and work in the Wilton Hotel, in Wilton Road, London SW1, a large busy hotel adjacent to Victoria Station, where she stayed until her retirement (she was still there in 1947 aged 66).

Without a family of her own, and only her aging older brother Geoffrey living across London in Hampstead Heath, there was no one to take care of her in her last years and by 1954, aged 73 she had moved into the former Marylebone Workhouse, by then converted to an NHS care home for the elderly (her brother Cuthbert, died on 8 March 1915, and her mother later died in London in 1940). It was here at Luxborough Lodge, in Luxborough Street, Marylebone, that Ruth Harwood Bowker passed away in 1956 aged seventy-five. Geoffrey died at 3 Denmark Street, Colchester aged 85 on 24 Jan 1965. Ruth had lived for a time with Geoffrey in Little Sutton in the Wirral in a cottage just on the corner of the A41, the main road passing north to south through the peninsular. By a strange coincidence she died at the other end of the A41, 200 miles away where it meets Marylebone in London.

Would she have spoken to her carers about her experience on the Titanic, or did the memory die with her? Memories of that fateful night were revived only two years after Ruth's death in obscurity, with the release of the film 'A Night to Remember', and many of the survivors were invited to attend special screenings. Several also enjoyed being interviewed by the media. The success of the film was to begin a revival of interest that has continued to the present day. The film was based on the 1955 book of the same name by Walter Lord, but in a documentary made in 1993 about the making of the film, Lord said that when he wrote his book, there was no mass interest in the *Titanic* at all. Lord was the first writer in four decades to attempt a grand-scale history of the disaster, synthesising written sources and survivors' first-hand accounts. The ship had been largely forgotten, and sadly it seems, so had Ruth Bowker.

Until now.

9

Liverpool Old Pals Regiment

The 17th, 18th, 19th and 20th Service Battalions of the King's Liverpool Regiment

As the eye drifts across the endless names on the panels, the summer breeze blows through the cavernous arches where the names still reach higher and higher. The images cannot help but drive home the futility of war and the desperate sacrifice made by so many men. In all, there are 73,367 names spread across the numerous panels set on every side of the supporting columns. It is heart-wrenching enough to walk among the cemeteries of Picardy, which seem to appear at every turn in the road, but these are names of the missing. A stadium full at Cardiff or Wembley. Breathtaking numbers. How can so many be missing? But the answer is too dreadful to contemplate; the nature of war, the weapons, the conditions, men swallowed up by the mud or quite literally blown out of existence.

It was late evening and the summer sun was still strong, shadows not quite long enough to cast the memorial in patterns across the lawns below. I was a solitary figure among the missing, where there are usually endless visitors. It was peaceful and so rare to be able take in the idyllic surroundings without the respectful background hum and trying not to get in the way of visitors

Some of the names of The King's Liverpool Regiment recorded on the Thiepval Memorial to the Missing, Somme, France

taking treasured photographs. The whole area is beautiful, rolling hills, pretty hamlets, larks singing above the dusty paths among the golden cornfields. And all in full colour. The black and white imagery in my head of trenches, craters, weary faces of soldiers staring at the camera among a desolate landscape, are completely at odds with the Somme landscape in front of me. It is quite impossible to imagine, to even begin to think of the dreadful events that took place here. It was the same at Auschwitz. A place you think will be in black and white when you get there. How can it be anything else? It has to be in monotone as that's how it was. Colour would just humanise it, or that's how the brain would react after decades of black and white imagery. But there the grass was green, the birds were singing, and from nowhere two hares raced across the beautifully mown grass and started boxing not ten yards away from the back of one of the still standing barrack blocks in Birkenau. A sight I had never seen in England, and I had to travel to that place to see it. Springtime. Life goes on. And so it was in Picardy, a place too beautiful for unspeakable horror. I was startled from my thoughts by the arrival of a coach. Passengers began to disembark and I resented their intrusion. Mostly men, some in their thirties and forties, but several seniors, all clearly military and most sporting regimental blazers.

They mounted the steps and as they passed, one or two accents sounded very familiar, they were men of The King's Liverpool Regiment, past and present. Such a strange moment. I had been studying the panels of their missing, looking for one of their men in particular only minutes earlier. This is why I had come to the Thiepval Memorial, one of many visits I had made over the years. They were making an annual pilgrimage to visit the sites where the 21 battalions of the King's (Liverpool) Regiment took part in the battles of the Somme, Arras and Passchendaele, a period of approximately 15 months, during which the Regiment lost some 10,000 men. They had stopped here to lay a wreath below the 2,058 Kingsmen looking down from the panels.

A few moments later, we were also joined by a small party of men from the First Honourable Artillery making a similar pilgrimage. They were accompanied by a bandsman in his red tunic and bearskin carrying a bugle (similar uniform to the Coldstream Guards to the lay observer). After they had spent some minutes walking below the arches and studying various names on the panels, an order was barked out and they quickly came to order at the top of the steps. The senior officer ran through procedure, before giving the order to begin the ceremony, which included words of remembrance, Binyon's verse, the laying of the wreath and a minute's silence. But it was their bugler playing the *Last Post* through those arches and beyond, so movingly, which will stay with me for eternity, and I was so grateful the coach parties had intruded on my moment of rare solitude at Thiepval.

Former servicemen on a private visit to Thiepval to pay their respects to regimental comrades

I returned to look for the name I was after earlier; Private William Caldicott, King's Liverpool Regiment. This was part of an ongoing project, tracing the men recorded on three war memorials back home - the village where I grew up, one near my work place and one in the village where I live now. I had made a great deal of headway on all of them, with the intention of not just photographing the grave, but to research and write about their lives too, with the results going on dedicated websites (see further reading). I had also discovered that both William and his younger brother Jack were part of the Liverpool Pals.

At the outbreak of war, the British professional army was badly equipped and tiny compared to the conscripted armies on the continent. It comprised just 450,000 men - including only around 900 trained staff officers - and some 250,000 reservists. While there were confident predictions that the war would be 'over by Christmas', Lord Kitchener, the newly appointed Secretary of State for War, was unconvinced. He warned the government that the war would be decided by the last million men that Britain could throw into battle. Conscription was still out of the question, so Kitchener decided to raise a new army of volunteers. On 6 August, Parliament sanctioned an increase in Army strength of 500,000 men; days later Kitchener issued his first call to arms. This was for 100,000 volunteers, aged between 19 and 30, at least 1.6m (5'3") tall and with a chest size greater than 86cm (34 inches). General Henry Rawlinson initially suggested that men would be more willing to join up if they could serve with people they already knew – people they worked with, or friends and neighbours. This idea was to develop into the units that became known as Pals Battalions. Lord Derby was the first to put the idea into practice and announced in late August that he would try to raise a battalion in Liverpool, comprised solely of local men. Within days, Liverpool had enlisted enough men to form three battalions, and by November it was four. So effective was Lord Derby's input that he was nicknamed *England's best recruiting sergeant'*. He even wrote to local businesses appealing to local employers to let their workers enlist.

When the volunteers turned up at 7.30pm on 28 August, 1914 at The King's Regiment (Liverpool) HQ in St Anne Street, the response was so overwhelming that there was enough men to form more than one battalion on that first day. Addressing the men Lord Derby declared,

> 'This should be a Battalion of Pals, a battalion in which friends from the same office will fight shoulder to shoulder for the honour of Britain and the credit of Liverpool…I do thank you from the bottom of my heart for coming here tonight and showing what is the spirit of Liverpool, a spirit that ought to spread through every city and every town in the kingdom.'

Three days later, St George's Plateau in Lime Street was swamped by the gathered throng of new recruits on parade, men that were taken from the offices and major companies across the city such as The Cunard Line, The Cotton Association and the dozens of banks, insurance firms and shipping offices in the commercial quarter. It took just a week for the enlisted figure to reach 3,000, and by November there were 4,000 - enough for four battalions, an incredible achievement in such a short time.

Winston Churchill also joined the local recruitment drive when he visited the city on 21 September 1914. Although he was the First Lord of the Admiralty, he was there to help encourage army enlistment and asserted that 'under the shield of the Navy this country could send an army which could settle the war. There need be no anxiety as to the result. In six or seven months' time, they could put in the field a million men who could turn the scale in our favour'. He was well received by the hundreds of men gathered in the Tournament Hall to listen to him speak and many more signed on at the end of the meeting. (A rather patriotic local newspaper report over-estimated there were over 15,000 men in the building).

The majority of local men were drafted in to the King's Liverpool Regiment. There were many divisions within the KLR, some of them being the Liverpool Scottish, The Liverpool Rifles, The South Lancashire Regiment, The Cheshire Regiment, The Royal Army Medical Corps and, of course, The Pals. Officially the Pals were named the 17th, 18th, 19th and 20th Service Battalions of the King's, but to many they were known as the 1st, 2nd, 3rd and 4th Pals. The Liverpool Pals Regiments were the first of all the Pal's Battalions to be formed in this country and this initial success inspired other towns to follow Liverpool's lead and form their own Pals regiments. They were also the last to be stood down. While many believe that the North of England's Pals battalions were wiped out on 1 July, 1916, the Liverpool Pals took all their objectives on that day. From then on, they fought all through the Battle of the Somme, The Battle of Arras, the muddy hell of Passchendaele in 1917, and the desperate defence against the German offensive of March 1918.

Whilst the War Office was pleased to see such a successful recruitment campaign, they were also quite happy to leave the city to resource its own troops. This was to be a massive undertaking to supply the men with food, clothing, and billeting. Training also had to be organised, and the new recruits would now be sent to a variety of local camps for rigorous preparation. Lord Derby arranged for temporary barracks in the old abandoned watch factory in Prescot, near his private estate (it was whitewashed throughout first, courtesy of the Cunard Line and White Star Line – many of their employees would benefit directly). Tents were erected on the Hooton Racecourse in the Wirral, in addition to the stables and barns already commandeered. Those assigned to train in Sefton Park either stayed in their own homes or were billeted in houses nearby. By late 1914, the grounds of Lord Derby's

Knowsley estate were ready, with their new barracks and facilities to take all the men of The Pals. This infantry brigade could now train together for the first time. Previously, many of these men had no physical fitness training whatsoever, never mind training for combat. They faced tough times even before they left these shores, and little did these brave enthusiastic souls know what horrors would eventually await them.

The Caldicott brothers were two such enthusiastic souls. The Caldicott family were originally from the Midlands. Their father, William Caldicott, was born in Newport Monmouthshire in 1856, but moved to the Wolverhampton area, where he married his wife Lucy who was born in Droitwich in 1861. They moved to Ettingshall in Bilston, south-east of Wolverhampton, a fast-expanding hub of the industrial West Midlands. Like most of the working men in the area, he was a sheet worker in the local Wolverhampton iron works. Their three children were born in Ettingshall; Esther (1884), William Francis (1889) and John Henry (1893), but in the early years of the 20th century, William senior uprooted his family and moved north to Ellesmere Port, although daughter Esther stayed behind to marry and bring up their children in Ettingshall.

The Wolverhampton Corrugated Iron Company was founded in 1857 and specialised in galvanised and black flat or corrugated sheets. In 1905 the company established the Mersey Ironworks in Ellesmere Port on the banks of the Shropshire Union Canal, adjacent to the main railway line. Across the line were their main competitors, Burnell's Iron Works, founded in the late nineteenth century, and until then the main employer. Ellesmere Port was little more than a village based around the canal terminus and its small dock complex on the Mersey, but the Jones Brothers, who owned the Wolverhampton works, chose Ellesmere Port for its commercially strategic position, with easy access to major ports, served by inland canals and railway, and because land was cheap.

The major part of the company's production was exported, and barges were used to carry finished products to ships in Liverpool and Birkenhead. Almost two thousand people would be employed at the new factory, but there were insufficient workers in Ellesmere Port and this was a catalyst for its pre-war expansion as hundreds of workers began to move in. Significantly, many of the workers came from Wolverhampton, Dudley and Bilston. Census records reveal that around 300 families made this migration en masse. Some of them walked along the Shropshire Union Canal towpath with their possessions to get to Ellesmere Port. Well-planned housing estates were built by the factory owners for their workers. The Jones Brothers also hired trains to move others over one weekend to get their business up and running. The nearby Wolverham housing estate was built to house many of the migrant workers, hence its name - other street names reflected their origins too, such as Wolverham Road, Dudley Road, and Stafford Road.

William Caldicott may have been encouraged to move by promotion, as he was now a timekeeper in the new Mersey Ironworks factory, and was later joined by his sons William and John Henry ('Jack') as iron workers, although William later moved to the John Summers mill, a larger concern, near the River Dee at Shotton, Queensferry.

When the war broke out, hundreds enlisted from Burnell's and the Mersey Ironworks. Many signed up to the local regiment, the Cheshires, but many Ellesmere Port families had close ties to Liverpool, and increasing numbers began to head over the Mersey. They were also attracted by the Old Pals recruitment drives. This certainly attracted the Caldicott boys – like many others they were not from the city originally, but worked close by, but it is also possible that they may have been influenced by an acquaintance, maybe in the factory, as on the Attestation Forms signed by both William and Jack on enlistment, they stated they had been encouraged by a Sgt Jones of the KLR.

The first Pals battalion to be raised was the 17th (Service) Battalion of the King's (Liverpool Regiment) on 29th August 1914. The Caldicotts were quick to heed the call and signed on together in Liverpool on 1 September, their service numbers issued were 15962 for William, and Jack was right behind him in queue as 15963. William was now aged 26 and Jack, twenty-one. Initially they returned home to wait for the call, but were back in Liverpool the following Saturday 5 September 1914, when they marched from their assembly point at West Lancashire Riding School in Aigburth, to St George's Hall in the city, where the local population had lined the streets and cheered them all the way. Within days, William and Jack were in the Prescot Watch Factory with the rest of the 17th. Several sergeants of the Grenadier Guards had been recruited to train the men in army discipline, foot drill and musketry, although it would be a few weeks before they all had regular uniforms and rifles. As news filtered back from France about the developing nature of warfare, the 17th, plus men from the rest of the Pal's battalions, moved onto Lord Derby's Knowsley Estate nearby and began to practice digging trenches.

At the end of April 1915, orders finally came to move out, and all four city battalions were entrained for Grantham on Friday 30 April, where the 12,000 strong Pals were quartered in a camp on the Belton Park Estate. During this period of training, and no doubt due to much tedium and frustration, William was twice on a charge, both for similar minor offences of arriving back late from local leave. Due back late the previous evening, William decided instead to turn up the next morning. For the first offence while still at Prescot on 4 April 1915 he was 'admonished', while the second one at Grantham on 11 August 1915 he was confined to barracks for 7 days. In addition, in both cases he lost a day's pay.

After 4 months of further rigorous training, the War Office formally took the Pals over as fully trained and equipped units of the British Army. It was a year to the day when Lord Derby had first raised the Pals. On 31 August 1915, they began to move out to Larkhill at Salisbury Plain, to join other regular units and practice large scale manoeuvres, with the 17th arriving on 5 September.

While at Larkhill, and with their embarkation for France looming, Will seems to have received a letter from his father telling him that the government were in desperate need of munitions workers back home, probably in a last attempt to keep his sons at home. Will wrote home in October 1915:

Dear Dad,

I know you will not blame me and Jack for the stand we have made in the endeavour to do what we felt strongly to be our duty. I know it would have been nice to have us both home again, but Dad, the honest truth is I know I could not be happy as a munitions worker after training thirteen months to be a good soldier.

I and Jack joined knowing that sooner or later we should be called upon to make a great sacrifice for our King and country, and for the life of me I can't help thinking that by backing out now we should not be playing the man. Dear Dad, whatever happens now no one can say that either Jack or Will Caldicott did not act up to what I hope they have always been – 'sportsmen'. As you used to say, 'chips off the old block'.

Your son,

Will

Jack wrote in a similar fashion, both sons clearly intent on making their father proud, even though there was a safer option open to them:

Dear Dad,

I told you I have put my name down as a skilled tradesman, and since then there have been fellows to interview us. I could have got my trade union rates, and if I was away from home working, I could have my Army allowance for mother as well, but I have refused to go, and I am sticking with the boys here. It was a splendid way of taking the easy way out, but I have refused to go. I do not think the money would compensate me for the misery I should go through if all my chums were in action and I was not with them.

Your son,
Jack

So, after just over a year to get all the units disciplined, trained and battle ready, the Pals finally began to move across the Channel to Boulogne on 7 November 1915, with the 17ths as senior battalion leaving first. After further intense training, the 17th were put in the front line with the depleted Royal Irish Rifles around Mesnil on the Somme on 18 December, where they stayed until the four battalions were withdrawn from the line in mid-March for rest and training.

17th Battalion, King's Liverpool Regiment (1st City Regiment)

Pictured here in the Dining Hall of the Prescot Watch Factory where they were billeted until April 1915
before leaving for further training in Grantham

*Private
William Caldicott*

After a short time back in the front at Maricourt in May 1916, the battalions were pulled back to Abbeville where they dug 7,000 yards of trenches in a replica of the battlefield they would soon be expected to attack. The 17ths returned to Maricourt on 17 June, which was now a hive of activity in preparation. The looming battle was the 'Big Push', the Battle of the Somme. On 24 June 1916, a fierce bombardment opened up over the German lines like never seen before, in readiness for the attack planned for 1 July. Masterminded by General Sir Henry Rawlinson, it was intended to pulverise the opposition trenches and wire defences to the extent that his infantry could walk into enemy lines without opposition. All four Liverpool Pals battalions were to play an integral role. The 17th, including the Caldicott brothers, were to the right of the 20ths and were the most eastern British unit next to the French. They were just north of Maricourt and were to attack the Dublin and Glatz Redoubt with the 20ths. Despite the appalling casualties on that first day alone (in total approximately 60,000 casualties, 20,000 fatalities), the 17th on the flank were relatively unscathed, taking all their objectives, and were dug in Dublin Trench by 8.30am. Three officers were dead or wounded and 100 other ranks killed and wounded. The Germans, of course, had not relinquished this land and battled hard over the coming weeks and months into the winter to try to retrieve it at the cost of many more thousands on both sides. Much of this was over the wooded areas of Trônes, Delville, High and Mametz.

The 17th Battalion spent the remainder of that first day and all of the second, in consolidating their captured Dublin and Casement trenches, with two companies of the battalion in each, and digging a communications trench between them. The battalion also reported the 3 July as a 'quiet day', although German shelling continued. Trônes Wood was proving especially difficult to overcome. By 10 July, four attacks had already been launched against the wood in an attempt to capture the whole of it, but no more than a foothold had been obtained in the southern end of the wood.

One company of the 17th Battalion had launched an attack against a German post situated where Trônes Alley entered the wood, but the attack was a failure and the Battalion suffered heavy casualties, including young Jack Caldicott, who was hit by shrapnel in the leg. Will saw his brother go down and frantically tried to reach him. Relieved he was still conscious, he carried him back across no-man's land and on behind the lines to the dressing station. Knowing he had left many more wounded in the wood, and satisfied his brother was going to be alright, he left to look for stretcher bearers to make the return journey. What happened next – and exactly when – is not quite clear, but Will did not return to the captured positions of the 17th Battalion at the end of the day. Nor did he return the following day, when he was eventually reported missing by one of the stretcher bearers who had been with him, who said he was hit by a sniper's bullet when they were taking a wounded man back to the dressing station. Officially he was 'Missing', but the stretcher bearer did not give any sign of hope, and it was a euphemism for lying dead out there somewhere in the mud. Although it was now the 12th, he was originally listed as *'Missing 10/12 July'*. It would be some time before his death was officially listed as 10 July 1916.

At the end of July, Will's parents received a letter they always dreaded arriving...

14 July 1916

Dear Mr and Mrs Caldicott,

I am very sorry to have to write to you to inform you that your son, Private William Caldicott was killed on the afternoon of the 12th July, being shot through the heart. He was away from the company at the time, helping to carry a stretcher with a wounded man on it down to the dressing station and no one in the company knew what had happened to him until the following day, when the man who had been with him reported in. He was a very gallant man and died a gallant death in getting a wounded comrade out of the danger zone. He was one of the most popular men in the company, being liked by everyone, and was always ready to do work, no matter how hard or how risky. I feel his loss very much. He was my orderly the night before he was killed, and we had many narrow escapes, yet he always passed them off with a laugh, and then to think of his being sniped by a Boche while carrying a stretcher makes one's blood boil and there is not much hope for the next Germans we meet. They'll pay for it.

I hope you take comfort in the bravery and care for others he showed when he was killed.
I remain your servant,

Captain Binnion

17th Battalion,
The King's (Liverpool Regiment)

On Saturday 12 August 1916, the *Chester Observer* and the *Birkenhead News* carried the headline *'Parting of Two Brothers - One Killed and the Other Wounded'* and recounted the sad events on the Somme, extending their sympathies to Mr and Mrs Caldicott while emphasising the 'supreme sacrifice' made by their local heroes.

But their torment continued, as over the following weeks the War Office's procedural correspondence was clearly giving them false hope, and they wrote asking for confirmation one way or another.

> 16 Briarfield Road
> Ellesmere Port
> Cheshire
> 13 August 1916
> Captain W. Nash,
>
> Sir,
>
> Will you explain the following different statements? On 30 July 1916, we received a letter from Captain Binnion of 17th Battalion Liverpool Pals that our son, Private W. Caldicott 15962 of the same Batt. was killed on 12 July 1916.
>
> On 7 August 1916, we received official notice from the War Office that he was missing after the engagement 10/12 July 1916 and again on 13 August have received a report that he is missing. Hoping to receive a reply to this and to end the terrible suspense under which we are at present undergoing.

We remain
Yours truly,

Wm & Lucy Caldicott

P.S. Sir, will you please note change of address as have moved from 20 Penn Gardens.

Despite this despairing letter, he was still posted as 'missing' in the columns of the local press on 9 September 1916.

While in France, the men came to rely on the boxes of supplies, food and clothing sent from the people of their home town known as the Comforts Fund. Jack wrote to them following the death of William.

*I hardly know how to thank you for your kind letter and expressions of sympathy. Hearing of my brother's death was the bitterest blow I have ever received in my life, for we were very much attached to each other, and I admired him as everyone did, and respected him for his grand, brave and generous nature, and I assure you the past months do show the best or otherwise in a man. We have been side by side at the Front for nine months, and had both refused promotion for fear we may have been parted, and almost the last action of my brother was to carry me from _____ * (censored) Wood to the dressing station, and I wished him God-speed* *and left him looking for stretcher-bearers to take back to the helpless wounded in the wood which we were clinging to, when I was hit and my brother killed on the same day. I shall cherish his memory and miss him as long as I live, and I am proud of him, for I know he died with his face to the enemy and doing his duty, and I know that is as he wished.*

I am pleased to say I am mending nicely, but the shrapnel which went through my thigh has broken some nerves and I find it difficult to brace my muscles yet, but I think my leg will get stronger soon. I should like to thank all of you and show my appreciation of the splendid work the committee and yourself are doing: it both cheers one and gives encouragement, which is a great help these days, and I know you have the thanks of every employee who is serving the Colours. Wishing the committee and yourself the best of health and success, and again thanking you.

Yours sincerely,

J.H. Caldicott

[*most likely Trônes Wood]

William's body was never recovered. His death was officially recorded as 10 July and today his name is among the missing of the Kings Liverpool Regiment on the Thiepval Memorial (Pier and Face 1D, 8B and 8C). A packet of letters and photos and his Parade Service book were all that was left to return to his parents. Brother Jack meanwhile, was brought back to England and recovered from his wounds in the Northern General Hospital in Sheffield. The 17ths were pulled out of Trônes Wood on 13 July and made their weary was back to Bois des Tailles to rest, the 19th and 20th having been relieved the previous day. Nevertheless, they were back in action by the end of the month when they were sent over the top on 30 July in the disastrous attempt to capture the village of Guillemont. At least Jack was spared this.

Nevertheless, as soon as he was fit enough, he returned to active service and was promoted to Lance Corporal. He was back in action again with the 17ths by Easter 1917, only to be badly wounded again on 9 April 1917, in the first phase of the Battle of Arras (known as the 'First Battle of the Scarpe'). Again, he was shipped back to England, but despite many months of treatment he was moved to Fazakerley in Liverpool, where his right leg was amputated in February 1918, following which he was also laid low by pneumonia. On 8 April, almost a year since he was wounded, he was sent to recover in Woolton Convalescent Home, in the leafy suburbs of south Liverpool. He was finally allowed home on 3 May 1918, although he would have to return to hospital for regular treatment. On 2 September, he was admitted to the Rock Ferry Military Hospital in Ionic Street, Birkenhead, for sixteen days, where he was said to benefit from the change. Again, he was allowed home, then more treatment followed in Alder Hey Hospital in Liverpool on 19 October.

Meanwhile in France, the Old Pals battalions were again in action from March 1918 in the last major German offensive and suffered heavy losses. Consequently, the 17th, 18th and 19th Battalions of Old Pals were reduced to cadre strength on the 14 May. After taking heavy casualties the 20th had already been disbanded on 8 February 1918 in France. Both the 18th and 19th were absorbed into the 14th Battalion KLR in June 1918, while at the same time the 17th Battalion was transferred to the 66th (2nd East Lancashire) Division. On the 30th they transferred to the 75th Brigade, 25th

Division and crossed to England, where the Brigade was retitled the 236th on 9 September. Then somewhat controversially, they sailed on 11 October from Glasgow for service in North Russia, where they remained until September 1919, the last serving Old Pals battalion. Of the four original Pals Battalions, which sailed to France in November 1915, twenty per cent were dead by 1919, but if the figures of wounded and those transferred to other units are included, the casualty figure is closer to seventy-five per cent.

Just days before the Armistice, Jack Caldicott was in Alder Hey and understandably suffering bouts of depression, but on the morning of 30 October 1918, he was well enough to leave hospital to return home for a few days. He was soon due to travel to Roehampton Military Hospital (founded in 1915 to help those who had lost limbs in the First World War) where he was due to be fitted with a prosthetic leg. After travelling over to Birkenhead, he boarded the 9.55am train at Woodside Station, and headed south on the Wirral line towards Ellesmere Port. As the train passed through Spital Station part way through the journey, Jack was looking through the window when his uniform cap blew off. When the train arrived at Hooton Station further down the line, he got off, crossed to the opposite platform and returned to Spital by the next train.

On alighting at the platform at 10.43am, he began to walk to the steps of the bridge, when the station master, Francis Bowles, asked him what he was doing. On explaining that his cap had fallen on the line near the signal box, and seeing Jack was on crutches, Mr Bowles told him to stay on the platform and kindly sent a porter down the line to fetch his cap. The station master then left Jack near the steps and walked on into the goods yard to carry on with his work. In the meantime, Jack walked down the slope at the end of the platform, crossed the rails and walked up onto the opposite platform. Resting a crutch on the bottom of the bridge he looked down the line where the porter had gone. No one saw what happened next, but a railway gas man working on the opposite platform saw Jack being dragged along under the trucks, before being left on the line after the train had passed, 27 yards from the slope. The station master heard the cries from his staff and rushed to Jack's aid. But he was dreadfully injured, his left leg practically severed, and with numerous lacerations to his head. An ambulance was called and Francis Bowles did what he could with a tourniquet and other first aid, before a doctor arrived. Jack was rushed by ambulance to the Borough Hospital in Birkenhead, but there was nothing further to be done, and he died only half an hour after admission.

His distraught father came to Birkenhead to identify his son's body, and the inquest opened the following week on 5 November. Evidence was heard before a jury from the doctor at the Borough Hospital who tended to Jack before he died, the station master, the porter, and the railway gas man. The train driver and his fireman told how astonished they were to be told of the accident when they arrived at the terminus, as they had seen and felt nothing as they went through Spital. The porter Charles Jones found Jack's cap 250 yards down the line and his crutches propped up leaning against the bridge wall.

The jury returned a verdict of 'Accidental Death', officially written by the coroner as death occurring as result of 'shock and haemorrhage consequent on compound fracture of the left thigh and injuries following the result of the deceased being accidentally run over by a Great Western Goods Train on the Joint Railway at Spital Station in the County of Chester on the 30 October 1918'.

This may have been kindness on the jury's part, but what was Jack's state of mind on that day? His hospital pal Fred Phipps declared to the court that Jack was in good spirits that morning when he left Alder Hey, while his father had stated he was quite normal on his last visit, despite feeling depressed over the previous weeks.

But the events of that day, although relatively unimportant, may have tipped him over the edge. The frustration at having to return to Spital station and having to cross footbridges and the line crossing, together with the humiliation of needing help from others, however good intentioned when he wanted to do it himself, may have been too much. He had lost his brother; he had lost his leg and probably his self-worth. The crutches were neatly propped together against the bridge. An accidental collision would have sent them sprawling too.

An extract from William Caldicott's war record, showing his service in France

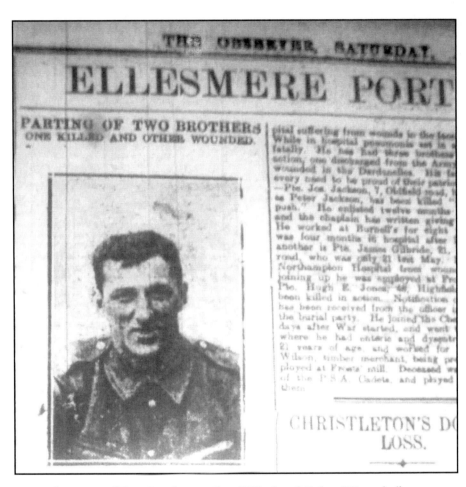

'Parting of Two Brothers – One Killed and Other Wounded'
Report on the death of William and injury to Jack on the Somme,
Chester Observer, 12 August 1916

THE KING'S LIVERPOOL REGT

PRIVATE	PRIVATE
BEVAN A.W.	CAIRNS J.P.
BIBBY J. 1451	CALDICOTT W.
BIBBY J. 37895	CALLAGHAN A.I.
BIGLANDS W.J.	CALLAGHAN J.
BILL E.	CALLAGHAN W.
BILLINGSLEY S.	CALLOW F.
BILYARD H.	CAMPBELL A.
BIMPSON S.	CAMPBELL C.
BIRCH A.	CAMPBELL J.
BIRCH T.A.	9911

Private William Caldicott recorded on the Thiepval Memorial to the Missing, Somme, France

Coroner's written verdict on the death of Lance Corporal J. H. Caldicott

Copy Verdict :-

The Cause of his death was :- Shock and haemorrhage consequent on Compound fractures of the left Thigh and other injuries the result of the deceased being accidentally run over by a Great Western Goods Train on the Great Railway at Bristal Station in the County of Chester on the 30th ulto.

Commonwealth war grave of Lance Corporal J.H.Caldicott,
Christchurch, Ellesmere Port

To add to the uncertainty, a letter from a Mr Robinson (signed 'Robbie'), a journalist friend of Jack on a Chester newspaper, was found near his body which said 'he (Robbie) was startled by the tone of his letter, but he (the deceased) would be held by them in as high estimation as before'. Unfortunately, illness prevented the attendance of Robinson at the court, so the jury were unable to hear the full contents of the original letter. The coroner also had a letter from the Chief Constable of Chester regarding the case, but the contents were not disclosed in his report. Did either have a bearing on Jack's state of mind? Had he confided in Robbie that he was suffering mentally as well as physically from his injuries? We will never know.

Jack was buried in a Commonwealth War Grave in Christchurch cemetery, Ellesmere Port, and with his brother William he is recorded on the War Memorial at the church entrance. They were both also remembered in their birthplace and are recorded on the Ettingshall memorial in George Street, Bilston - the street where the family lived before moving to Ellesmere Port. They are also listed in Hall of Remembrance in honour of the King's Liverpool Regiment in Liverpool Town Hall.

Sometimes when we look back at the histories of these great forces and the immense events they were involved in, among the platitudes we sometimes overlook the intensely personal stories of honour and bravery combined with tragic loss and the very real tearing apart of families. In this way, the Caldicott brothers were typical of many. Missing, never to be found. Rescued, patched up, sent back out, badly damaged again, very slow physical recovery, hidden mental scars not healing at all. Two Liverpool Pals, brothers, who were encouraged to join up together, to fight together, to look out for each other on the battlefield, and to be tragically split up for all eternity.

Further Reading

Maddocks, Graham, *Liverpool Pals: 17th, 18th, 19th, 20th (Service) Battalions, The King's (Liverpool Regiment)* Pen & Sword Military

Royden, Mike, *'Tracing Your Liverpool Ancestors - A Guide for Family and Local Historians'*, Pen & Sword (see www.roydenhistory.co.uk)

Mileham, P. *Difficulties Be Damned - The King's Regiment 8th 63rd 96th, A History of the City Regiment of Manchester and Liverpool*, History of the combined Regiments, 1685 - 2000

Wyrall, E. *The History of the King's Regiment Liverpool 1914-19*, (3 Vols. 1935, reprinted 2002)

McCartney, Helen B. *Citizen Soldiers. The Liverpool Territorials in the First World War;* Cambridge UP (2005)

Captain Noel Godfrey Chavasse
VC & Bar, MC

10

Captain Noel Godfrey Chavasse VC & Bar, MC

9 November 1884 – 4 August 1917

'There never was a man who was better loved by officers and men alike; there never was a man who gave himself more unsparingly in the in service of others'

– Colonel A.M. McGilchrist

After a very long day touring around the former World War One battlefields of the Salient surrounding the Flemish town of Ieper (Ypres), I gratefully arrived at the Vlamertinge Cherry Blossom B&B where I would be spending the next couple of nights. Owned by English couple Jon and Liz Millward with their teenage son, they were so interested in the history of the war and had spent so much time here, that they decided to sell up in England and move to Flanders. I was on the trail of my great-grandfather Charles Royden, a bombardier in the Royal Field Artillery, who was killed in action in 1918. A few days earlier I had travelled from my home to The National Archives at Kew in London where I had discovered his battalion war diary and I was able to trace his progress from January 1915 until his death, just outside Arras on

22 March 1918. Sitting in my car in the car park at closing time I was armed with a wealth of information about his movements; I'd found his soldier's war record, his soldier's pension records and medal card. This was at a time before these records were made available online and a visit to Kew was essential. I was ecstatic and eager to discover more about his experience at the Front. By chance I had my passport with me and decided to head straight to Dover. By 9pm I was on a ferry to Calais. On disembarking I had resolved to follow Charles' route as best I could, following the entries in the battalion war diary. After a gradual approach along a myriad of minor roads and lanes, where in 1915 the battalion had marched and billeted overnight in fields, barns and churches, I had reached their destination – the Belgian front, the Salient around Ypres, and using trench maps tried to pinpoint the location of his gun emplacement.

So, lacking sleep and food, the events of the last few days had caught up and I was glad to get to my room for a shower and change of clothes. It was a little early for dinner, so Liz's son offered to show me the three Commonwealth War Graves cemeteries located at the end of the road. In fact, they were only 50 yards away. I had arrived at the B&B from the minor lanes reaching down from the Salient ridge, and I now realised where I was. We were adjacent to the main N38 Noorderring road from Poperinge to Ypres (now known as Ieper) where I had travelled several times before, and these were the 'Military Cemeteries' of Brandhoek; 'New', 'No.1' and 'No.3 New Military Cemetery'. During the First World War, the Brandhoek-Vlamertinge area was comparatively safe from shell fire, and the site of Casualty Clearing Stations and a base for field ambulances. Inevitably, this also meant provision for burials, and until July 1917 burials had been made in the Military Cemetery, but the arrival of the 32nd, 3rd Australian and 44th Casualty Clearing Stations in preparation for the new Allied offensive launched that month made it necessary to open the New Military Cemetery, followed in August by the New Military

Cemetery No.3. At the end of Grote Branderstraatwe we turned left into Zevekotestraat to visit New Military Cemetery No.3 just a few yards away. I could not believe how close this was to the B&B, as I had intended visiting this cemetery before leaving Ypres.

The Commonwealth War Grave of Captain Noel Chavasse V.C. and Bar, M.C. in New Military Cemetery No.3

Among the 530 Commonwealth burials and 28 German war graves dating from July and August 1917 is the grave of Captain Noel Chavasse, VC and Bar, MC, one of only three men who have won the Victoria Cross twice. It was not difficult to locate his grave and it wasn't necessary to use the documentation which is available on site in a small compartment at the entrance to an all Commonwealth cemeteries. This is one of the most visited on the Western Front and the concentrated mass of small wooden

233

crosses bearing poppies placed by visitors in front of the headstone clearly revealed its position. All war graves are uniform in size and appearance, but this grave stone is quite unique as it has not one, but two images of the Victoria Cross carved side by side into its Portland stone surface. Below the regimental crest of the Royal Army Medical Corps was carved:

Captain N.G. Chavasse V.C. and Bar, M.C.
Royal Army Medical Corps
4th August 1917

Greater love hath no man than this,
that a man lay down his life for his friends.

(The verse was taken from the King James version of the Bible, John, Chapter 15 Verse13 and chosen by his father). I had waited a long time to stand in this spot.

After a hearty evening meal with Liz and her family, where the conversation was enlightened and informative especially regarding their local knowledge of the battlefields, they offered to show me a local memorial to Noel Chavasse during their evening stroll while walking the dog.

Crossing the N38 thoroughfare, we turned right towards the garden of the village church at Brandhoek where there was the memorial set up by the Flambertus History Society of Vlamertinge in 1997 to mark the 80th anniversary of his death.

The memorial is of contemporary design in local brick and acrylic with a Union flag on the adjacent flag staff. It was unveiled in 1998

Left: The Flambertus History Society of Vlamertinge memorial to Noel Godfrey Chavasse

by Captain Edgar Chavasse. A party of about 60 members of his battalion, the Liverpool Scottish, went over to Ieper to see this memorial unveiled.

I explained to Jon and Liz that it wasn't only his memory and links with Liverpool that had brought me here, but the fact that I was also lecturing in Local History in the Continuing Education Faculty at the University of Liverpool which was based in his former Chavasse home in 19 Abercromby Square in Liverpool. He is well remembered in Liverpool and this was a pilgrimage I had wanted to make for some time.

Number 19 Abercromby Square was designed by William Culshaw for C.K. Prioleau, a American Confederate merchant, and was part of the prestigious laid out square of beautiful late Georgian/early Victorian terraces, now owned in its entirety by the University (the History Faculty is located in the row of terraces on the opposite side of the square). Number 19 became The Bishop's Palace in the 1880s and today is regarded by many as the grandest surviving 19th century house in Liverpool. It was here that the Chavasse family came to live in 1900.

Francis James Chavasse, an Anglican minister, and his wife Edith Jane Maude, had seven children, and among them were their twin sons, Christopher and Noel, born on Sunday 9 November 1884 at 36 New Inn Hall Street, Oxford 1884. The twins had an older sister Dorothea, and they would be followed by another pair of identical twins, Edith (Majorie) and Mary (May), and younger brothers Francis (Bernard) and Aidan. Noel was educated at Magdalen College School in Cowley Place, Oxford, until 3 March 1900, when Reverend Chavasse was offered the Anglican Bishopric of Liverpool. And so came the move to The Bishop's Palace. Noel and Christopher went to school at Liverpool College, where their academic progress was initially slow, no doubt affected by the move. Nevertheless, they excelled at sports, which would continue to greater heights after they left. In 1904, the twins were both admitted to Trinity College where they returned to Oxford to study Medicine. Noel graduated with First Class Honours in 1907, but Christopher failed and suffered a nervous breakdown trying to cope with the pressures as he studied to retake his exams.

Their interest and dedication to sport continued throughout their time at University, especially in rugby and athletics, and their highest achievement was in 1908 when they were both asked to represent Great Britain in the Olympic Games in the 400 metres. Both finished in the top three in the heats, but their times were not quick enough to proceed to the semi-finals.

By July 1909, Noel had finished his studies in Oxford and was elected a Fellow of the Royal College of Surgeons. Returning home to Liverpool, he was then sent to spend a short placement working at the Rotunda Hospital in Dublin, before transferring to the Royal Southern Hospital in Toxteth, Liverpool, continuing his medical studies under teachers such as the eminent orthopaedic surgeon Robert Jones. He passed his finals in January 1912, being awarded the first prize - the Derby Exhibition, and in the summer, Noel registered with the General Medical Council on 22

July becoming a qualified doctor-surgeon. In early 1913, he was accepted by the Royal Army Medical Corps (R.A.M.C.) and after being referred by one of his mentors, Dr McAlistair, Surgeon-Captain of the Liverpool Scottish, he was attached to the battalion as Surgeon-Lieutenant on 2nd June, 1913. This wasn't his first taste of the military, as he had been a lance-sergeant in the Oxford University Officer Training Corps Medical Unit which he had joined in January 1909.

The Liverpool Scottish was originally formed as an infantry battalion on 30 April 1900, in response to the Boer War crisis. It was raised from among educated and professional young Scotsmen in Liverpool as the 8th (Scottish) Volunteer Battalion, The King's (Liverpool Regiment). By 1910, it was a Territorial Battalion following the Haldane Reforms the previous year, and it was regarded across the city as not just for local Scots, but the battalion for the more educated class, professionals, white collar management, rather than the labouring class. (The Haldane Reforms modernised the army, reorganising the BEF and the Territorials). During this pre-war period, many also felt it was a way for advancement both socially and also in the business world. For a great many men from the city it was a way to bring excitement and adventure into their lives, an opportunity for travel, and trips away to camp at a time when holidays were rare.

(In fact, I had another personal link here, as on this battlefields trip I was also researching the movements of Charles Royden's brother, my great-uncle William Royden, who had enlisted with the 10th Battalion, Liverpool Scottish (The King's Liverpool Regiment) on 22 June 1910, and who served with Noel Chavasse, both during peace time and in action). His black and white studio photograph I had with me showed him in the battalion's dress uniform of traditional highland attire including kilt and sporran, and if in colour would reveal a khaki tunic with scarlet collar and facings, together with a feather bonnet or Glengarry).

Private William Royden
10th Battalion, Liverpool Scottish, The King's Liverpool Regiment

Noel had been in the Liverpool Scottish for little more than a year when war broke out on 4 August 1914. He was keen to serve on the front, but in fact it was his brother Christopher who was the first member of the family to make it to France, becoming Chaplain to Number 10 General Hospital at St Nazaire. He had spent the time after his studies at Oxford to move into the ministry under his father's guiding hand. His two younger brothers would also follow him into war service, while his sister May left the family home to serve as a VAD at a hospital at Etaples in France.

It wasn't long before orders were through for the Liverpool Scottish to move out, which came on 9 October 1914. The 1/10th were ordered to move to Tonbridge Wells in Kent for final training and equipping, before heading overseas on 1 November 1914, arriving at Le Harve the following day. By 27 November, they were in the front line near Kemmel, where they spent the winter on the Salient in defence of Ypres at the northern section of the Western Front. Noel was faced with dozens of cases of trench foot resulting from the battalion standing for hours, freezing in the flooded trenches. In March 1915, they were moved a short distance along the line to Hill 60 to take part in the Second Battle of Ypres. Poison gas was used for the first time, although the battalion were not directly affected. Noel was able to meet up with his brother Christopher behind the lines at this time as his unit was stationed nearby.

On 16 June 1915 the Liverpool Scottish were involved in their first major engagement, The Battle of Hooge. Officially known as 'The First Action at Bellewaarde', it was designed to pin down German reserves while other Allied forces were trying to gain the advantage further down the line. Although it was regarded as a success, casualties were heavy, only 2 officers and 140 men came through unscathed from the 23 officers and 519 other ranks of the Liverpool Scottish who went over the top. For his work during the battle Noel was recommended for the Military Cross by his Commanding Officer, but not one of the battalion, including

Noel, received any recognition for their actions as the official recommendations were lost. Consequently, the usual citations did not appear in the London Gazette. Nevertheless, he was promoted to Captain following the battle in August 1915 and Noel was finally was awarded the Military Cross on 14 January 1916, but it was not until April 1916, before he was granted leave to receive his award from King George V. Unfortunately, the ceremony was postponed, and after many delays he finally went to Buckingham Palace on Tuesday 7 June 1916, almost a year since the Battle of Hooge.

By now, the reconstituted Liverpool Scottish had moved south to the Somme in France in mid-July 1916 to relieve the 18th King's Liverpool Regiment ('Liverpool Pals') near Montauban on the 31st. This was the height of the Battle of the Somme. They were pinned down for six days under constant artillery fire while carrying out auxiliary duties around Bernafay and Trônes Woods before they were moved further down the line to Mansel Copse in preparation for the assault on Guillemont, where the Liverpool Scottish were ordered into battle on 7 August. This attack was made over the same ground attacked by three battalions of Liverpool Pals on 30 July 1916 who had suffered enormous casualties. It must have been doubly difficult for the Liverpool Scottish to cover the same ground where so many men from their home city had been annihilated. This too would be a costly failure; out of twenty officers and about 600 men who began the action, five officers were killed, five were missing, and seven wounded. Of the men, sixty-nine were killed, twenty-seven missing and 167 wounded. Noel was one of the wounded, but despite this, he showed enormous bravery helping to save the wounded stranded in no-mans-land.

On 26 October, the London Gazette announced that Noel Chavasse had been awarded the Victoria Cross 'for the most conspicuous bravery and devotion to duty'.

'During an attack, he tended the wounded in the open all day, under heavy fire, frequently in view of the enemy. During the ensuing night, he searched for wounded on the ground in front of the enemy's lines for four hours. Next day he took one stretcher-bearer to the advanced trenches, and, under heavy fire, carried an urgent case for 500 yards into safety, being wounded in the side by a shell splinter during the journey. The same night he took up a party of trusty volunteers, rescued three wounded men from a shell hole twenty-five yards from the enemy's trench, buried the bodies of two officers and collected many identity discs, although fired on by bombs and machine guns. Altogether he saved the lives of some twenty badly wounded men, besides the ordinary cases which passed through his hands. His courage and self-sacrifice were beyond praise'.

By now the Liverpool Scottish had returned north to an even more battered Ypres Salient, this time to the Weiltje sector. It was here that the rest of the battalion learned the news of his award, and in addition, two of Noel's stretcher bearers had been awarded the Distinguished Service Medal, and two more the Military Medal. To celebrate the award, Noel's fellow officers gave him a dinner in the chateau at Elverdinge on 28 October.

In February 1917, he was granted 14 days leave in England, during which time he went to Buckingham Palace to receive his Victoria Cross from the King. The medal was brought back to Liverpool by his sister Marjorie for safe keeping in the Bishop's Palace, and during his break from the Front he became engaged to his long-time sweetheart and first cousin Gladys Chavasse (she was the daughter of Rev Chavasses's younger brother, Sir Thomas Frederick Chavasse).

On his return to the Liverpool Scottish, now enduring the depth of winter, he found himself treating numerous cases of frost-bitten knees, a condition peculiar to kilted battalions in icy weather. A few weeks later on 9 April, he heard that his sister

May had been mentioned in Sir Douglas Haig's despatches for her services at Etaples, while the youngest Chavasse brother, Aidan, was transferred nearby to the 17th Kings Regiment, one of the Liverpool Pals battalions where another brother Bernard was Medical Officer. Meanwhile, on 20 June, the Liverpool Scottish moved to Zudausques, a village west of St Omer where they had a long stay training for the forthcoming Salient offensive, the Third Battle of Ypres (Passchendaele). By the 1 July the 17th King's were in the front line at Observatory Ridge, about 5 miles from Ypres and a mile from Hooge. A small raiding party of nine men was sent towards the German lines with Lieutenant Aidan Chavasse among them, but on engaging an enemy patrol Aiden was wounded and didn't return to the trenches. A rescue team were sent out which included a distraught Bernard, but his young brother was never found. Today, Aiden's name can be found among the 55,000 Salient missing on the Menin Gate at Ieper. Meanwhile, Christopher brought further distinction to the family after being awarded the Military Cross. He would later be awarded the Croix-de-Guerre and a military OBE.

On 20th July, the Scottish moved away from their training camp and back to front line they knew so well at Weiltje (including my great uncle William Royden). Over the next few days they lost over 150 men to German shelling before being relieved on 24 July. But their respite behind the lines was very brief, and they were back in the line making ready for an assault by 29 July. The incessant rain began again and turned the already devastated area into a complete quagmire. The attack started at 3:50am on 31st July. The Scottish were already in open ground by this time and made good progress, and by 7:45am all the battalion's objectives had been taken. As the gains were made, so Noel moved his aid post forward, until he was able to secure more cover under intense fire in a captured German dug out at Setques Farm. As he stood up to wave to let the men know the location, he was hit in the head by a shell splinter. He went back to the Weiltje dugout where the wound was dressed, but he may have suffered a fractured skull. Nevertheless, despite being strongly advised to stay in the dugout, he returned to his aid post, where he found the stretcher bearers had been constantly engaged in bringing back the wounded. As darkness descended, and after an exhausting few hours treating the men, he collected his torch, and in the rain and mud he went searching for survivors.

The following day Noel worked with a German captive who was a medic, treating wounded men in the appalling conditions of mud, blood and ditch water. As he went to the entrance of the dugout to call in the next man, a shell flew past him killing the man who was waiting to be carried away by the Field Ambulance. In the confusion, it is thought he received another head wound, but still he refused to return behind the lines, and continued to treat the wounded, with little sleep or food while enduring intense pain. Then at around 3am on the morning of Thursday 2 August 1917, while Noel was collapsed in a chair, finally able to try and get some rest, a shell hit the first aid post killing or seriously wounding everyone in the vicinity. Noel was hit by several pieces of shrapnel, but more serious was the abdominal wound from which he was losing a lot of blood. He crawled up the stairs and out along the muddy path until he slipped into a dugout containing British soldiers who sent back for help. He was now in a very serious state and was taken directly to the Casualty Clearing Station No.32 at Brandhoek, which specialised in abdominal wounds, and he was operated on immediately. Despite all the shell splinters being removed and regaining consciousness, he died peacefully at 1pm on Saturday 4 August, 1917. The war had been going for exactly three years.

Noel's brother, Bernard, was only a mile south of the Liverpool Scottish on 5 August when he was told of his brother's death. He was able to get to CCS 32 on 6 August, but Noel had already been buried the day before. There were no formal arrangements, but despite this, the whole battalion had paraded and every Medical Officer at the hospital attended the funeral. Bernard was comforted to discover that Noel was nursed in his final hours by Sister Ida Leedam who had worked with him at the Southern Hospital in Liverpool. Later she wrote to the Bishop to tell him of the time spent with him. (Bernard would also receive a Military Cross, which was gazetted on 29 September).

At home the news was greeted with great sadness, and obituaries appeared all over the press. Many messages and letters were received by the family including one from King George V. Early in September a letter arrived from Lord Derby,

'I signed something last night which gave me the most mixed feelings of deep regret and great pleasure, and that was the submission to His Majesty that a Bar should be granted to the Victoria Cross gained by your son. There is no doubt whatsoever that this will be approved and while it cannot in any way diminish your sorrow, still from the point of view of those who are your friends, it is a great pleasure to think that your son in laying down his life laid it down on behalf of his fellow countrymen, and that it is recognized, not only by those who knew him, but by the King and Country as a whole. In all the records of Victoria Crosses given I do not think there is one that will appeal to the British Public more than the record for which this Bar is to be given, and as I said at the beginning of my letter, it was a great pleasure to think that this recognition of his services is thus recorded'.

The award was announced in the London Gazette on 14th September, 1917;

'Though severely wounded early in the action whilst carrying a wounded soldier to the dressing station, he refused to leave his post, and for two days, not only continued to perform his duties, but in addition, went out repeatedly under heavy fire to search for and attend to the wounded who were lying out. During these searches, although practically without food during this period, worn with fatigue and faint with his wound, he assisted to carry a number of badly wounded men over heavy and difficult ground. By his extraordinary energy and inspiring example was instrumental in rescuing many wounded who would have otherwise undoubtedly succumbed under the bad weather conditions. This devoted and gallant officer subsequently died of his wounds.'

The headstone over Noel's resting place in Plot 3, Grave B15 Brandhoek's New Military Cemetery is the only headstone in the world to have two Victoria Crosses engraved on it. Across the road is the memorial outside Brandhoek Church, raised on the 80th anniversary of his death, while in July 2000 a new memorial to commemorate the men of the Liverpool Scottish who fell near Bellewarde Ridge in the Third Battle of Ypres in 1917 was unveiled.

In addition to the memorials in Flanders, there are several in the UK where he is believed to be commemorated by more war memorials than any other individual. Currently the UK National Inventory of War Memorials lists twenty-three, four of which are in Oxford, one in the Scottish Wood at Hightown near Formby and eighteen in his home town of Liverpool. Practically every establishment that had a connection with Noel has some form of commemoration, and as the son of a Lord Bishop, he is also entered on the House of Lords memorial. Both Noel and Aiden are remembered in their school, Liverpool College, and there is a bust of Noel in Liverpool Cathedral, where he also appears in the Book of Remembrance. He is also listed among the 13,000 Liverpool men recorded on Liverpool Town Hall's Hall of Remembrance, while in 2001, English Heritage placed a Blue Plaque commemorating Noel Chavasse on the front wall of the Bishop's Palace. A stained-glass window dedicated to Noel and Aiden Chavasse was presented to St Saviours Church in Falkner Street, near to their Abercromby Square home. After the church was demolished it was donated to the Museum of Liverpool on the Pier Head.

Yet, despite the numerous memorials, there did not exist a public piece of art, such as a statue, that could be recognised as a main object of focus for the people of Liverpool.

This was to be realised on Sunday 17 August 2008 after many years of campaigning, petitioning and fundraising, when a permanent memorial to Noel Chavasse, and, it must be remembered, fifteen other Liverpool V.C. recipients, was finally unveiled in Abercromby Square, a few yards from the former Chavasse family home. Designed by local sculptor, Tom Murphy, the bronze statue depicts Captain Chavasse and a Liverpool Scottish stretcher bearer rescuing a wounded soldier. Chavasse draws the soldier's right arm across his own back and supports the soldier under the left arm as he strides forward. The stretcher bearer kneels beside the wounded soldier's lower body, his right arm around the soldier's waist and his left reaching towards the soldier's legs. According to Tom Murphy,

> 'Noel Chavasse is extremely highly regarded in the city, and it's amazing how many people out there are interested in the sacrifices these people made all that time ago. There's been a fantastic job fundraising and I feel very proud to be asked to do the sculpture'.

Over £120,000 had been raised due to the support of a small number of local businesses, donations from regimental and other associations, plus countless locals. The driving force behind the statue was Bill Sergeant, of the Noel Chavasse VC Memorial Association, which gifted the statue to the University, who said;

> 'The statue provides brave men of the city who lost their lives in the two world wars with the recognition and gratitude they so richly deserve. Abercromby Square is a great location for people to come and see the statue and our memorial service will still be held here every year too.'

The unveiling service was conducted jointly by the Reverend John Williams, chaplain to the Forces, and the Very Reverend Paul Chavasse, a distant cousin of Noel. Ann Clayton, Chavasse's biographer, read an extract from the funeral oration of Pericles. There were families of several of the Liverpool VC winners present, including nearly 50 members of the Chavasse family, in a crowd that must have been over a thousand strong despite the poor weather. A large number of Liverpool Scottish glengarries were present, including serving soldiers and pipers. Also in attendance were the Pipes and Drums of the Liverpool Scottish Association, while the actual unveiling was performed by Lt Commander Ian Fraser VC and Lance Corporal Johnson Beharry VC.

The panels contain the following:

Liverpool Heroes
This sculpture commemorates the life and deeds of Captain Noel Godfrey Chavasse VC & Bar MC, RAMC, Medical Officer to the 10th Battalion (Liverpool Scottish) King's Liverpool Regiment and fifteen other recipients of the Victoria Cross who were born in Liverpool and whose names appear across the base.

Captain Chavasse, son of the second Bishop of Liverpool, was the only man to be awarded two Victoria Crosses during World War I and died on 4th August 1917 of wounds received in Flanders.

Several of the others named also made the supreme sacrifice. May this memorial remind us all of the debt we owe to such men.

"Greater love hath no man than this, that a man lay down his life for his friends"

---

3 O'Clock Face, base and 9 O'Clock Face, base:

(Names of some of the Liverpool V.C. winners)

12 O'Clock Face, base:

Erected with the support of many ordinary citizens of Merseyside and beyond who acknowledge the bravery of such men as these.

To all of you and to those Regimental Associations, local businessmen and organisations who contributed, we, and the families of those named are eternally grateful.

We do not seek to glorify war but rather to show the suffering, sacrifice and incredible valour which war demands and will always demand.

Noel Chavasse VC Memorial Association 17th August 2008
Sculptor: Tom Murphy, Liverpool

Chavasse and Liverpool VC Memorial, Abercromby Square, Liverpool

A second significant memorial was unveiled in the summer of 2011. Chavasse Park was originally laid out in the 1980s as a three-acre plot on the site of the old pool of Liverpool, bound by Canning Place and the Dock Road, and was named in commemoration of the Chavasse family for their work and dedication to the city. After extensive reconstruction, it is now an integral part of the Liverpool One retail development, and now covers over 5 acres of elevated green space, rising in terraces overlooking the historic waterfront. Re-opened in Autumn 2008, it provides a calm and tranquil escape from the vibrant city centre. However, it was missing a dedicated formal memorial, but after the developer Grosvenor worked closely with the Noel Chavasse VC Memorial Association, their architects went to work. They created a memorial eight metres long and two metres high, engraved with words which give an insight into the events and experiences of the life of Noel Chavasse. Guy Butler, the Grosvenor projects director commented said, 'Creating a fitting memorial for Noel Chavasse was a challenge given the recognition that is already made elsewhere in the city. To compliment what exists, we wanted something that was contemporary, but that also explained his story, and getting the balance right was essential.'

In fact, the memorial's design fits the shape of the buildings which surround the park and the steel is weathered to reflect the existing sand stone walls and foliage colours throughout. Mr Butler added,

> 'It was important that the surrounding environment had time to establish before we made a decision on how the memorial would look – something that looked out of place would not have the longevity that we hope this will. Now is the perfect time to unveil this memorial. Chavasse Park is brimming with people enjoying the green space – and they will now able learn a little more about such an inspirational man.'

Around 100 people gathered in the park on 4 August 2011, the 94th anniversary of the Noel's death, to watch his great nephew,

David Watson, who had travelled from Herefordshire, to perform the unveiling ceremony. A bugler sounded *The Last Post*, which was followed by a minute's silence in a poignant ceremony attended by cadets, serving and retired military personnel, and family members.

In November 2009, Noel Chavasse's Double VC was sold for a world record price of nearly £1.5 million. The purchaser was Tory Peer Lord Ashcroft, whose lifelong interest in awards for bravery has resulted in a collection of 160 VCs - over 10% of the medals in existence. Noel Chavasse's service and gallantry medals were left by his family decades earlier to St Peter's College, Oxford (founded by Captain Chavasse's father, the Reverend Francis Chavasse), although they were given on permanent loan to the Imperial War Museum in February 1990 in the presence of HM the Queen Mother. The College issued a statement which declared, 'St Peter's College welcomes the opportunity this sale will provide for the medals to be seen by the public in their proper context. The sum received for the medals will be applied for the educational purposes of the college, which was founded by the Chavasse family in 1929.' The Chavasse medals now have a place of honour in the Imperial War Museum's Lord Ashcroft Gallery, which houses his collection of VCs. The VCs and George Crosses already owned by the museum are also on display in the gallery.

After the First World War, Bishop Chavasse retired with his wife to Garsington Rectory in Oxford in 1923. Mrs Chavasse died in 1927 aged 76, and the Bishop in 1928 aged 81. Christopher returned to continue his work in the Anglican Church and rose through the ranks to become Bishop of Rochester in Kent in 1942 where he served until his retirement on 30 September 1960. He died on 10 March 1962 aged seventy-seven. Christopher's eldest son Noel, served with Field Marshal Montgomery in World War II and also won a Military Cross. Bernard survived the war and returned to Liverpool to become a renowned ophthalmic surgeon.

He was killed in a car crash in 1941. Twin sisters May (Mary) and Marjorie (Edith) also had distinguished careers. May served as a VAD in France while Marjorie worked for the Dr Barnardo's charity setting up children's homes. Both received telegrams from the Queen on their 100th birthday in 1986, and at the time they were Britain's oldest twins. Marjorie died a few months later, and May in 1989 aged 103.

It is fitting that the final words should be those of the regimental historian of the Liverpool Scottish, reflecting on what Noel Chavasse meant to those who knew him, those he served with and cared for in the most inhuman and terrifying conditions.

> 'It is difficult to finds words to express all that 'The Doc's' life and example had meant to the Liverpool Scottish. There never was a man who was better loved by officers and men alike; there never was a man who gave himself more unsparingly in the service of others. His bravery was not of the reckless or flamboyant type but the far finer bravery that sprang from his determination that nothing should stand in the way of whatever he considered his duty. More than once he was offered the less dangerous work at a Casualty Clearing Station or Field Hospital to which his long service as a regimental medical field officer entitled him, but he preferred to remain with the men he knew and admired. The award of two Victoria Crosses – a distinction gained by only one other – was the official recognition of his work; the Battalion's is in the hearts of those who served with him.'

- (McGilchrist, 1930, p128)

Further Reading

Clayton, Ann *Chavasse: Double VC.* Leo Cooper (1992)
Gummer, Selwyn. *The Chavasse Twins: A Biography of Christopher M. Chavasse, Bishop of Rochester, and Noel G. Chavasse* (1963)
Murphy, James. *Liverpool VCs.* Pen and Sword Books (2008)
Ed. Ann Clayton, *Liverpool Heroes Book 1* (The stories of 16 Liverpool holders of the Victoria Cross, including Chavasse)
McGilchrist, Colonel A.M., *The Liverpool Scottish 1900-1919* (1930) reprint by Naval & Military Press
Arthur, Max, *Symbol of Courage – A History of the Victoria Cross,* Sidgewick & Jackson (2004)

On the Net

Ian Jones *Captain Noel Godfrey Chavasse VC & Bar, MC*
www.chavasse.u-net.com/chavasse.html

Double VC Holders

Noel Chavasse is one of three Double VC Holders, the others are:

Lieutenant Colonel Arthur Martin-Leake received his first VC in 1902 during the Boer War while serving as a surgeon captain in the South African Constabulary attached to the 5th Field Ambulance, and the Bar whilst serving with the Royal Army Medical Corps near Zonnebeke, Belgium in 1914.

Captain Charles Upham of the 2nd New Zealand Expeditionary Force (NZEF) Canterbury Battalion, to whom Chavasse was related by marriage, for actions during the Battle of Crete in May 1941; his Bar as a captain during First Battle of El Alamein in July 1942. (Captain Upham's VC was purchased by the Imperial War Museum, but since New Zealand law prevents the export of such historic treasures, it is on "permanent loan" to the National Army Museum, Waiouru).

Both the above also had links to Chavasse - Lieutenant Colonel Arthur Martin-Leake was with the 46th Field Ambulance which brought Chavasse back to Brandhoek, and Captain Charles Upham was distantly related to Chavasse by marriage.

Liverpool police during the 1919 strike

11

The Liverpool Police Strike of 1919

On Thursday 20 May 2012, the biggest demonstration by police officers the country had yet seen was held in London, when more than 30,000 officers marched through the capital demanding that the government halt its cuts and 'privatisation' of the service. According to the Police Federation, it was the only action they were legally entitled to take, in a show of defiance against budget cuts and proposed changes to the service. One detective constable from the Metropolitan Police, who did not want to be named, said: 'Our problem is we don't have a union, so this march is the strongest action we can take. I think there are a lot of us wanting full industrial rights, and the right to strike. If you take away our job security, we should have the right to defend our jobs.' They had marched only two years earlier when they numbered around 20,000, but numbers had now swelled, as frustration and anger had grown among the rank and file, with officers faced with cuts to their pay, pensions, and changes to their working conditions. Some officers even wore T-shirts demanding full industrial rights. The last time officers went on strike was in 1919, but the government banned them from taking such action again.

A police force on strike seems unthinkable, but it did happen, not just in the capital, but on the streets of Liverpool too, and it is astonishing to think they were striking for similar demands almost a century later.

Responsibility for regulation of the Police Forces were local borough 'Watch Committees', which were established by the Municipal Corporations Act of 1835, where each region had to appoint constables to preserve the peace. Relations between officers and the Watch Committees were often strained, even in the Victorian Period. For example, in 1870 in Newcastle, officers were in dispute over conditions of work and low pay, although there was no withdrawal from duty. It was for similar reason that 179 men of the Metropolitan Police refused to report for duty in 1872. Sixty-nine men were swiftly dismissed for refusing to come into work, while the rest were allowed back after apologising for their conduct. Nevertheless, a precedent had been set for the effectiveness of such collective action, as there was an improvement in pay and conditions, although it did not result in the formation of police union.

The Metropolitan Force came out again in July 1890, despite the previous sackings. The dispute this time was over police pensions, and despite the government arguing that it could not be held hostage by police workers, it drafted the Police Pensions Bill and rushed it through Parliament in a matter of weeks.

By September of 1913 there was still enough discontent for there to be support for a union. An anonymous letter appeared in the *Police Review* of September that year informing officers that a union was formed, and the ranks secretly began to sign up, as anyone found to be a member would be instantly dismissed. By 1918, out of 12,000 officers in the Met, 10,000 were in the union. In fact, the National Union of Police and Prison Officers (NUPPO) had been formed in 1910 by John Syme, a former inspector of the Metropolitan Police. He was dismissed from the service after he supported two constables who had been sacked.

The Chief Commissioner again reiterated the official stance against the union and membership, while the hostility of the government was also made clear, the Home Secretary believing that instant dismissal and loss of pension was an adequate deterrent. But by August 1918 there was growing anger at the refusal to recognise the union and when a prominent member of the union was sacked, matters finally came to a head. Their strength and anger was underestimated by the top brass, who were taken by surprise by the action. Union leaders were vociferous in their demands, seeking a pay increase, improved war bonuses, extension of pension rights to include policemen's widows, a shortening of the pension entitlement period, and an allowance for school-aged children. Key to their demands was the ongoing desire for the union to be officially recognised as the representative of the police workers. They wrong footed the authorities when they set a deadline for their demands to be met at midnight on the 29 August, or they would call a strike. When the deadline came and went, support was solid, and 12,000 men, virtually the entire Met, came out on strike. Troops were deployed at key points across the capital in response.

At the time of the strike the Prime Minister, Lloyd George, was in France dealing with matters of war, but called a meeting with the union executive for the 31st. Determined to crush police unionism, Lloyd George solemnly declared to Conservative leader Bonar Law, 'Unless this mutiny of the Guardians of Order is quelled, the whole fabric of law may disappear. The Prime Minister is prepared to support any steps you make take, however grave, to establish the authority of social order'.

Little time was wasted, and terms were settled later that day, ending the strike almost as swiftly as it had begun. The country was still at war and there were more pressing matters demanding the attention of the government. The union gained most of its demands – there was an increase for all ranks of 13 shillings [65p] per week in pensionable pay, raising the minimum to 43 shillings [£2.15]. The right to a pension was reduced from thirty years' service to twenty-six years' service, and widows were awarded a pension of 10 shillings [50p]. A war bonus of 12 shillings [60p] per week was granted, and a grant of 2 shillings and sixpence [12½p] for each child of school age was given. Even Constable Theil, the sacked officer at the centre of the strike was reinstated. Yet, the key demand was not secured – the official recognition of the union.

The government had nipped the strike in the bud at some expense, but they had headed off any chance of a national strike, and even when Manchester officers threatened the same, they were offered and accepted the same terms given to the Metropolitan Police. Over the next couple of months several other police forces around the country had been given pay increases, which may have reassured the government with such a measure of success, but union membership had jumped at the same time from 10,000 in August to 50,000 by November 1918. Lloyd George may have refused to recognise the union at time of war, but by his very action of negotiation with the union leadership and what they saw as his capitulation, this was recognition by any other name.

The resolution of the strike was the death knell of the career of Sir Edward Henry, the Commissioner of the Metropolitan Police, who resigned on 31 August. He had been away on leave at the time of the strike, and felt let down by his men and by the government who he felt were encouraging trade unionism within the police – which he totally opposed – but he was still viewed as a scapegoat for the failures of the government.

His replacement was General Sir Nevil Macready, still a serving soldier, who lost no time in reorganising the command structure of the police. Given the circumstance surrounding his appointment his attitude towards the union was to have nothing do with them, and to break their stranglehold. The days of the NUPPO, as far as he was concerned, were numbered. He wasn't interested in talks and he refused to recognise both their president and general secretary, the union was unofficial and they were lucky to have had their grievances settled.

There was no escaping the fact that the resolution of the August strike had been a quick fix and there were still problems to be addressed regarding the force as a whole as the unrest continued into 1919. The government consequently decided to form a committee to look into all aspects of policing across England Wales and Scotland. Headed by Lord Desborough, the report of the committee confirmed what everyone knew already, in that there was no uniform pay structure, and that there was inconsistency in pay across the country - even the average pay of unskilled labourers and agricultural workers exceeded police wages. In fact, the committee were quite sympathetic with the plight and grievances of the police, and drew attention to the fact that the pay for the average constable serving in a provincial force with five years' service who was married with two children would earn 2 pounds 15 shillings [£2.75], including all their allowances, such as rent and a child allowance, while they also highlighted comparative pay of ten menial manual workers such as street sweepers who earned a similar wage or more. They were clear in their recommendations of a generous increase in pay.

The Desborough Report was clear in its recommendation that pay should be standardised throughout the country and substantially increased, which meant a rise of about one third for Liverpool constables. A new representative body, the Police Federation, was to be established as a channel for the airing of grievances. However, questions of discipline and promotion affecting individuals, a major sources of grievance in the Liverpool force, were to be completely excluded from its jurisdiction. Significantly, membership of a trade union was to be made unlawful for officers. Central to any strike action would be the very survival of the police union itself.

Yet, the government had good cause to be worried about general labour relations across the country. Strike action was on the increase and general union membership had tripled between 1910 and 1919, while days lost due to strike action increased by 6 times in 1919 compared to the previous year as militancy increased. Paranoia gripped the British press as they declared the arrival of the Bolshevik revolution. As the First World War was moving to a close, worker's unrest had begun to spread through Britain. This was only months after the Russian Revolution of 1917, and various factions of the proletariat were waging pitched battles on the streets in Berlin in 1918. In Britain, disaffection and unrest wasn't confined to one trade or area, as those taking industrial action between 1917 and 1919 included miners, railway and transport workers, engineers, bakers, cotton spinners and munitions workers.

Given that the police were essential in helping to maintain the stability of the social order and existing class relations, how could it be feasible to rely on the loyalty of a force which could disobey authority while following orders of their union? The government also feared an unhealthy relationship would develop from the potential integration of the police union into the labour movement, which could clearly prove a conflict of interest and prevent police order being maintained in future industrial disputes. Any industrial action taken by the police therefore, would be view by the government as disloyal and an abdication of their allegiance to the state.

To head off any such moves, the Police Act of 1919 was pushed through Parliament, which outlawed the NUPPO and banned them from joining any other union. Instead, under Lord Desborough's recommendation, it established the Police Federation as an officer's representative body. In its death throes, the resultant NUPPO strike was futile, when despite the view that the new organisation would be a toothless tiger, only 1,156 men out of the 18,200 strong

Met came out on the call for strike action.

Nevertheless, the NUPPO were confident their fight for Union recognition would become a national strike, but again this was not the case. Action was taken in Birmingham, but the strike found most support on Merseyside, where officers failed to report for duty in Liverpool, Birkenhead, Bootle and Wallasey. In Bootle only 14 officers out of 77 failed to strike, while in Liverpool 954 took action out of 1,874. The strikers were thoroughly fed-up with their local Watch Committee, which had ignored their complaints for years. Even the forces in the rest of England knew how much worse conditions were in Liverpool.

It hadn't always been this way. In late nineteenth century, as trade unionism was gathering strength across the country, the local Watch Committee revised Liverpool officer's pay scales making them one of the better paid forces in the country. By 1912, there were further increases to weekly pay of constables by one to three shillings, according to length of service, and to encourage recruitment. But even that pay award hadn't gone smoothly, as there was still a discrepancy regarding pensions where Liverpool bobbies had to work 4 years longer than other forces to receive their maximum pension, while a deputation of sergeants approached the head constable with their grievances concerning inadequate differentials. Following adverse publicity in the local press their original pay rise of one shilling a week was doubled.

However, as wartime wage stringency began to take hold, the pre-war equality in starting pay of Liverpool constables in comparison with local labourers had come to be eroded, and had even fallen below that of many unskilled workers leading to the unrest at the end of the war.

But their grievances were not just centred upon pay. A major complaint was the excessive range of duties. In addition to their normal functions, wartime conditions had led to the additional workload of enforcing lighting restrictions, undertaking enquiries regarding army and navy pensions, and enforcing the National Registration Act in Liverpool. The latter required the registering of many thousands of aliens in the largest scheduled 'prohibited' area in the country relative to the size of its population. During wartime, officers had also lost their weekly rest day and were given one day off per fortnight (on the same day without variation), and to add insult to injury, the Watch Committee had failed to compensate for the loss. Even after 1916 they were only paid time and a half, with nothing for the days lost prior to that.

Thus, the Liverpool police had major grievances concerning earnings levels and hours of work which they felt were worse than other forces, furthermore, despite the generous pay award in 1919, they were still determined to take strike action due to long-standing issues, such as the internal work environment, job and promotion opportunities, unjust treatment by superiors, and the pursuit of equity in the administration of discipline. It was these grievances which had accumulated over a long period which had driven their continued allegiance to the union, and their fight to save it.

Department store Owen Owen of London Road, boarded up during the Police Strike in 1919

Tanks on St George's Plateau, Liverpool
*Called in by the authorities to help keep order on the streets,
early August 1919*

MOB RUNS RIOT AT LIVERPOOL.

Man Killed and £300,000 Damage To Property.

Liverpool and district have proved the storm centre of the disturbances arising out of the police strike. In Liverpool the rioting necessitated the calling out of the military and the reading of the Riot Act. The mob were repeatedly charged by the military with fixed bayonets, and the loyal police with batons, while the soldiers fired shots over the heads of the mob. Many people were injured, and one man has since died.

A good deal of damage was done to property, the sum involved at Liverpool being about £250,000, while Birkenhead has suffered £50,000 damage.

There were no trams running in Liverpool to-day, the men having gone on strike over the long-standing question of wages. The dispute has no connection with the police strike.

Riot headlines in the Sheffield Evening Telegraph 4 August 1919

LIVERPOOL POLICE STRIKE

NOT A SINGLE STRIKER TO BE REINSTATED.

Not a single police striker in Liverpool will be reinstated, said the chairman of the Watch Committee yesterday, with reference to the threat of three days' general strike next week to enforce the reinstatement of these men.

The Chairman remarked that the Police Union leaders would doubtless do their worst, but the authorities would remain firm.

Over 450 recruits have now been sworn into the Liverpool police force, 95 per cent. being ex-Army men.

MORE PAY FOR POLICE.

LORD DESBOROUGH'S REPORT ADOPTED IN LEEDS.

The Leeds Watch Committee yesterday adopted in their entirety the recommendations of Lord Desborough's Committee for police pay and conditions.

The new rates, which become operative on the first day after the next meeting of the City Council, are retrospective as from April 1st.

They are as follows:—Constables, 70s. to 95s. a week; Sergeants, 100s. to 112s. 6d. a week; Sub-Inspectors, £299 to £312 per annum; Inspectors, £320 to £360; Chief Inspectors, £375 to £415; Superintendents, £450 to £530; Chief Superintendents, £550 to £625. War bonuses are merged in the new increases. An important concession is made as to rent aid. A flat rate will be made as follows in cases where no house is provided:—Superintendents, 12s. a week; Inspectors, 10s.; Sergeants, 8s.; Constables, 7s.

The existing pension conditions remain in force for present members of the force, but for new entrants there will be some alteration.

*Report on the fate of Liverpool Police strikers,
Leeds Mercury, 16 August 1919*

THE LIVERPOOL POLICE STRIKE RIOTS.

SENTENCES AT THE ASSIZES.

Arising out of the Liverpool police strike, and the rioting and looting which supervened, Mr. Justice Avory began trials yesterday, at the Liverpool Assizes, of persons under arrest. Counsel for the Crown detailed the incidents of attacks upon loyal police which took place, and the "sacking" of bottling stores and also a warehouse. In connection with the former Thomas Ward, music-hall artist, and Michael Whelman, fireman, were sentenced to six months' hard labour; and John Threlfall, labourer, and thomas Murphy to three months' hard labour.

His Lordship said that although it was a serious disturbance of the peace, he made allowance for the fact that the absence of police from duty was a temptation to persons evilly disposed. Prisoners would probably not have dreamed of doing what they did if the police had been on duty in the neighbourhood.

In the warehouse case it was stated that £2,730 worth of property was stolen, and damage done to the build- amounting to £3,379. Two youths received three months in the second division, and another was bound over.

Looters and rioters dealt with by the courts with the judge making allowances for temptation in the absence of police, Yorkshire Post, 7 November 1919

On the day of the strike, numerous police stations across the city were the scenes of striking officers protesting outside and confronting those who were reporting for duty, especially those who were union members. It is not known how many young officers, approached whilst on their beat, were bullied into joining the strike. It was even rumoured a Sergeant in one Bridewell locked a number of his officers in the cells to prevent them joining the strike.

But of course, this type of strike action would inevitably begin to uniquely affect the city in ways that other social unrest would just be designed to cause inconvenience. As the local forces began to become seriously stretched, wayward elements soon took advantage, and looting and rioting broke out in numerous areas. It would be several days before working officers, bolstered by the military wielding rifle butts and bayonets, would be able to regain control. Meanwhile, the Watch Committee gave an ultimatum on 1 August 1919, that those men who have failed to parade for duty by 8.00pm that night would be dismissed. The majority ignored the order and only around 50 men turned up for parade. Support came from the ranks, while no plain clothes or CID staff refused duty. One of the striking police officers who returned to work was PC Joseph Wright Teesdale Smith, who later became the Chief Constable of Liverpool in 1960.

Within hours, gangs began smashing shop windows and looting anything that was moveable, using prams, carts and wheelbarrows to shift the booty. Over 400 premises were looted and frequently torched in four days of anarchy. As the undermanned force was still quick to respond, whilst they were at one location, similar events were taking place elsewhere. In response, the City Council called on the business community to volunteer as special constables. Those who took up the offer were given a duty armlet and a baton. They were further boosted by the arrival of police officers seconded from other parts of the country.

The government acted swiftly and despatched the battleship *HMS Valiant* from Scapa Flow, as well as two destroyers, *Venomous* and *Whitley*, which steamed up the Mersey to an anchorage off the Pier Head. Almost 3,000 troops were drafted in and encamped in St Johns Gardens, behind St George's Hall, while around the other side of the Hall on St George's Plateau, tanks rolled into place on 3 August. *The Times* called central Liverpool a 'war zone', while the *Liverpool Echo* declared it 'rather reminiscent of the early occupation days in some of the Cologne districts'.

Whatever the impression, Liverpool was effectively put under military occupation, while soldiers patrolled the streets with guns loaded and bayonets fixed, as they protected key public buildings and brutally restored order. Many were injured by baton-charges, and one looter was shot dead trying to take a rifle from a soldier. Live rounds were also fired at a gang looting a bonded warehouse. As crowds began to gather in Everton on the third night of disturbances, a magistrate read the Riot Act from the safety of an armoured car. He declared, that in the name of the King, all citizens were to disperse within one hour, giving the authorities the right to clear the streets by whatever means after the hour's grace. An hour later the Army fired a volley over the heads of rioters.

Pat O'Mara later recalled some of the events in his *'Autobiography of a Liverpool Slummy'*,

> 'The bobbies were on strike! There were no bobbies! That could only mean one thing, and that thing happened. I was coming out of the Daulby Hall with Jackie Sanchez (having mooched the entrance fee from him) at the time when the first fever caught on. We went across the street to Skranvinsky's chip-and-fish shop and listened to speculations over this new and strange strike. As we stood in the crowd a couple of bucks walked in, ordered in some chips and fish and refused to pay for them, suggesting to the hysterical Mrs Skranvinsky that she'd "get a bloody bobby!".

Then they walked out, followed by others not yet paid up, who had taken the hint. Some leaned across the counter and grabbed handfuls of chips and fish and scallops, and without waiting to salt them, continued brazenly out into the street. Only Mrs Skravinsky's screams kept those on the outside at bay...

Looting fish and chips has its elements of farce, but actions elsewhere were becoming more serious as Pat witnessed walking through town,

'...On the corners here and there stood the bobbies, grimly passive and, to signify the fact, with no official labels on their arms. Excited groups of hooligans eyed them wonderingly. A jewellery window just down London Road crashed in, and, as bobbies smiled, wonder vanished from the hooligans. Another window crashed in. It was the Lusitania [riots] all over again, only much more intense, since now there was no restraining hand at all. Hands were out grasping through the jewellery store windows. Inside other stores whose windows were bashed in, respectable-looking men and women joined with the slummies to gather up loot and flee homeward. Every store with anything worth stealing was broken into and the furnishings wrecked in the frenzy to get the best stuff available. I did not have anything like good luck, until Ben Hyde's pawnshop farther down London Road was reached. After the windows were bashed in, the place was ransacked, lockers pulled out, pledged articles tucked into aprons. I got hold of a couple of muffs that struck me, in my innocence, as very expensive things and once outside, fearing the riot would be short-lived, I skipped away from Jackie, tucked two precious furs under my coat, and sped along the comparatively quiet streets for home'.

News of the riots soon spread across the country and Liverpool correspondents swiftly dashed off their copy to the major broadsheets, as this report in the *Leeds Mercury* of 4 August testifies:

MAD ORGIES BY MOB AT LIVERPOOL

RIOTERS FIRED ON

**OVER 200 SHOPS WRECKED A PILLAGED
WARSHIPS IN MERSEY
SOLDIERS AND TANKS GUARDING THE CITY
MOB VIOLENCE
SHOPS SMASHED AND DEBRIS SET ON FIRE**

UGLY SCENES AT LIVERPOOL

The Police strike at Liverpool has been followed by serious consequences. On Saturday night, a large number of shops were broken into and looted. Bonfires were lighted in the streets and rioters indulged in wild orgies.

SAILORS AND SOLDIERS CALLED IN

In response to an appeal by the Lord Mayor, troops, accompanied by tanks, were sent into the city to maintain order. The battleship *Vigilant* and two destroyers were also sent to the port, with crews, to guard the docks.

RIOTERS FIRED ON

Matters took an ominous turn yesterday afternoon when systematic raids on bottling stores and spirit warehouses were made.

A number of looters were smartly captured by soldiers, but the crowd made a hostile demonstration against the troops. Shots were fired and a young man was seriously wounded. Another one was admitted to the hospital suffering from bayonet wounds.

Liverpool, the unhappy storm centre of hooliganism on many bygone occasions, is once again suffering the devastating experiences of mob law, for which the police strike is directly responsible. During the last two nights owing to the paucity of police protection, the rowdy elements of the city's population emerged from obscurity and indulged in a campaign of rioting, which led, not only to the destruction of thousands of pounds' worth of shop property, but to the pillaging of their contents.

In a tour of London Road and Scotland Road, the principally affected districts, which I have just completed, nearly two hundred wrecked shops stand as monuments of the ruthless crowd's activities overnight and early this morning. A couple of pianos standing derelict on the sidewalk denote the purposelessness devilry of the rioters.

PUBLIC HOUSES SPARED

All establishments were alike victims of their frenzy, save public-houses for mysterious reasons, remained immune. Grocers' shops are standing empty, general stores have been denuded, boot makers, pawnbrokers' establishments, wine sellers' premises and clothing shops were indiscriminately looted, and the thoroughfares previously mentioned present a picture of desolated property.

The presence in the city of a large force of military had little apparent effect on the disorganised gangs who were noticeably aggressive shortly before midnight, when following the rioting, which to place early yesterday morning, the Lord Mayor's appeal to the authorities was answered by the despatch of nearly a thousand soldiers to the city from neighbouring camps. It was anticipated they would be in a position to at once quell any recurring disturbances, but in the outbreaks this morning there appears a disinclination to use the soldiers other than in a parade of potential force.

RIOT ACT READ SOLDIERS FIRE OVER THE HEADS OF THE CROWD

After the first outbreak in the neighbourhood of the Rotunda Theatre, where a shop was attacked and looted, it had been answered by the reading of the Riot Act, where a body of soldiers had fired a volley of shots pointing their rifles over the heads of the crowds. Thereafter they paraded in the districts, where the mob were threatening activity, without, however actually interfering.

Passivity being cunningly used, no sooner were they out of sight, than shop windows were smashed and lawbreakers, young women prominently included, pressed forward to help themselves to the contents.

War tanks which moved in yesterday afternoon to support the men of the Derby, Notts and Stafford regiments who composed the occupying military force, stood silent sentinels on St George's Hall Plateau. Almost within a stone's throw away, scenes of lawless effrontery were witnessed. A batch of men stole a horse and cart, drove up to a big drapery establishment, piled up the cart with stuff and got away.

BONFIRES IN THE STREETS

Individuals carrying piles of looted commodities, walked calmly by the military and away to their homes. In Scotland Road, shop fittings were hacked, thrown out into the streets, and made into bonfires, by the light of which was dancing to the tunes of stolen musical instruments. For over two hours, hooliganism held supreme sway and gave vent to its passions in sheer wanton damage and wholesale robbery.

To a great extent, the police were powerless, being grotesquely outnumbered. There were 951 of the full force of 1880 available, the remaining 921 being on strike. The strikers, it should be stated, were in no way identified with lawlessness. As soon as the trouble began, detachments of regular police, augmented by drafts from the six hundred odd special constables enrolled yesterday, were despatched to the scenes of operation. Several ugly baton charges took place, and numerous minor injuries are reported both among police and rioters. There was, however, a remarkable absence of serious injury as the result of the early morning collisions between forces of law and disorder.

NUMEROUS ARRESTS

Numerous arrests were made, however, and included over sixty persons taken into custody during yesterday's disorder, a tremendous list of persons awaits police-court prosecution. Police charges continued over a period of nearly three hours, at length had the effect of dispersing the rioters, and at four o'clock this morning, some semblance of order had been restored and the overworked constables secured a much needed rest.

Today, the city is comparatively unpoliced and a variety of minor disturbances and shop robberies are repeatedly occurring, while the open prevalence of gambling in the streets accurately reflects the state of disorder to which Liverpool is reduced.

DRUNKEN ORGIES

Meanwhile, trouble has spread to Birkenhead, where one third of the police force of 225 is out on strike. Here, unlike Liverpool, the public-houses have suffered heavily, and the spectacle of whole groups of drunken people lying helpless in the streets was a feature of this early morning's occurrences. Scores of shops have been wrecked in the centre of the town, and the loyal police and specials have arrested upwards of fifty raiders. The neighbouring borough of Wallasey remains unaffected, but Bootle, where half the police are out, has suffered from a great deal of disorder. All along the docks stealing has been rife during the weekend, huge quantities of food-stuffs having been removed due to lack of adequate protection.

One 'capture' of nine men has been recorded at Collingwood Dock, where they ransacked a whisky store, but fell into the hands of special guards when getting away with the loot. All local banks, by the way, were guarded throughout the night by their staffs, who were sworn in a specials for the purpose. The battleship *Vigilant* and two destroyers arrived in the Mersey this afternoon, with crews, who will be detailed to guard the docks where necessary. As though to lend additional emphasis to Merseyside's position of gravity, a baker's strike is announced to be now in operation, and a large section of tramway men have decided to leave work tonight pending the settlement of grievances. The bakers' declare that unless their strike is settled not a loaf of bread will be available in Liverpool on Tuesday.

Leeds Mercury, **4 August 1919**

Police tactics that weekend included transporting officers in motor lorries to disturbances, where they quickly organised themselves into a baton charge running at the rioters, inflicting a high rate of injuries. By Monday 4 August, the city was quieter, as the as the police were finally taking control. Later that morning, 350 people appeared before the Liverpool Police Court charged with looting and rioting, while that same day the Watch Committee wasted no time in recruiting new officers. Newspaper adverts were printed, and replacement officers were accepted from all over the UK, with very few accepted from Liverpool itself. Yet within 12 months, quite a few of the new recruits had left the force, either dismissed or disillusioned.

LIVERPOOL CITY POLICE

Recruits are required at once to fill up vacancies. Wages commencing £3 10s. per week, Uniform and Pension. Apply personally or by letter to

HEAD CONSTABLE,

Police Offices,

Dale Street.

Recruiting advert placed in the local press, August 1919

273

For those who failed to parade on duty the punishment exacted by the Watch Committee was harsh. Every one of the 954 striking officers was sacked and lost their pensions, without any right of appeal. The strikers still considered their action was still active into mid-August, but any hopes of union recognition or reinstatement of officers was completely futile. Numerous constables were also summoned before local magistrates to be given eviction orders from their police homes. The leader of the strike was a notable casualty. Sergeant Robert Tissyman was the local NUPPO Leader and organiser of the union's eight branches in the city. An officer with a long service award from the Watch Committee, he was a passionate believer in the officer's cause, and with only eight weeks to go to his pension he led the men out on strike. He lost everything, his job, his pension and his home. He continued to fight for the working class, and became a city councillor two years later.

The strikers tended to find no animosity from their former colleagues but such toleration was rarely mutual as many strikers were extremely bitter towards those who hadn't come out with them. Considering the contemporary socialist movement and actions across the country and in Europe, the Liverpool officers also felt particularly let down by the lack of support from the local Labour movement in their fight for reinstatement, and consequently the morale of the Liverpool strikers collapsed completely after the third week. Such support had been pledged in the preceding months, and the police union claimed that they had been assured that in the event of a police strike, the vast majority of organised workers would down tools in support. But when it came to decisive action, meetings were split, as many of the union rank and file were wary of too close a relationship with officers. These were the same officers they felt, who at any other time, would be so quick to break up local union activity and demonstrations, and many of these union men had been on the receiving end of police brutality during the Liverpool transport strike of 1911 -

and consequently held the police with contempt. Even the local trade unions were now doubting the true authenticity of a 'police union'. Furthermore, orders had not been received from their own national executive in London, and most trade unionists in Liverpool were not prepared to strike without them.

The representatives of the strikers even announced publicly that they now regretted their action, they would leave the union, and, bowing to authority, 'respectfully begged' the Watch Committee to give them their jobs back. The response was blunt and heartless, being told not to 'cringe and whine', but 'to take a licking like men'.

Many former officers found it very difficult to find work in the city, as businesses were frequently paid a visit by non-striking officers, who 'encouraged' them not to employ strikers. It also became common for many Liverpool firms to advertise jobs with the stipulation that dismissed police officers need not apply.

Paradoxically, a collection was started for the officers who remained loyal. The Head Constable refused to allow his officers to take the money, so instead they were given a silver ring to place on their truncheon, inscribed: 'Liverpool City Police Riots August 1919' alongside their name. Sergeant's uniform chevrons were broadened and made of silver wire thread, whilst the Inspector's Cap Braid was silver thread, as opposed to the traditional black. This is a tradition that Merseyside Police still retains today.

Strike action certainly benefited those still in the force. Officers received a pay increase that doubled their wages, and the government was forced to take notice of their issues with the establishment of the Police Federation. The two strikes also sent a clear message to the government regarding the importance of the police in terms of the government's own stability. After 1919, the police were never again taken for granted, as they had been in the years before (although this sentiment may have evaporated in the present atmosphere). It would, however, be some years before the Liverpool federation had any measure of effectiveness. By the mid 1920s, constables on maximum pay received around 60 per cent more than the earnings of the average male worker in industry and more generous scales of leave were introduced, universal rent allowances paid, and in Liverpool, daily hours of duty were reduced to eight for all ranks except detectives and the mounted police. A more selective recruitment policy was adopted, and many of the strikers were replaced by returning ex-servicemen, already made suitable by their army training and discipline.

The ruling class saw the defeat of police militancy as a significant victory and a hammer blow against militant labour generally, during a time of broad socialist unrest. The Lord Mayor of Liverpool was quick to capitalise on the outcome, describing how Lloyd George 'looked on the Liverpool police strike as perhaps the turning-point in the Labour movement, deflecting it from Bolshevist and direct actionist courses to legitimate Trade Unionism once again. Had Liverpool been wrongly handled, and had the strikers scored a success, the whole country might have very soon been on fire' - whatever the cost to men like Robert Tissyman who never gave up the fight against injustice. Clearly, it was essential to the government that they had a loyal and reliable police force – soon to be tested and proven during the General Strike of 1926. Such a relationship and reliability has been maintained to the present day.

Police Bill, page 544

THE POLICE & PRISON OFFICERS' MAGAZINE.

THE OFFICIAL ORGAN OF THE NATIONAL UNION OF POLICE & PRISON OFFICERS

EDITOR: E. R. RAMSAY. [Registered at the G.P.O. as a Newspaper

VOL. I., No. 33. WEDNESDAY, OCTOBER 8, 1919. ISSUED WEEKLY Price 2d.

The Police Strike

TRADE UNIONISTS OF BRITAIN

This Fight is Your Fight.

The Government has Forced this Strike on the Police and Prison Officers.

Shortt has Slammed the Door. Lloyd George has Bolted it.

If the Government succeeds in Defeating Us, it will deal with You Next.

The Government is out to Smash the Trade Union Movement.

The Government tried to Reduce Your Wages.

By Reconstruction the Government means Restoration of pre-war Sweated Wages and Conditions.

The Press poured forth a Stream of Lies and Abuse about the Strikers.

If the Policemen Fail, Trade Unionism has Failed.

STAND BY YOUR BROTHERS!

All enquiries respecting advertisements should be addressed to Mr. S. F. Devitt, Advertisement Manager, Wardrobe Chambers, 146a Queen Victoria Street, London, E.C.4

As late as October 1919, the organ of the striking police was still appealing for support across the trade union movement

Further Reading

Bean, Ron, *'Police Unrest, Unionisation, and the 1919 Strike in Liverpool'*
Journal of Contemporary History, Vol. 15 (1980)
O'Mara, Pat, *The Autobiography of a Liverpool Slummy*
Sellwood, A.V, *Police Strike 1919,* W.H. Allen (1978)

On the Net

Rothwell, Shaun R., *Liverpool Police Strike 1919*
liverpoolcitypolice.co.uk

Jones, Owen, The 'Spirit of Petrograd'? The 1918 and 1919 Police Strikes
- *What Next?* Marxist Discussion Journal (online)
www.whatnextjournal.co.uk (Vol. 31, 2007)

12

Frank Hornby and his Factory of Dreams

Every boy's hero (and, let's face it, every man's, even those well into retirement) must surely be Frank Hornby. I don't get *Top Trumps,* I don't get *Pokemon,* or anything that needs to have fifteen buttons pressed incessantly at the same time, while glued to a screen without seeing daylight for the whole of August. Ok, I'll admit to the odd game of FIFA on the Xbox, but I can't score a goal to save my life against my two sons, who have the world championship sown up by lunchtime. When they were younger they had their Dinky cars and several Thomas the Tank Engine trains running on their Hornby train set, which incidentally I had carefully laid onto a hinged board, complete with double tracks and numerous sidings for the important shunting manoeuvres. It may lay folded up in the garage, while they were temporarily distracted by these crazy fancy button games, but I do know they will return to it if they have sons of their own, or nephews, or any excuse to get the train sets out once again. Too uncool while they had the Xbox, but they will come back. I know it.

So our hero, Frank Hornby, with no formal training in engineering, became a visionary in manufacture and development of toys, and was responsible for the invention and production of three of the most popular lines of toys based on engineering principles in the twentieth century: *Meccano, Hornby Model Railways*, and *Dinky Toys*.

Frank Hornby was born on 15 May 1863 in 77 Copperas Hill, Liverpool. An exotic sounding place, but just an ordinary street, reaching up the modest rise from the end of Lime Street alongside the first Adelphi Hotel, to its summit just behind the station approach. Most of the buildings lining the road were rows of terraces built in the previous century. There were numerous tradesmen, including a small community of watchmakers, centred in this street. Frank's parents were John Oswald Hornby and Martha Hornby (née Thomlinson), and his father operated a small business as a wholesale provisions dealer.

Copperas Hill in the nineteenth century

While not a salubrious area, it was still a cut above the streets of densely packed labourer's housing that lay around the docksides. But now the expanding family needed more space, and by October that year, they had moved to Mill Street in Toxteth. Frank was christened shortly afterwards on 25 October in nearby St Simon's. By 1871, they were across town in St Anne's Street, Islington, followed by another move to 20 College Street North in Everton by 1881. Frank went to school until the age of sixteen – a reflection of the modestly higher social standing than much of the surrounding local population. This was still the decade before the introduction of the Education Act of 1870. Nevertheless, he revealed later that he was unhappy at school and often played truant. Far more inspiration seems to have been gained from a book called *Self-Help* by Samuel Smiles, which he read constantly.

On leaving school, he started working as a cashier in his father's business, while he followed his love of music by joining the Liverpool Philharmonic Society in the 1880s. The original Liverpool Philharmonic Hall opened in 1849, but the Liverpool Philharmonic Society had already been in existence for nine years prior to that. Liverpool architect John Cunningham had been appointed to provide a concert hall to house their orchestra of 250, plus space for an audience of 2,100 and 'refreshment and retiring rooms'. The result was a building that was regarded by many as one of the finest and best adapted to music of its day. So it was here that a young Frank Hornby attended concerts and also met his future wife, schoolteacher Clara Walker Godefroy, a daughter of a customs officer. Frank was a tenor and Clara a contralto, both also being able to play piano. They regularly sang at local informal concerts and soon struck up their relationship. They were married on 15 January 1887 and had two sons, Roland (1889) and Douglas (1890).

In 1899, John Hornby died, and it was decided to close the business. Frank became a bookeeper for David Hugh Elliot, who ran a meat importing business located among the commercial office quarter of James Street. This was close to the Pier Head, a hive of business activity where dozens of shipping companies, banks, importers and exporters had their office premises. At the bottom of the street the famous White Star Line, would be relocated at the end of the century from its premises in adjacent Water Street. Frank would later make dozens of journeys across the Atlantic on their vessels.

As a white collar worker on a reasonable income, he was able to move away from the city centre and relocate to the leafy village of Maghull to the north, a mile or so past Aintree. Their house, 'The Hollies', was in Station Road, making it an easy commute by train to the city. (The house later became the first building outside London to be awarded a blue plaque.) So it was in this suburban home with two young boys that Frank began to think of ways to keep them entertained, and began to tinker with the idea of making small components that could be made into larger models. A moment of inspiration came on the train journey home from work. He said later, 'we were stopped opposite a goods yard and there was a small crane there. It occurred to me that I could make a crane like that for the children using strips of steel. I sat in the carriage dreaming about it. New possibilities kept coming; I saw what this new game could mean. I was drunk with delight when I got out of the train.'

Frank was speaking in the early 1930s, when Meccano magazine published 'The Life Story of Meccano: the Romance of the World's Greatest Toy', in which Frank thought back to this early period, 'my thoughts turned in the direction of interchangeable parts that could be used for a variety of purposes, instead of parts that had to be made especially for each particular job. Looking back over those days I can trace in those vague ideas the germ of the Meccano system'

He began experimenting with a few of his ideas, some of which entailed cutting small parts from sheet metal. The early structures were models of trucks, cranes and bridges, but as yet the parts were not interchangeable. Toys would soon outlive their interest, and a child's boredom with a once exciting toy was inevitable. What if the toy could be dismantled and rebuilt into something just as worthwhile, just as exciting? It could be a learning tool too - there were many educationalists at that time, following the Education Act of 1870, who were looking towards the value of learning through play. Coupled with the legislation, social and economic change was also increasingly promoting the notion of childhood. The Factory Acts had put paid to the exploitation of child workers, and by the 1890s it was illegal to employ children until they were 12 or 13, although the new school hours often saw working class children being sent out to work before or after school. So by the end of the century, commercial toy makers were on the increase, and more and more toys and children's books began to appear.

Yet this type of toy didn't exist. Was that because there wasn't a market for it, or because it just hadn't been thought of? As Hornby developed parts that could be bolted together, it enabled them to be easily dismantled to be put away, so on another day they could be reconstructed into something else entirely.

He worked on the presentation of a marketable boxed model kit and included an eighteen page manual, which placed great emphasis on the educational aspects that children would gain by playing with the toy. He called it 'Mechanics Made Easy', and, no doubt due his lack of professional training, he sought approval from trained engineers, sending them samples and drawings. He received a brief, although positive reply from Professor H.S. Hele-Shaw, the first professor of engineering at the University of Liverpool, a recent red-brick foundation. Hornby treated this endorsement as a testimonial and reprinted it in the front of the manual.

Walker Engineering Laboratories
University College Liverpool
Nov 5th 1901

Dear Sir,
Thank you very much for the photographs of your clever and useful form of toy. When it is on the market I shall certainly buy a set for my little boy, and feel sure it will afford many hours of enjoyment both to father and son. With a little ingenuity and exercise of the imagination, it should be as good as a fairy story, and what can one say more!

Yours truly,
H.S. Hele-Shaw

(*Much later in 1934, Frank Hornby would proudly show Hele-Shaw around his factory during a visit of the Institute of Mechanical Engineers, and tell him he was able to borrow £5 on the strength of his letter.*)

He began to cut metal strips by hand from copper sheets. They were regular in pattern, half an inch wide with holes for bolts spaced at half inch intervals. These regular perforations in different sized strips allowed for the interchangeable element to be introduced, and with the addition of axles and shafts, more complex structures could be constructed with a simple method.

The early attempts were understandably crude, but the basics were there. By January 1901, he had built a set of sufficient quality that he began to consider trying to market it. He didn't have enough capital of his own, and he even had to borrow £5 from his employer

David Elliot to cover the patents consultation fee, which had only been forthcoming once he had shown him the letter from the professor. With professional advice now in hand, he lodged his final patent specification in October 1901 as '*Improvements in Toy or Educational Devices for Children and Young People*'. The patent gave detail on the nature of the system, and also on the type of models that could be constructed, most of which related to railways, although the idea for Hornby model railways was still some way in the future.

But there were many teething troubles getting the first kits into manufacture. Initially, he farmed out production to a number of suppliers, but this caused endless problems and a centralisation of the business was inevitable. He was now a businessman and not a designer - 'from being an inventor I became a manufacturer', he said later. But his life was to change considerably more.

Frank was now Chief Clerk at Elliot's, and mutual trust and a friendship had formed between the two men. Hornby even gave his daughter Patricia, born in 1905, the middle name of Elliot. Consequently, as Frank had now outgrown his home workshop, Elliot came to his aid, formed a partnership between them, and provided rented premises next door to his business at 18 James Street, as well a providing most of the much needed investment to get the business off the ground.

The earliest '*Mechanics Made Easy*' kits to go on sale in late 1901/early 1902 had only sixteen different types of parts, with instructions on how to build twelve models, and it was going to be some years before Hornby could draw a salary from the company or for Elliot to see a return on his investment. Nevertheless, the signs were encouraging. Between 1901-03 they sold around 2,000 kits. Despite his enthusiastic moves into advertising, too many retailers were not taking up options on the kits. Many thought them crude and unattractive in appearance, and he was frequently faced with emphatic rejections, but with a marketing agreement made with Philip, Son, & Nephew, with their branches in Liverpool, London and Stoke, sales slowly improved. In 1903, interest and sales were boosted by the idea of a model building competition which wisely also included a school entry.

By 1905-6 the kits had expanded with an increase in the range of parts, and the company moved into profit, although meagre, for the first time. Elliot was now able to take back some of his investment and reduce his liability, while Frank now able to resign from his full-time position in Elliots and begin to look for larger premises. *Mechanics Made Easy* was now selling well with retailers across the country, and he had even broken into the French market.

In 1907, he signed a three-year lease on a one room factory among the warehouses of the dock trading area of Duke Street. *'Elliot & Hornby, Machine Tool Manufacturers'*, were now installed in 12 Duke Street; lathes, presses and milling machines were purchased and the workshop fitted out, thereby enabling more of the parts to be manufactured on site and less reliance on erratic suppliers.

The name *'Meccano'* was coined – much snappier than *'Mechanics Made Easy'*, and according to Hornby, a play on *'make and know'*, and easier to pronounce by people of all nations. Other origins of the name refer to it sounding like a cross between mechanics and dynamo, with potentially more universal appeal. Whatever its origins, it was a success and sales of Meccano had risen to 8,000 over the next two years, bring in a four-figure profit for the first time.

Hornby was now confident enough to approach Elliot's bank, Hill & Sons, with the plan to launch as a limited company – Meccano Limited. This was set up with seven shareholders:
Arthur Hooton, a bank manager from Liscard;
George Jones, a photographic manager from Tranmere;
Owen William Owen, Hornby's solicitor;

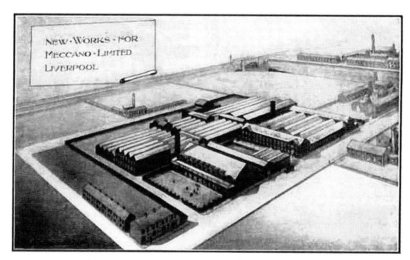

*Above: Artists impression of the new purpose built
Meccano works in Binns Road, Liverpool 1916*

Below: Inside the Binns Road Factory

Montague and Leonard Hill representing the bank;
Edward Holt Diggles Wary, a bank cashier from Birkenhead; and
of course Hornby himself.

Elliot retired from the company although he received £1,600 worth
of shares. He sold them in 1911 and it appears he had played no
further role in the business after its re-launch. Meanwhile, ever
mindful of the business advice he had first paid for, Hornby began
to register the new company and their patents across the world
to protect the ideas and assets. Nevertheless, the company would
spend much time and resources over the next sixty years battling
to remove some very blatant imitations, both in the brand name
and the product itself.

The Duke Street works was far too small to cope with the latest
expansion, and production moved to a larger site into an old
carriage works in West Derby in 1909, while the kit boxes were
rebranded with the Meccano Boy on the cover, together with a
rather large model. The kits were advertised as a 'fascinating
hobby for all ages', although it was clear that marketing was
directed at boys, despite the girl on the cover on the boxes, who
seemed to have wandered on there by accident. They were quick
to act on early flight too, as following Bleriot's Channel crossing
in 1909, aeroplanes appeared on Meccano publicity by 1910.
Attention turned to crack the US market, where 10% of sales was
to be re-channelled into advertising. Within seven years £100,000
had been spent, as the business swiftly expanded and reaped the
benefits. Hornby's sons Roland and Douglas joined the firm during
this pre-war period, having both been educated at the Liverpool
Institute and periods abroad, Roland in France and Douglas in
Germany - consequently they took charge of the offices in Paris
and Berlin.

By 1914, the company had outgrown the West Derby carriage
works, but Frank was now intent on securing a site for a purpose

built factory, and a piece of land in Binns Road, in the Old Swan area of Liverpool, was secured for the new building. It would be the company headquarters for the next sixty years. During the First World War both his sons enlisted and survived the hostilities, but in 1919 the family were devastated by loss of the Hornby's only daughter Patricia, who died aged 14 of Poliomyelitis. It was made all the harder as Frank and Clara were away on holiday at the time, Patricia passing away at her boarding school in Liverpool, with only Roland at her side.

The immediate post war boom in the market and rising success of the business was little consolation. The workforce had now reached 1,200 and a new wing to the factory in Binns Road was added for the construction of clockwork trains.

Yet this boom was to last only two years as recession approached. By 1922 the workforce was down to 453. Gradually, the company recovered through the twenties, and by clever marketing Frank had become a kind of 'Scouse Santa' to the boys who bought his products. The company was unique in its relationship with its young clients, as from 1916 a magazine (featuring their mascot 'Mecanno Boy') was regularly produced for them, full of hints and tips, plus they were encouraged to write in for replacement parts and helpful advice.

The most iconic boys' toy, the train set, first appeared in 1920. It seemed a natural progression, as many of the suggested Meccano models were trains. The first sets were in 'O' gauge and were clockwork powered, with either two or four feet of circular track. They made an immediate impact and were marketed with similar educational qualities of Meccano, and of course, in similar fashion they could be endlessly added to. A Hornby set would never be complete. Accurate representation of the stock, liveries and dozens of accessories just added to its authentic appeal.

Meccano Magazine (February 1937), with its evocative front cover featuring the 'Three Graces' on the Liverpool Pier Head waterfront, with the added futuristic elevated airfield – to be built from Meccano of course.

Most of the factory workers were young unmarried women working on a conveyor belt production line. Those familiar with the 'downstairs' domestic servant life in the homes of the wealthy, will be all too aware of the treatment towards any young working class female staff who wished to be married – it was the job or a new husband, but not both. This was still the same approach towards the Binns Road women in the 1930s, and those wishing to get married were forced out.

In 1930, domestic sales of Hornby train sets eclipsed Meccano sets for the first time. Further miniaturisation of train sets in 1938 to '00' (*Dublo*) broadened their appeal still further. These kits were electric, and 80% of homes were now receiving an electric supply. But at the beginning of the 1930s, at a time in life when most people of Frank's age were content to ease up a little and enjoy retirement, Frank started to step up a gear. He entered politics and was elected Conservative MP for Everton, and served in the coalition of 1931. Each week on late Friday afternoons, after arriving by train in Lime Street directly from Parliament, Frank was then whisked straight to the factory in his 'Roller', always keeping his Binns Road staff on their toes. But the schedule was gruelling, and inevitably began to take its toll on Hornby's health, but still he worked on. While competitors consolidated, or went under during the depression, Hornby went public in 1932 raising £300,000 to fund expansion. Two years later, following a plan of diversification to ensure continued growth, the company expanded and introduced *Dinky Cars* in 1934. By 1935 his health had deteriorated to such an extent, that he left the running of the company to his co-directors and staff, while his stay in politics was cut-short, having to resign his parliamentary seat before the 1935 General Election.

Back in 1920, Hornby's increasing fortune had enabled him to purchase a large mansion and estate in Maghull known as '*Quarry Brook*', not far from '*The Hollies*'. He continued to travel abroad and made frequent trips to the United States, often travelling alone on company business to the American offices, but he also enjoyed taking cruises with Clara. Ironically, it was while Clara was travelling alone on a Mediterranean cruise when Frank was taken ill at home. On 5 September 1936, Clara had left Southampton on the *Arandora Star* with her niece and other companions, on a cruise to improve her own health, while Frank had to stay at home due to his work commitments. They had been looking forward to planning their golden wedding anniversary celebrations in January 1937, and he was planning the programme when he was suddenly taken ill. He had been suffering from heart trouble for some time, as well as diabetes which had badly affected his sight, and on Friday 18 September 1936, he had an operation at the David Lewis Northern Hospital in Great Howard Street. Although he survived the surgery, he passed away three days later on Monday 21 September. He was seventy-two.

Poor Clara had no idea, and the news was kept from her, despite it being announced on the ship's tannoy. Roland met her seven days later to break the news, and to tell her that she had also missed the funeral, which had taken place on the Thursday after his death. Frank was interred in the family grave alongside his daughter Patricia in St Andrew's Churchyard, Maghull.

The Hornby Family Vault, St Andrew's Churchyard, Maghull

Considering his impact on the toy world and the enjoyment brought to so many youngsters across the world, there is surprisingly little to commemorate his life in his hometown. The Catholic Sisters of Mercy purchased *Quarry Brook* from Clara in 1949 where they established a school for 5-11 year olds. By the end of the 1950s, a purpose built Catholic grammar school had been constructed in the adjacent grounds. Today the house is still *in situ* as part of the Maricourt High School. Clara took a suite at the Adelphi, before retiring to the south coast, where she died aged 92 on 13 October 1953. She was laid to rest alongside Frank in the family grave in Maghull.

Roland inherited the company at a difficult time. Despite the initial hopes of the 1930s, turnover was down by more than half the 1930 figure, and the outbreak of war placed further stresses on production. The company struggled on into the fifties, but by 1963 Meccano was trading at significant losses. This led to a takeover by Lines Brothers in 1964, and Roland and his sister-in-law Una were forced off the board. To add to the pain, it was Walter Lines who had asked Hornby to buy out his struggling company in the thirties - such a reversal of fortune must have been hard to swallow. Hornby products were broken up and *Airfix* acquired the Meccano name, but numerous takeovers have been witnessed since then. Production in Liverpool finally ceased in 1979, with the closure of the Binns Road factory.

Overflowing with nostalgia, TV presenter James May brought Meccano back to its home city in 2009 in his *Toy Story* series. In a homage to some of Britain's best loved toys, he developed a number of projects which entailed making life-size constructions – which also included a programme on Hornby trains. The 'Meccano challenge' was to construct a bridge, entirely from standard size Meccano, over the new Leeds and Liverpool canal extension on the Pier Head in front of the Liver Building (just opposite the site of the futuristic elevated air strip on the magazine cover!). James May engaged Hayden Nuttal, Design Director of Atkins Structural Engineering, as chief design engineer, together with the help of a number of student engineers from the University of Liverpool (and help from the North East Meccano Guild). It took approximately 100,000 normal, half inch-wide Meccano strips, girders and bolts, and more than 1,000 man-hours to build the structure across the 40 foot wide Leeds-Liverpool canal. Dr Tim Short, from the University of Liverpool, said:

'We've taken inspiration from James May, the design proposal from the architecture students, and the design drawings from Atkins, added an enormous amount of Meccano, and created a bridge that is unique and impressive. It is fitting that Meccano has been brought back to Liverpool as the city was home to Meccano for more than 70 years until the Binns Road 'Factory of Dreams' in Wavertree was finally closed in 1979'.

James May and the Meccano Bridge at the Pier Head, Liverpool

James May was just as enthusiastic, 'This is a really impressive structure and it shows just what can be achieved with Meccano, which was the first - and some say the best - construction toy.' He proved the success of the design by walking across the bridge, which took his weight without problem, as he continued his piece to camera in the final scene of the programme. A triumphant return by an invention from humble beginnings over a century earlier.

Today, just a few yards from where the bridge was built, a small section in the Museum of Liverpool on the Pier Head waterfront is dedicated to Frank Hornby, while the Museum has also given support to the Frank Hornby Trust, which is trying to raise enough money to create a permanent Frank Hornby Heritage Centre exhibition in Maghull based in the Meadows Leisure Complex. Liverpool Museum have pledged to help Maghull's trustees to obtain Heritage Lottery funding and will loan items for the Meadows museum.

It seems remarkable that given the success and fame that Hornby achieved, that there is no major memorial to him to be found in the city. Yet this lack of a substantial memorial in Liverpool doesn't really matter. Hornby's memorial is what he produced. So many industrialists, engineers, scientists and academics have testified to the influence and impact that his toys made upon their early lives. Can't quite see that from the button-pushing-game-console generation. Sir Harry Kroto, the Nobel Chemist, used Meccano to work out the shape of the Carbon 60 Molecule and bemoaned the decline in popularity of Meccano declaring, 'it has been a disaster for the education of our young engineers and scientists'. It is hard to see the skills gained from pushing buttons on a game console as comparable to those gained by trying to build a three-speed gearbox as a small child. No doubt if Frank was still alive his 'Hornby Game Console' would have been in kit form and you couldn't play it until you had put it together yourself - and written the programme for the game play.

Hornby's legacy lives on today with thousands of enthusiasts all over the world, still building Meccano models, running Hornby Train sets, and collecting Dinky Toys.

Here son, pass me that spanner will you.

Further Reading

Gould, M. P. *Frank Hornby - The Boy Who Made $1,000,000 With A Toy* (1915, reprinted 2004)
Gamble, J., *Frank Hornby – Notes and Pictures* (2001)
McReavy, A. *The Toy Story – the Life and Times of Inventor Frank Hornby* (2002)
Brown, Kenneth D., *Factory of Dreams – A History of Meccano Ltd 1901-1979* (2007)

On the Net

Frank Hornby's Life and the History of Meccano
www.frankhornby.com

Short Pictorial History of Frank Hornby
http://replay.waybackmachine.org/20060215002421/
http:/www.toyman.co.za/history/hornby.html

Meccano Magazine
http://pdfmm.free.fr/ (*an extensive collection available for free download covering the years 1916-1981*)

13

The Murder of Julia Wallace 1931

On the case files of Liverpool City Police, there still lies a murder dating from 1931 recorded as 'undetected'. Yet at the time, the Force thought they had their man, who was tried, found guilty, and sentenced to hang in April 1931. The following month he was freed on appeal – the first time in criminal justice history that a conviction for murder was overturned, and the accused released. The case was that of the gruesome murder of Julia Wallace, and the man arrested and tried was her husband William. It has fascinated crime writers and amateur sleuths ever since, some even going as far to call it the 'perfect crime'.

William Herbert Wallace was born in the small Cumberland town of Millom in 1878. His first job on leaving school at fourteen was as a draper's assistant in Barrow-in-Furness. When he finished this apprenticeship, he moved to Manchester where he obtained a position with Messrs Whiteway Laidlaw and Company, who were outfitters to the H.M. Armed Forces and the Colonial, Indian and Foreign Services. He spent five years there, before being transferred to their branch in Calcutta in 1903. There he remained for two years, until he was contacted by his brother Joseph in Shanghai, suggesting he come and join him there, and in 1905 he was able to transfer to Whiteway Laidlaw's branch in that city. Not long after his arrival, he was laid low by a recurring kidney problem, and he left China for England in 1907 in order to have it treated at home. It was serious enough for his left kidney to be removed at Guy's Hospital, and after discharge he went for convalescence to live with his retired parents and sister, who had relocated to 9 Belmont Road in Harrogate. When he was able to return to work, he became an election agent for the local Liberal Party, and around this time he met a local girl, Julia Dennis, to who he was married in March 1914. Born on 28 April 1861, she fifty-two, seventeen years his senior, William being thirty-five.

William Herbert Wallace

A few months later, he found himself out of work, a victim of the suspension of elections due to the outbreak of the First World War in August 1914. Given his age and health problems, war service was not going to be the obvious path for William, however, he was helped back into employment by his aged father, who used his contacts in his former employment in insurance to secure a position of collections agent with the Prudential Assurance Company in Liverpool. William and Julia moved to Liverpool in 1915, first to 26 Pennsylvania Road, Clubmoor, then to 29 Wolverton Street, a quiet cul-de-sac in Anfield, four months later. He was a cultured man with a scientific mind, and set up a home laboratory for chemistry experiments in the rear bedroom. Such was his knowledge, that he was engaged as a part-time lecturer in Chemistry at Liverpool Technical College, while he also attended lessons to improve his violin playing so he could accompany his pianist wife at home. But it was his hobby as a keen chess player that would play a significant role in the events that would follow.

It was on Monday 19 January 1931, that Wallace was in the Central Chess Club in the basement of Harrington Chambers at 24 North John Street, at a meeting of the Liverpool Chess Club, where he was taking part in a scheduled game. While he was there, a telephone message was passed to him, which had been received 25 minutes before his arrival. It was a request from a R.M. Qualtrough, asking him to call at 25 Menlove Gardens East, Liverpool, at 7.30pm the following evening to discuss insurance. Although a little puzzled by the call, he pocketed the note as there was always the chance of earning 20% commission.

Tuesday was a normal day at work, helping customers, collecting cash, travelling home, arriving just after 6pm. He had just enough time to grab a bite to eat and freshen up, before saying goodbye to his wife, reminding her to lock the door after he had gone.

He walked the three miles to the junction of Lodge Lane and

Smithdown Road, where he picked up a tram to Allerton, alighting close to his destination. He then made his way to Menlove Gardens, an area of leafy suburban housing in south Liverpool just off Menlove Avenue (this main road would become famous in the sixties, as it was where John Lennon grew up with his Aunt Mimi). He found Menlove Gardens West, and a North and South, but bizarrely no Menlove Gardens East. He even knocked at 25 Menlove Gardens West, but the name of Qualtrough was unknown. He walked back towards the nearby Allerton Road, a busy thoroughfare where the local shops were situated, and asked about the mysterious road at the newsagents, also asking several passing locals, then a policeman on his beat, all to no avail. After around 45 minutes he gave up and returned home.

The gruesome murder scene at 29 Wolverton Street, Anfield

Yet as he tried his key in the front door, it wouldn't budge, nor could he force the back door, accessed via a back alley. The Johnstons, his next-door neighbours, were on their way out and paused awhile to help. He tried the back door again, which now gave way after extra force. The scene that greeted him in the sitting room was one of shock and horror – his wife Julia lay face down by the fireplace, brutally beaten to death. He screamed to the Johnstons to come and see the awful sight.

The scene was soon one of intense activity, as the detectives went about the necessary procedures, while the word went out to look for a man covered in blood stains. In the kitchen, the cabinet door had been wrenched off, lying in two pieces on the floor. Wallace checked the Prudential cash box on the top shelf, which was found to be missing its contents of around £4. Julia's handbag on the chair still had money and some silver in it. The five pounds kept in a jar upstairs had not been touched. At five past ten, Detective Superintendent Hubert Rory Moore, the head of Liverpool Special Branch (CID) and detective Sergeant Adolphus 'Dolly' Fothergill arrived and were immediately brought to the murder scene.

After making a statement into the early hours of the morning, Wallace moved in with his sister-in-law Amy Wallace, at 83 Ullet Road while the investigation and man hunt was underway. It would not take long. Three weeks later on 2 February there was a knock at the door, and in walked three officers - Superintendents Moore, Thomas and Detective Inspector Gold, who arrested Wallace on suspicion of the murder of his wife.

The Police suspected that 'Qualtrough' was in fact William Herbert Wallace. Superintendent Moore considered there'd been no break in, no murder weapon left at the scene, and questioned why a thief would go to the trouble, whilst under pressure of time and having made a possible noise, to take four pounds from the tin after breaking the doors on the cabinet, then replace the lid and even put the tin back on the top shelf. The police were also convinced that it would have been just possible for Wallace to murder his wife and still have time to arrive at the place where he caught his tram. They made several different journeys to test out the times involved, but it would hinge on a very fit young man to make the connections – Wallace was a 52-year-old, not in the best of health.

The trial of Wallace began on Wednesday 22 April, and was held at St George's Hall. To a hushed court room, Edward George Hemmerde KC opened the case for the prosecution and swiftly began to tear apart Wallace's tale about his 'arranged meeting' with 'Qualtrough'. Over the next two hours he ridiculed the very idea that the events of the night in question had unfolded in a completely natural manner - the phone call to the chess club, the tram rides, asking directions from passers-by, the newsagent and most conveniently – the bobby on the beat – who incidentally he also asked the time – clearly to pinpoint the exact moment that he was on the other side of town and well away from the crime scene. And not forgetting, of course, the locked back door that conveniently gave way once the neighbours were there to witness it. 'Do you believe a tale like that?' said Hemmerde turning to face the jury. He also revealed that a mackintosh was found under Julia's shoulder. This, said Hemmerde, was worn by Wallace during the murder, who was naked underneath, which explained why there was no blood on his clothes.

The mysterious Qualtrough was never found. Hemmerde put it to the jury of 10 men and 2 women that Wallace made the "Qualtrough" call himself to avert suspicion. Beattie, who took the call in the chess club, said the voice on the phone was 'gruff but ordinary'; the prosecution argued that surely Beattie would have recognized Wallace's voice. The call had been made from the public call box on the corner of Rochester Road and Breck Road, only 400 yards from Wallace's home and nowhere near the Menlove Avenue area where it might be more likely to have been made if Qualtrough and his home actually existed.

Regarding the timings of Wallace at home that night, he told the police that he had been home between about 6:05 and 6:45. A 14-year-old milk delivery boy said he saw Julia Wallace take in the milk at 6:30pm, and the evening paper had been delivered at 6:35pm, which was later found spread on the kitchen table. The sighting of Julia threw doubt on the accuracy of the pathologist evidence who had given the time of death at around 6.00pm.

Attention turned to Mr Justice Wright, who began to summarise the case and give the jury direction. He told them that there was only circumstantial evidence against Wallace, there were no eyewitnesses, there seemed to be no motive, nor was there a murder weapon. There was the testimony from Samuel Beattie, the chess club captain, who was adamant it was not Wallace on the other end of the phone line, not to mention the extremely tight, if not impossible, timing needed for him to commit the murder. Advising the jury, Justice Wright strongly suggested that he considered the case not proven.

Nevertheless, with indecent haste, taking them little more than an hour, the jury returned to deliver their verdict of guilty. It was left to Justice Wright to pass the only sentence available to him – that of death by hanging.

Yet, legal history was about to be made. Wallace was returned to Walton Gaol after the trial to await his execution set for 12 May, but by Monday 27 April, plans for his appeal were already well under way. Public opinion was on his side, most feeling surprised by the conviction and an appeal fund was set up to help him meet the costs.

Wallace's defence team took the case to the Court of Appeal, and in London on 19 May 1931, the jury's verdict was quashed on the grounds of insufficient evidence. This was unprecedented in the British legal system. No convicted killer had ever had his or her conviction overturned.

William H. Wallace was now a free man. After a short break in London with his brother Joseph, Wallace returned to Liverpool by car on Thursday 21 May. At the Prudential, he was given a month's holiday to recuperate. He spent time in Broughton-on-Furness, again with brother Joseph. He tried to return to his usual routine and circumstances, but public opinion seemed to have reversed and he found society against him. He was met with antagonism on his collecting round and was harassed by people on the street, even the local children taunted him with rhymes about the murder. With great sympathy for his predicament, his superintendent at the Prudential, Joseph Crewe (who had taught him violin in the 1920s), transferred him to a desk job in the clerical department at the company head offices in Dale Street.

His lawyers also successfully contested several libellous actions against those who had defamed Wallace in print, and with the proceeds he was able to move into a bungalow in Bromborough on the Wirral for a quieter life. He continued to commute to Dale Street, but he was now increasingly suffering from a crippling abdominal condition. On 9 February 1933, he was rushed to Clatterbridge Hospital in the Wirral, where surgery revealed his remaining kidney to be in a poor state. His condition deteriorated over the next few days and he died on 26 February. He was buried in the same grave as Julia in Anfield Cemetery on 1 March. It seemed a final message to those who doubted his innocence.

And that could have been the end of the matter, but this was, to many, the perfect crime. This case began to fascinate the general public and more significantly, a whole slew of criminologists well before the ink was dry on the overturned verdict.

There have been at least ten substantial publications since 1931, and the age of the case, just as in the Ripper murders, has not dimmed the interest, but seems to have made the search for a solution even more vigorous. There have been dozens of essays, journals and magazine articles, and now with the advent of the internet, there are numerous dedicated websites, plus a hive of activity on criminologist and local history forums, exchanging relevant detail, photos, archive reports, and a plethora of posts suggesting new theories. Each new book claims to be the definitive version, no doubt at the insistence of the marketing people, rather than the outlandish claim of yet another amateur sleuth who has found the missing evidence, or has interviewed the prime suspect that everyone else has overlooked. Few sit on the fence - it was either Mr Wallace in the lounge with the lead pipe, or one of the two or three oft repeated names that have been put forward from the time of the case.

Richard Gordon Parry

So, if it wasn't Wallace, then who? A number of researchers have put forward Richard Parry. He was a 22-year-old insurance agent at the time of the murder, and had previously taken on Wallace's round when he was unwell and working for the Prudential. He would call at the Wallace home to deposit his takings and to see how Mr Wallace was keeping. Consequently, he got to know the interior of their home and where the money was kept, even the stash upstairs as he would pop up to Wallace's room to see how he was.

Yet he was always short of money, and Parry began to blacken his own character following a number of petty misdemeanours, eventually resulting in his dismissal from the Prudential. Collected policy contributions would go missing, and his accounts were short on more than one occasion, which including money from Wallace's round when he was covering for him. Once, William confronted him, Parry apologised, claiming it was an oversight and made up the difference out of his own pocket.

But later, Wallace learned that this was not the first time that this had happened, as some months earlier Parry had been short when paying into the Prudential's head office in Dale Street. It was brought to the notice of the Prudential Superintendent Joseph Crewe, who decided to contact his father, rather than sack Parry on the spot. Parry's father William bailed him out and his son was given a final warning. This must have been very embarrassing for both men, as William Parry was a Liverpool Corporation treasury official – he would later rise to Assistant City Treasurer by the time he retired in 1950, while Richard's uncle, George H. Parry, was chief Librarian in 1929 during a career lasting nearly forty-five years. However, in 1929 Richard stretched his employer's tolerance by one theft too many, and he 'left to take a position with a competitor'. In reality, he had been given the ultimatum - resign or be fired. Richard must have brought great anxiety and distress to the family over the next few years as his brushes with the law increased.

After being convicted of attempting to steal a Liverpool councillor's car in 1932, he was convicted of car theft in Aldershot two years later and sentenced to 3 months with hard labour. The following year came another conviction for theft – working as a salesman in Willesden he was again embezzling money from his employers, this time taking £2. 7s & 3d. He was bound over for a year. In 1936 he was in court for a more serious crime, accused of assaulting a woman he had offered a lift home to, but it was dismissed without sufficient evidence.

After the Wallace trial, criminologists believed Parry knew more about the case than had come out in court and began to search for his whereabouts. When he was eventually found, he steadfastly refused all approaches to talk about the Wallace case, even telling Jonathan Goodman and Richard Whittington-Egan who had tracked him down in London, 'not if you were to offer me £2000'. Much later he was working as a switchboard operator in Colwyn Bay Hospital, but after a heart attack he died in his North Wales home in April 1980 aged 71.

Could he have made the call on the night of the murder? He was known to be a good mimic of voices and had spent time in amateur dramatics. He had a track record for theft and he knew where Wallace stored his daily takings, as well as the layout of the house. Later, on the night after the murder, Parry turned up at William Atkinson's all night garage and taxi business on Moscow Drive, where an acquaintance, 24-year-old John Parkes had not long begun his night shift. A local bobby on the beat had already called that evening and spoken of the murder – Parkes knew the victim to be Parry's friend. Parkes later told the police about the reason for his early hours visit to the garage - Parry was pacing around, very agitated, pressing Parkes to hose his car down inside and out. Parkes thought it was quite clean already, but did as he was requested. On finding a leather glove inside he noticed it was covered in blood. According to Parkes, Parry grabbed it, declaring 'If the police found that, it would hang me'. Then he spoke about a bar which he'd dropped down a grid outside a doctor's house on Priory Road, a stone's throw from the Wallace home.

The grave of William and Julia Wallace, Anfield Cemetery, Liverpool

Before he left his shift the following morning, Parkes told his boss Atkinson what had transpired in the early hours. 'Don't have anything to do with it', said his boss, who even advised him to change his route into work. However, they did agree that the police should be told if Wallace was convicted. Parkes kept his word and did call the police, but by that time they had their man and were dismissive of Parkes' story. Nevertheless, John Parkes continued to maintain his story even saying the same on a local radio interview in 1981 during the investigation by Roger Wilkes. Police also believed Parry's alibi for the time of the murder to be 'unshakable'. The alibi was provided by a woman with whom he was having a relationship, but when this ended, she offered to swear to Wallace's solicitor that the alibi had been false. It covered the later part of the evening, but also threw the alibis for the time of the murder into doubt. Others pointed this was just the actions of a woman scorned. Other crime writers have suggested Parry had an accomplice who carried out the actual murder, while other suspects with less convincing evidence have included his next-door neighbours, the Johnstons.

But this, of course, is all too late for William Wallace. The case is still officially 'undetected' and interest is unlikely to wane considering the fascination with the unresolved, which both the researchers and the eager readership continue to display. As Justice Wright commented, the case *'must be almost unexampled in the annals of crime murder so devised and arranged that nothing remains which will point to anyone as the murderer'*.

Crime writer Raymond Chandler declared,

> 'The Wallace case is the nonpareil of all murder mysteries ... I call it the impossible murder because Wallace couldn't have done it, and neither could anyone else... The Wallace case is unbeatable; it will always be unbeatable.'

The perfect crime.

Further Reading

Wyndham-Brown, W.F., *The Trial of William Herbert Wallace* (1933)
Rowland, John, *The Wallace Case* (1949)
Bridges, Yseult, *Two Studies in Crime* (1959 and 1970)
Goodman, Jonathan *The Killing of Julia Wallace* (1969)
Hussey, Robert F., *Murderer Scot-Free* by (1972)
Wilkes, Roger, *Wallace The Final Verdict* by (1985)
Marshall Cavendish magazine partwork - *Murder Casebook 25: The Wallace Case* (1990)
Waterhouse, Richard, *The Insurance Man* by (1994)
Murphy, James, *The Murder of Julia Wallace* (2001)
Bartle, Ronald, *The Telephone Murder: The Mysterious Death of Julia Wallace* (2012)
Gannon, John, *The Killing of Julia Wallace* (2012)

On the Net

There are various short articles and discussions, but the best start point is a summary article by Mark Russell and Ged Fagan, *'The Wallace Murder Case'* which has a detailed discussion including commentary on the latest research.

http://inacityliving.blogspot.co.uk/2012/11/the-wallace-murder-case.html

Available on DVD

The Man From the Pru' – Film (1989)
(starring Jonathan Pryce, Anna Massey, Susannah York and Tom Georgeson).

A drama-documentary, *Who Killed Julia Wallace?* was made by Yorkshire TV in 1975, with Eric Longworth playing William Herbert Wallace.

The devastation of Huskisson following the SS Malakand explosion

14

Exploding Munitions

Captain Kinley and the May Blitz 1941

Liverpool endured a harrowing time in the Second World War as a major target for the enemy, suffering great devastation, both in her communities and infrastructure. In the first week of May 1941 alone, Liverpool experienced the heaviest bombing of the war in Britain outside London. The docks were the main target, but 3,000 people were killed and 11,000 homes completely destroyed. The first German bombs landed on Merseyside on 9 August 1940 at Prenton, Birkenhead, and in the following sixteen months, German bombs killed 2,716 people in Liverpool, 442 people in Birkenhead, 409 people in Bootle and 332 people in Wallasey. The worst periods of bombing were the 'Christmas Raids' of December 1940, and the 'May Blitz' of 1941, and these enemy raids continued for months, until the final bombs were dropped on 10 January 1942.

As the most important port outside London, Liverpool had become a crucial route for military equipment and supplies into the country, and consequently the 'Western Approaches Command' headquarters based in Plymouth were transferred to Liverpool in February 1941. The purpose of the Command was to co-ordinate intelligence information from the Admiralty and the Air Ministry, and to protect supply ships on their approach to the Mersey. This move was instigated by Winston Churchill, and an underground complex was constructed, known locally as the 'Citadel' or 'Fortress'. Located underneath Derby House in Exchange Flags (to the rear of the Town Hall) it was designed to be bomb proof and gas proof, with a 7ft. thick roof and 3ft walls, and 100 rooms covering an area of 50,000 square feet. The decoding room was home to the Enigma decoding machine, which had been recovered from a sinking U boat. (The headquarters have been reopened to the public as the Liverpool War Museum). In the docks were sited important munitions factories, while naval U-Boat hunters were stationed at Bootle. As the German campaign of destruction to immobilise London's docks became more intense, and the Mersey became more important to the British war effort, it was inevitable that Merseyside would soon become a target for the Luftwaffe. Evacuation would be essential.

When war broke out in September 1939, 95,000 people were evacuated to escape the threat of bombing. 57,000 of these were school children, and 31,000 were mothers and children under five years of age. Yet, as the 'Phoney War' convinced many that this threat was minimal, around 40% of the children were returned home by January 1940. Lancashire, Cheshire, Shropshire and Herefordshire received a total of 51,000 Liverpool evacuees, while another 44,000 were sent to live in Wales. A second programme of evacuation followed the 'Christmas raids' of 1940, when 1,399 children were rushed out of Liverpool between 20-22 December. Yet more children were evacuated during the 'May Blitz' of 1941.

During the summer of 1941, the threat of bombing seemed to lessen, and increasing numbers of children began to return home. More came back to the city in late 1944. But in many cases the upheaval changed the destiny of families forever. Some of the evacuated children did not stay in Merseyside when they were returned. There were cases of some children returning with their foster parents to live together in Liverpool. In other instances, family bonds had been irreparably broken, or parents felt their child would have better prospects if they grew up with their foster parents in their place of evacuation. Other foster parents were known to have funded their evacuee's education even after they had returned to their Merseyside homes. Paradoxically, by January 1942, Liverpool had taken in more evacuees from other parts of the country than it had children staying elsewhere.

If the docks were vulnerable from enemy action, then so were the local population with labour housing in close proximity, with cramped court housing and endless rows of terraces spreading in regular rows away from the dock road, both north and south of the city centre. Consequently, it became Dock Board policy that if munitions trains arrived too late in the day to be accepted by the docks then they would be shunted back to the nearest available sidings, which was a compromise between being safely away from the docks, but near enough to get on with the job of unloading in the morning. The Breck Road sidings, about three miles away near Anfield, were deemed most suitable.

And so it was, that such a train arrived too late on the evening of 3 May 1941, and was directed to the Breck Road sidings. However, this was to be the most intense night of the Blitz over Liverpool, as the docks and city centre endured a third night of pounding.

As enemy aircraft flew away from the targeted area, they frequently offloaded any remaining bombs to lighten their payload for the journey home, and it is generally believed that this is what happened as one such plane flew over the Breck Road sidings. It was an unlucky hit in a quiet residential area around midnight. The bomb landed on the track next to the munitions trucks, setting them alight, and soon the trucks began to explode one by one. Meanwhile, adjacent houses (mainly Worcester Drive, Pensylvannia Road) were suffering fire damage caused by the blasts and they were evacuated, as well as their Anderson shelters. George Roberts, a 34-year-old goods guard, was among a group of ten LMS railwaymen (London, Midland and Scottish Railway) who acted with great heroism that night. Together with several emergency teams of signalmen, ARPs (Air Raid Protection Wardens) and firemen, he tried to manhandle the trucks away, but had to call for the help of a locomotive.

The men who went off for the engine fetched a shunter from Edge Hill, two miles further south. On the way back, they met a goods train and decided to bring that instead. However, as they approached, they came across a bomb crater impeding their way, and realised they could not get near the sidings. In the darkness of the blackout, one of the men even fell in the crater and had to be rescued. In spite of their efforts, they could not get near the munitions train and had to settle for saving other trucks, mostly containing Spam and corned beef, which they uncoupled and shunted away. The situation had not improved by dawn, and the fires raged throughout the next day into 4 May. The munitions trucks continued to explode at regular intervals during the day, leaving a 250-yard trench gouged out along the main line, and blast damage leaving the nearby houses uninhabitable for some time afterward.

George Roberts recalled later,

'We were in the guards' waiting room at Edge Hill when we heard that Breck Road had been bombed. We went there by train to find the place an inferno. The Auxiliary Fire Service was already there doing a great job, but they were running out of water. Huge pieces of debris were flying all over the place and the whole of the area was alight with fires. There were 32 waggons on the train, each containing at least 10 tons of explosives. A bomb had dropped right in the middle of the train and the ammunition in the waggons was going off like squibs. After working for some hours, we managed to uncouple the waggons and shunt them into a siding.'

The Breck Road sidings are circled, centre right

315

Three men received the BEM, while George Roberts was awarded the George Medal in recognition of the leading part which he played in this heroic mass life-saving affair. Amazingly, no one was killed.

My own mother Hazel Royden (then Hazel Wiggins) lived nearby in Daneville Road. She had told me the story as a youngster, but coincidentally the *Making History* programme on BBC Radio 4 had asked me to research the events of that night and I pressed her for as much as she could recall.

'It was a horrific night, there were blasts going off everywhere – we were in the Anderson shelter throughout the continuous bombing. It was so terrifying to a little girl. We had no beds in the shelter, so my dad had taken our bedroom doors off and made them into bunk beds, but I hated the shelter and I can smell it now just talking about it, the mustiness, the damp earth, it brings back frightening memories. My parents were in the house with my youngest sister, and I, as the eldest aged 10, was looking after my two younger sisters and brother. I was so terrified that I screamed outside the back door to make them come out and come into the shelter with us, even though I risked a telling off.

In the morning, we emerged to find our house damaged - the windows were blown in, but then my father said "Look at this - it's not even part of a bomb, it's like iron plate off a train". He had found a big piece of iron or steel - it had sliced straight through our front door and taken it clean off the hinges. But we were lucky, as apart from the windows, it was the only real damage our house sustained in the war. It had been blown over from the sidings. We were always up between 5 and 6am to collect shrapnel out of gutters to take in to school for recycling. I remember there were loads more that morning. Later that same day my father and I walked to the siding - we didn't know what had happened – there were rumours abound, so we went to see. It felt a long way for my little legs, but in reality, it was a short distance. All the trees were covered in what looked like cotton wool, and it made everywhere look like there had been a snowfall. Maybe it was some kind of packing off the munitions. Many high explosives had dropped - there were huge holes cordoned off in the roads. I can remember hoping the Clubmoor Picture House - where we children went to regularly - hadn't been bombed, and luckily it was unscathed. As we approached the siding, we were not allowed near, there were big white tapes and we were stopped by the ARP's from going any further. Later there was a great fuss over why the train was there in the first place - I remember heated discussions between the adults. But then, the bombs could have hit the Royal Ordnance Factory at Stopgate Lane near Aintree - only a mile away. They did hit a munitions ship in the docks that night which was the greatest explosion ever heard in the area.'

After the events of 3/4 May there was a great deal of discussion over how best to handle the import and export of high explosives through the city and the port. The LMS promised never again to hold ammunition trains overnight at Breck Road sidings - only to be caught doing it again within three months.

The munitions ship that was hit was the *Malakand*, and as my mother described, it was by far the worst explosion Liverpool experienced, not just during the Blitz, but the entire war. The *S.S. Malakand* was a steamer owned by Thomas Brocklebank of Liverpool. Built by Lithgows, Port Glasgow, and launched in late 1918, the *Malakand* was operated as a cargo vessel of 7649 tons, 170 feet in length, with a breadth of 58 feet. She was part of the supply convoys to the Middle East, and on the night of the 3rd she was lying in Huskisson Dock No.2, with over 1000 tons of shells and bombs in her hold. She was under the care of Captain Howard Cooke Kinley, a 43-year-old Londoner, with ten other shore-relief officers and a Lascar crew of sixty-one.

Howard Kinley had inherited the seafaring instinct from his father, although tragically he never knew him. Howard Cooke Kinley was born in West Ham in London in 1897, the son of William Kinley and Esther Rogers. The family had moved from Liverpool where they had six children before relocating to Upton Park in London where William's Merchant Navy career had now taken him. Although he had met Esther in Liverpool, William was a Manxman, his father Edward being a farmer in Bradda, on the hillsides above Port Erin. The usual alternative to working on the farm for young men on the island was to be a fisherman or a mariner. When William was old enough he chose the latter, moving to Liverpool to the dockside area of Toxteth, in 61 South Chester Street. It was here he met Esther, the daughter of a dock labourer, and they were married in St Philemons in Toxteth on 14 April 1879.

After the move to London, William had signed on as chief engineer on the SS *Mohegan*. The ship had originally been launched as the *Cleopatra*, having been constructed as a mixed passenger liner and animal carrier by Earle's of Hull for the Wilson & Furness-Leyland Line. She had accommodation for 120 first-class passengers, plus stalls for 700 cattle, complete with an improved system of sanitation 'rendering the cattle carrying quite free from annoyance to passengers' However, before she went into service she was purchased by the Atlantic Transport Line, and sailed on her maiden voyage from London to New York on 31 July 1898, arriving on 12 August 1898. A number of defects were quickly revealed, blamed on a rushed construction. Her water system feeding the boilers malfunctioned and there were a number of serious leaks as the crew struggled to keep the ship operational. It was certainly bad enough for the passengers to lodge their protests to the company about the poor condition of the ship, although they exonerated the crew, acknowledging they had tried their best. The vessel returned to London at half speed, received extensive repairs, was trialled, inspected and passed by the Board of Trade and re-emerged as the *SS Mohegan*. So she left Tilbury at 2.30pm on 13 October 1898 with 53 passengers on board, seven cattlemen and 97 crew, carrying a general cargo including antimony and spirits under the command of the 42 year old Captain Richard Griffith. Her pilot left at Dover later that same evening, and the report on the progress so far was dispatched with him, addressed to the engineering superintendent of the Atlantic Transport Line. A few minor leaks and electrical failures were reported, but otherwise all was well, although the new team of firemen complained of a shortage of steam and that she wasn't 'up to the mark'. The author of the report was the Assistant Engineer William Kinley, Howards' father.

The *Mohegan* continued her voyage through the English Channel en route for New York, hugging the Cornish coast on her way to the Atlantic, but she took a wrong bearing not far from Falmouth Harbour, and as she approached the Lizard came in too close to the coast and ran on to the Manacle Rocks. One of the survivors described the moment,

> 'Suddenly there was an awful sound as though the ships bottom was being torn out....no one seemed to know what was the matter.... Stewards continued to serve dinner, and it was only when Charles Duncan (the father of Isadora), who was on the ship, shouted out "To the life preservers!", that we realised a serious accident had happened.'

Despite the ship carrying six steel lifeboats and two of wood, few were successfully launched. Within only twelve minutes she had gone down with the loss of 106 lives, including the Captain and all his officers. Howard's father, assistant engineer William Kinley, was one of them. He was only 43 – the same age his son would be when he was on the *Malakand* – and he left his wife aged 40 with their large family, although the eldest were now making their own way in the world. Nevertheless, there may have been some support from a relief fund, but life was going to be very difficult from now on. For young Howard there was more than a glimmer of hope when it was recommended he take advantage of The Royal Merchant Navy School, an institution founded in St George in the East, London, in 1827, before moving to Hermon Hill, Wanstead in 1862. The new building provided board and lodging for 300 orphans of British Merchant Navy seamen, and an education sufficient to enable them to obtain 'suitable employment'. Young Howard was taken in as a full-time boarder and by 1913, at the age of 15, he was at sea in the Merchant Navy. By 2 June 1919 he had gained his Second Mates Certificate, which was followed by his Masters Certificate on 7 February 1924. He was clearly a man up for a challenge as during this time he also left the Merchant Navy for a time to join the newly fledged Royal Flying Corps, before being demobilised in 1920 with an honorary commission as a Second Lieutenant. But now back in the Merchant Navy with a decent wage, he proposed to his girlfriend Kathleen Green, and they were married at St Agnes in Ullet Road, Sefton Park. By the 1930s, he was a regular First Mate on Cunard-White Star vessels such as the *Markhoor* travelling from Calcutta to Boston, while Kathleen looked after their new home on Queens Drive in Mossley Hill, looking forward to his return after months at sea.

When war broke out, he soon found he was needed on the supply convoys and was in command of the *Malakand* on the night of 3 May when she was berthed in Huskisson. Several hundred bombers began the enemy raid on the city at around 10.30 that evening, to continue the assault that had begun two nights earlier. Visibility was good and docks and industrial works, storehouses and business centres, were soon hit. The Liverpool Daily Post reported,

'Merseyside experienced on Saturday night its worst air-raid of the war. Considerable damage was done to commercial and other buildings, whilst residential property again suffered extensively, and it is feared the casualties will be heavy.

The S.S. Malakand

Howard Cook Kinley's Master's Certificate 1924

The German News Agency describes the attack as 'one of the heaviest ever made.' The combination of R.A.F, night fighters and anti-aircraft gunfire, however, made their night over Britain the most expensive ever for the Luftwaffe, the fighters claiming 14 raiders, and the gunners two.

A number of cultural buildings, famous business premises and shopping centres in Liverpool, were among the property seriously damaged, while hospitals, churches, hotels, schools and many houses were hit. Gallant work was performed throughout the raid by the police, firemen, A.F.S, and all the voluntary services.

This being the fourth successive raid on the area this morning, German bombers for some hours made circuits of the area and dropped large numbers of bombs. This morning's raid was on a considerably smaller scale than Saturday nights. Each bomber on arrival was met by an intense barrage, which forced the raiders to a great height and, as the results showed, baffled them in their quest for objectives. Most of the fires started were quickly extinguished. The loss of life is not expected to be serious.

Saturday night's raid on Merseyside was the severest yet experienced, thousands of fire bombs rained on a wide area followed by high explosive bombs, which were dropped in some cases on the burning buildings and among the fire fighters as they strove to quell the flames.'

At around 11 o'clock that night a barrage balloon, which had become partly deflated and had broken away from its moorings, had become snagged in the foremast of the *Malakand*. It flopped down over No.1 hatch as a shower of incendiaries were dropped, three of which landed on deck, one landing only a yard or so from the balloon material flapping in the wind. The crew rushed forward to cover the flames with sand, but the balloon swept across them catching fire before exploding and sending sheets of flame upwards and across the deck. The crew battled to extinguish the deck fire which they succeeded in dousing after 15 minutes. It had been an intense fight, but the raid was still going on and high explosive bombs were going off around them, two of which hit the dock side shed closest to the vessel. Here too the men on the dock side had been trying to cope with incendiaries, but the high explosives caused numerous fires to break out along the row of dock warehouses which stood only six feet from the edge of the quayside. It must have been so frustrating for the men of the *Malakand* to suffer this new threat, as the flames fanned by a strong wind, began to shoot across the decks. The wooden lifeboats caught fire first then the wooden top deck. The heat and smoke were soon too intense and the Lascar crew were sent ashore by Kinley.

Meanwhile, he also despatched the 3rd Officer, Mr Cullen, to supervise and also see if there was any chance of help from the hard-pressed men of the AFS at the end of Huskisson Dock No.1. Captain Kinley was now faced with the serious dilemma of what to do with his blazing ship. If she were cut adrift it was highly likely that the wind would push her to the other side of the dock with the potential danger of spreading fire there. The option of scuttling her was no longer on due to the intensity of the flames making it impossible get below to set any such action in motion. The fire was also spreading to the last remaining gangway, so the order was given by Kinley for the last of the crew to abandon ship.

Once on the dockside, Kinley hurried down to the fire station at the end of North West Huskisson 1 only to find it empty. A few minutes later he found the senior officer fighting a shed fire. This was Section Officer John Lappin of the AFS, a master stevedore (who had seen service with the Royal Navy at the Dardanelles). Kinley swiftly told him the desperate position of the *Malakand* and her dangerous cargo, whereupon Lappin immediately called his HQ for assistance, with the inevitable reply that very few pumps were available, so Kinley also informed the Naval HQ in the Liver

Building. In the meantime, all they could use was a small portable pump, but it broke down after only 20 minutes. Nevertheless, an engine arrived at 1am, having been driven through the city from Speke. Starting up several hoses, all they could do was make little impression on the shed fire and couldn't get anywhere near the *Malakand* due to the heat and flames.

The Royal Navy made an attempt to help by sending their salvage boat down river from where she was on stand-by at the Liverpool Landing Stage, but as she reached the dock gates at Sandon Dock, (the entrance to Huskisson), the tide was still too low and they couldn't gain access. Not giving up, the captain jumped onto the sea wall to try and get around to see what could be done, but the way was blocked, explosions had begun to go off near the vessel, and he decided to get back to his own ship and help out elsewhere on the river. It now looked as though no more help would be forthcoming and the one fire-appliance from Speke was all that could get through. This was the worst night of the Blitz and despite the serious threat to the inflammable cargo of the *Malakand*, services were stretched right across the city as never before.

The shed fire was huge – an eighty-foot-wide blaze had to be controlled before they could get anywhere near to the stricken vessel. They still hadn't given up on assistance, but the quarter master, who they had sent on a two-mile journey for help, had returned. The dock road was impassable, and he had to take cover under the Overhead Railway all the way, before reluctantly giving up. This wasn't how it had become known as the 'Docker's Umbrella', as what he was sheltering from was rather more dangerous than rain. On the return of the quartermaster, and realising hopes of assistance had stalled, Kinley and Lappin jumped into a car and headed to Hatton Garden in the city centre, the H.Q. of the local fire service. Bursting in, they were shown in to the Chief Officer himself, where in no uncertain terms they briefed him on the seriousness of the situation and the urgent priority of diverting appliances from less serious conflagrations. Kinley asked Chief Officer Owen if something could be done to sink her from the offside, by either cutting holes or even a shot in the engine room. They decided that the second option was unworkable, so an appliance was despatched with oxy-acetylene burning apparatus. Kinley also tried to contact the Dock Board and the Navy while they were in the control room, but unknown to them the main Telephone Exchange in South John Street had been hit and 22,000 lines were down.

Back at Huskisson, the struggle continued with whatever equipment was to hand - there was even one report of a policeman helping out with a bucket. So desperate was the situation across the city in those early hours, that no further firefighters nor appliances arrived before the 'all clear' sounded at 5.20am, and by then the *Malakand* and the sheds had been burning for over five hours.

Courage was in abundance that night on the dockside, all hands knowing what cargo was on board, and yet not knowing if they could prevent it going up. But the crew, firemen and dock watchmen continued to battle on with impossibly limited resources. Lappin and his men were now in a state of exhaustion – and in their desperation arguments began over what to do next. At one stage they thought of towing the *Malakand* out into the river, but they decided against it as she could blow as they were passing through Sandon Dock gates, thereby putting the whole complex out of action. Kinley then wanted to withdraw - their efforts seemed futile, his men were exhausted and still in mortal danger - but Lappin convinced him to fight on. However, by 7.30am, Kinley felt his men could do no more and the risks were increasing, and he called them off. It was a timely decision - minutes later the *Malakand* exploded. Those at Huskisson may have expected it, but it certainly took everyone else by surprise, as it had been impossible to notify everyone in the surrounding area. It was a terrible, violent explosion. Huge pieces of debris rained down in the immediate dockside area, some of it crashing onto the decks of neighbouring ships, while a wave was created which swept around the dock complex causing vessels to surge and shift moorings. One of the crew of the nearby *Clan MacWhirter*, was heading to his bunk, completely exhausted after a hard night, and described what happened,

> 'As I was nearing the wheelhouse it happened — a terrific 'whoosh' came from the next basin and the whole sky was blotted out by a dirty yellow fog... For a full minute, metal of all shapes and sizes came raining down. A steel plate crashed through the engineer's cabin, just missing the sleeping occupant and completely wrecking it. In that one minute we received more damage than we had all night.'

Other vessels nearby were very badly damaged by the blast, one being completely covered by the steel doors off the dockside sheds, while Charles White, a dock gateman, had just come on duty, only to see one of the crane drivers thrown into the dock. Showing great courage, he jumped in after him, despite the hail of debris still raining down. He managed to grab him and got him to hold onto the anchor line of the *Busiris* berthed alongside until help arrived, while they were buffeted by the shockwaves.

As the smoke and dust cleared, a scene of complete devastation was revealed. Several dockers walking towards the dock estate about to 'clock on' were hit, several losing limbs. Huskisson had been demolished, thick stone walls turned to rubble, the Overhead Railway nearby badly damaged and nearby sections were even covered with a cargo of green Lever Brothers soap. Some of the steel plating off the *Malakand* was found two and a half miles away. One of her 4 ton anchors was blown 400 yards on top of dockside machinery. Kinley and several men were injured, but one of the firemen off the Speke appliance was killed.

Yet Lappin and his men continued fighting the fires, while others bravely attended to the removal of the dead and injured, rescuing many of the wounded, and organising their removal to hospital in improvised ambulances. But the horrors of this brutal struggle were not yet over. In the midst of the rescue as nine o'clock approached, there was a second explosion, and debris was again thrown across the dock, with twisted metal flying in all directions. A Lascar on the nearby vessel *Clan MacWhirter* was killed by a flying shed door, and a married couple driving home along the dock road were killed instantly when a huge section of steel plate crashed onto their car. Another flying shed door was blown out of the dock complex and sliced a carthorse in two on a dockside road almost a mile away. Numerous buildings and warehouses along the dock road near Huskisson were also badly damaged, although later it was difficult to assess which could be attributed to the heavy bombing and that caused by the explosions. Furthermore, this was not to be the end of the destruction as it would continue for several more nights. It would take another seventy-four hours for the fire to burn out.

Later, several men involved in the events that night were honoured. Lappin was awarded the George Medal and Landau the BEM, which was also awarded to several of his colleagues. Captain Kinley was given a Commendation, while his officers Allan and Exley were later awarded the MBE.

Afterwards, the dock was drained to begin salvage. Incredibly, 1,350 bombs were recovered from a relatively intact hold in the *Malakand* by the Navy and despatched to the RAF for disposal. The lower hull of the *Malakand* still lies below Huskisson.

Kinley, who was hospitalised to treat his injuries, was discharged three weeks later. His first job was to take a ship up the Manchester Ship Canal. He was well known among his crews for his membership of the Magic Circle, and he was most concerned that an injury to his finger might have impaired his skill as a conjurer. He stood on the bridge practising sleight of hand with a matchbox to get his touch back again, and the Canal pilot was so fascinated by his skills that he nearly ran them aground. Months later he was back at sea in command of the *SS Fort Ville Marie* sailing from Immingham for New York as part of the Atlantic Convoys. Due to the heavy losses suffered by the Allied Merchant Navy Ships in the early months of the war, a large-scale ship-building programme was begun. Ships were commissioned from Canada and U.S.A. for management by British shipping companies. Most were run on a lend-lease basis. Ninety *'Forts'* – vessels built in Canada, were bought by the U.S. War Shipping Administration and leased to the British Government, who were then responsible for supplying and equipping the vessel with all fuel, chandlery, hardware, paint and other expendable supplies. The *SS Fort Ville Marie* was one of those vessels and operated by Cunard-White Star. In 1944, he also captained the *Mahout* to Calcutta, the vessel which was lying next to the *Malakand* on that fateful night where many of his Lascar crew had taken cover.

After the war, Captain Kinley continued to have a full career with T & J Brocklebank (owned by Cunard-White Star) and captained many of their cargo vessels, mainly to India, such as *Mahanada* in 1953, the *Maturata* (1956) and the *Maipura* (1959), before enjoying his retirement in Ness on the Wirral. He passed away aged 67 on 5 May 1965.

But the night of 3 May and the role of those brave men will never be forgotten on Merseyside. Damage in the city centre was considerable with some of the city's best-known buildings destroyed, including the Customs House, the Cotton Exchange, the Rotunda Theatre and Lewis's department store, while many of the outlying neighbourhoods were reduced to rubble. The main City Museum and Library and their collections were also badly damaged, while many roads, railways and tramlines were made unusable. Many vital services were quickly restored, but other damage often took years to repair. The damage to Huskisson was just part of the extensive destruction to the dock system. By the end of the 1941 Blitz, 69 out of 144 cargo berths were closed, there were serious losses of ships, food and fuel, and had the bombing continued for just a couple more nights, the docks could have been totally disabled.

The Prime Minister Winston Churchill came to see the damage for himself in May 1941, touring the city and the surrounding area, before declaring, 'I see the damage done by the enemy attacks, but I also see the spirit of an unconquered people.'

Seventy-two years later, on May bank holiday weekend in 2013, these unconquered people and the men who braved the seas were remembered in several events to mark the 70th anniversary of the Battle of the Atlantic. Twenty-five warships sailed into port to mark the milestone, and on Sunday 26 May, Liverpool was bathed in glorious sunshine as huge crowds made their way to the waterfront. Many were at the Pier Head to witness the Princess Royal lay a wreath at the British Merchant Navy Memorial. The Princess also paid her respects to the other three Merchant Navy memorials close by, which include plaques to the Belgian, Dutch, and Norwegian merchant navies. The final tablet on behalf of the Polish merchant navy had been unveiled two days earlier. These free Allied merchant fleets were crucial in supporting Britain's war effort in its greatest time of need, before, and during, the Battle of the Atlantic. After a memorial service at the Anglican Cathedral, Princess Anne stood outside to take the salute, as Battle of the Atlantic veterans and those from other conflicts, international warships' companies and other naval groups, including cadets, marched past the steps. Out of a pure blue sky above, flew the veteran Fairey Swordfish bi-plane of the Royal Fleet Air Arm Museum, accompanied by four modern helicopters, for the Royal fly-past. Captain Andrew Burns, master of the Royal Navy's flagship *HMS Bulwark* - moored in Alexandra Dock, Bootle, for the Battle of the Atlantic event, said:

> 'It is vital that we are here to show our continued support for the maritime community past and present. It is also important for my ship's company to reflect on the commitment and sacrifice made by those in the Battle of the Atlantic and what it means for us to be here today.'

The decimated docks of Huskisson, following the fateful night of 3 May 1941

Huskisson No.2 Branch looking towards the dock road
On the right are the sheds of Huskisson No.1, while the wreckage of the Malakand is to the left. In the distance beyond is the Overhead Railway, with the Van Olney berthed in front.

Unexploded bombs being hoisted out of the wreck of the Malakand

The devastation of the city caused by the Blitz is clear, as this view of Lord Street (left) and South Castle Street clearly shows, while the bomb sites are in the process of being cleared and made safe.

Further Reading

Whittington-Egan, Richard, *The Great Liverpool Blitz* (1987)

Hughes, John, *Port in a Storm – The Air attacks on Liverpool and its shipping in the Second World War* (Nat. Museums and Galleries on Merseyside 1993)

Whitworth, Rodney, *Merseyside at War – A day-to-day diary of the 1940-41 Bombing*; Scouse Press (1988)

Wade, Beryl, *Storm over the Mersey* (1990)

Liverpool Daily Post & Echo, *Bombers Over Merseyside*, (1943) Facsimile edition of this work was issued as:

Spiegl, Fritz ed., *Bombers Over Merseyside: The Authoritative Record of the Blitz, 1940-1941*; Scouse Press (1984)

Johnson, Arthur, *Merseyside's secret Blitz diary: A remarkable personal account of Liverpool at war* (Liverpool, 2005)

Royden, Mike, *'A History of Mill Road Hospital'*. (Liverpool 1993) - Chaper 6 *'The May Blitz'* contains a harrowing account of the direct hit on the hospital and maternity wards with numerous personal recollections.

Royden, Mike, *Merseyside at War 1939-45* (Pen & Sword 2018)

Ayers, Pat, *Liverpool Docklands*; Liver Press (1999)

Collard, Ian, *Mersey Ports: Liverpool and Birkenhead*; Tempus Publishing, (2001)

Alois Hitler and his wife
Bridget Dowling

William Patrick Hitler

15

The Hitler Family of Liverpool

Of family and history I have no idea. In this respect I am completely ignorant. Before, I did not know that I had relatives. Only when I became Reich Chancellor I learned this. I am a totally unfamilial creature. That does not suit me. I belong only to my people.

– Adolf Hitler. *Monologues,* 1942

There is a Liverpool urban myth that surfaces from time to time, which meets with a flurry of activity between believers and disbelievers, then disappears until enough time has lapsed for the story to gather 'credibility' again and demand attention from new readers. And it is this: *'Adolf Hitler lived in Liverpool before World War One with his half brother Alois'*. It conjures up many images - the young artist studying the architecture, improving his mind, learning the language, standing on the Kop. In fact, what has been published is even more ludicrous; loafing around his brother's house, ranting about German politics in a Toxteth back kitchen, learning about his future with an astrological mystic neighbour, followed by a reconnaissance trip to the waterfront to make a note of the shipping using the port – just for future reference you understand, should Germany ever go to war with, say, Britain for example. So aside from the elaborations, is there any truth at all in this story? Much of the interest has stemmed from the publication in the 1970s of a memoir written thirty years earlier, supposedly by

Bridget Hitler, the wife of Alois, Adolf's half-brother. This was met with wide reportage in England, especially in the Liverpool press. It also influenced local writer Beryl Bainbridge to produce *Young Adolf*, a fictionalised story about his visit to Liverpool as told in the memoir. She followed this in 1981 with a drama commissioned by the BBC called *The Journal of Bridget Hitler*, with Maurice Roeves, Siobhan McKenna and Julian Glover in the lead roles. This television play portrayed the 'pre-war visit' by Adolf to his half-brother's Liverpool home.

Since then, there have been many corruptions of the story, including a version by a local writer who also featured a fake photograph on his web site of a young Hitler standing in front of the William Brown Street Galleries and Library buildings, just to muddy the waters still further.

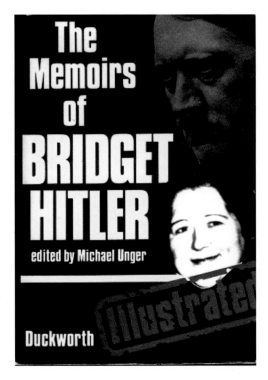

The 1970s edition of Bridget (Dowling) Hitler's memoir edited by Michael Unger, former editor of the Liverpool Daily Post

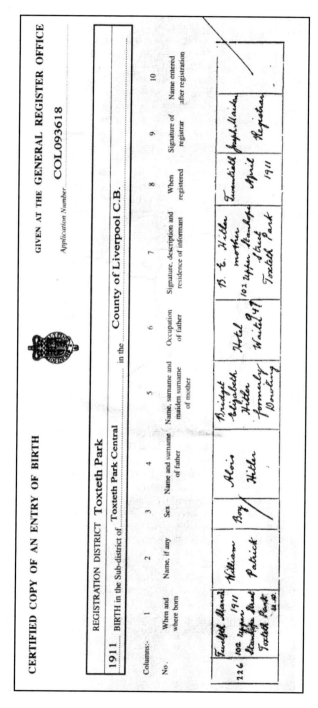

Birth certificate of their son, William Patrick Hitler, in 102 Upper Stanhope Street, Toxteth Park

The 1911 census record for 102 Upper Stanhope Street, Toxteth. Entry 4 reads Anton (Alois) Hitler, 6 is Cissie (CeCe) and 7 William Patrick their son

CENSUS OF ENGLAND AND WALES, 1911.

Before writing on this Schedule please read the Examples and the Instructions given on the other side of the paper, as well as the headings of the Columns. The entries should be written in ink.

The contents of the Schedule will be treated as confidential. Strict care will be taken that no information is disclosed with regard to individual persons. The returns are not to be used for proof of age, as in connection with Old Age Pensions, or for any other purpose than the preparation of Statistical Tables.

The story came to the fore again in 2002, when David Gardner, a former crime writer and senior foreign correspondent on the Daily Mail, published a book entitled *The Last of the Hitlers*. Although it deals primarily with his story of how he traced the last remaining relatives of the Nazi dictator, he discusses the Liverpool connection, and this was shortly followed by a Channel 5 documentary which consequently reawakened interested in the story.

The following year in December 2003, the story was featured on Radio 4's *Making History*, where an objective approach was taken to get to the truth of the matter and involved myself in the making of the programme, together with Liverpool Record Office archivist Roger Hull, Hitler's biographer Professor Sir Ian Kershaw, and producer Nick Patrick. This had a knock-on effect, resulting in my further participation with numerous radio features on Radio 4, and local radio (Merseyside and City) and a few television appearances, including Stuart Maconie's *'TV Towns'*. Most bizarre was filming and appearing in a Dutch programme, *'Mission Unfindable'*, a series where the presenter, Dutch celebrity Katja Schuurman, was sent each week on a new mission. That week she was given the task of finding the living relatives of Hitler. The previous weeks she had to try to discover the closely guarded recipe for Coca-Cola and the whereabouts of Osama Bin Laden, which gives an idea of the realms the programme makers were living in. But then, this was the country that gave us *'Big Brother'*. I met Katja and the film crew outside Liverpool Central Library and we spent the day filming in the Picton Reading Room, (as a 'front' for Liverpool Record Office), then later in Upper Stanhope Street. There was an interlude in Dale Street where Katja went off with a handy cam (with the crew in tow), in search of where Alois Hitler may have worked and where the Hitler's might have sunk a few beers. I tried to put them off. Point that camera at someone with questions thrown at them, such as 'Did Hitler used to drink around here?' and, well, you can imagine the situation and the

Scouse wit that would follow. 'Oh yeah, he useter drink in d'pub round d'corner wid me arl feller' was the first response, and it quickly went downhill from there.

But I digress.

The crux of the story is that in pre-First World War Liverpool, young Adolf, still hoping for a career as an artist, came to stay at the house of his half-brother and his wife Bridget in Upper Stanhope Street, in Toxteth. There he stayed for around six months, before returning to the men's hostel in Vienna. As the only source for this is Bridget's own memoir, it has inevitably undergone thorough analysis.

According to an interview given to the *Daily Express* in the thirties, Bridget Dowling may have met Alois at a staff dance at the Royal Hibernian Hotel in Dublin. This contrasts with the version she gave in her memoir, where she states she met Alois for the first time at the Dublin Horse Show in 1909. There, she said her father and neighbour began talking to a stranger. The young man cut a dashing figure in his smart suit and his waxed, turned up handle bar moustache. He introduced himself as Alois Hitler from Austria, and with his 'fine foreign manners and his debonair Viennese ways' he made a great impression on the teenage Bridget. 'He fairly won my heart with his sugary talk and foreign ways', she declared.

They agreed to meet, and a close friendship soon developed between them. However, Alois had already created suspicion in the family with his fancy talk about being in the 'hotel business', and that he was there on a 'fact finding trip' covering France, Belgium, and the British Isles, to study the trade. It wasn't long before they discovered he was actually a waiter at the Shelbourne Hotel, in the centre of Dublin, sent there by a London employment agency. Despite this, Bridget was 'head over heels in love' and they began to see more of each other.

The Dowlings clearly did not approve of the relationship, especially once they became aware of his true station. Having decided to marry, the couple eloped to London, where they were married at Marylebone Registry Office on 3 June 1910. William Dowling, Bridget's father, a farm labourer from Kilnamanagh, was so incensed he even wanted the police to arrest Alois for kidnapping.

'My father - rest his soul - was a real Irishman', wrote Bridget. 'He would not hear tell of a wedding to a foreigner. Alois and I used to meet every afternoon in the museum and make plans to elope. Four months later when Alois had saved enough money we went to England on the night boat and came to London. I wrote to my mother and said I would not return until we got permission to marry. She talked my father around and he gave his consent'.

Bridget was reunited with her father the following year, when she presented him with a new grandson. By now the Hitlers had relocated to 102 Upper Stanhope Street in Toxteth, Liverpool, where their baby was born on 12 March 1911. He was christened William Patrick, and the birth was also officially registered (as was their marriage in London). In the census of April 1911, they were recorded living in a flat in No.102, where there were several more boarders occupying the other flats. It is likely the information was given by Alois, although his own name was recorded as Anton – was that intentional, or had the enumerator misunderstood his accent? Bridget's surname was, at first, declared as Dowling before the mistake was realised, causing the enumerator to cross it out and start again. Alois gave her first name as 'Cece', this was his pet name for her after a painting of St Cecilia which he admired (according to her memoir). The official misheard, and wrote it as 'Cissy'. Their one month old son is also recorded as William – Bridget preferred Patrick, whereas Alois called him William, further suggesting it was Alois who spoke to the official.

His occupation was recorded as Chief Waiter at the Lyon's Café (possibly the State in Dale Street, owned by Lyons).

Alois found it difficult to settle in Liverpool, and changed his source of income four times in their first two years of married life. According to Bridget, he ran a restaurant on Dale Street, a boarding house on Upper Parliament Street, and then a hotel in Mount Pleasant. When he became a salesman for a disposable razor firm, he began to have grand ideas about developing his own business in the same field. This, he hoped, would involve his sister Angela, and brother-in-law Leo Raubal back in Austria [was Bridget confused again? – Leo died in 1910]. He then sent them money to cover their travelling expenses in the hope they would come to Liverpool for a visit where he could discuss his ideas further. According to Bridget, '...we were looking forward with pleasure to their visit. When we went to Lime Street Station to meet them, I eagerly scanned the couples descending from the 11.30 train, wondering if I would recognise our relatives. Instead of Angela and Leo Raubal, however, a shabby young man approached and offered Alois his hand. It was my husband's younger brother, Adolf, who came in their place'.

A row then broke out between the brothers and Bridget left them to it. When they returned to the flat later that evening the tension was gone, and once Adolf had retired to bed, Bridget berated her husband for the way he had treated him. What then followed was a diatribe against Adolf and how Alois portrayed himself as the classic mistreated step-child, while all favouritism went to the true offspring of the mother. He described to his young wife his unhappy childhood and the way he was constantly beaten by his father, especially when he came home the worse for wear after yet another night at the local tavern. Despite his uncomfortable memories, Alois was not going to turn his half-brother away, and this was to be the beginning of a stay that would keep Adolf in Upper Stanhope Street for almost 6 months, from November 1912 until April 1913... according to Bridget. Alois did have a difficult childhood. Alois senior, the natural father of both Alois and Adolf, was born on 7 June 1837 to Maria Anna Schickelgruber, a forty-two-year-old cook and the unmarried daughter of Johann Schickelgruber from the village of Strones in Lower Austria. The entry made that same day in the baptismal register of Dollerscheim parish, shows that the baby was christened Alois Schickelgruber. The space in the register for the father's name was left blank, and despite much speculation has remained a mystery ever since. In 1842, Maria Shickelgruber married a journeyman miller named Johann Georg Hiedler. The marriage lasted only five years as Maria died in 1847. Young Alois was taken in by his step-father's brother Johann Nepomuk Hiedler, who raised him like his own son. Why this was so is unclear, but Johann Georg may have returned to his travels to support himself.

At eighteen, Alois senior entered the Austrian civil service and by 1875 he had risen to the position of customs inspector in Braunau am Inn. The following year he had cause to have his name changed. It would not appear to be due to his illegitimacy, as he had never attempted to conceal it, rather, it may have been due to a legacy from his adopted father Johann Nepomuk Hiedler, who, having no heir, required Alois to legally take the family name.

As a consequence, his birth records were altered to read Johann Georg Hiedler as the name of his father, despite the fact he had been dead for nearly 20 years. In fact, it was 'misspelled' as 'Johann Georg Hitler' in the process. The parish priest was also persuaded to strike out Schickelgruber and to change 'out of wedlock' to 'within wedlock'. There was also marginal note: 'The under signed confirm that Georg Hitler, registered as the father, who is well known to the under signed witnesses, admits to being the father of the child Alois, as stated by the child's mother, Anna Schickelgruber, and has requested the entry of his name in the present baptismal register'. Three illiterate witnesses added their marks to the statement. The statement was clearly false, but his natural parents were no longer around to object. From January 1877 Alois Schickelgruber called himself Alois Hitler. [Hiedler, Huttler, Hietler, Hutler, Hitler, were all phonetic spelling of the same name on documents of the 19th century. The name means 'smallholder']

Alois, who was now a much-respected customs official, was to marry three times. Firstly, to Anna Glassl, a woman much older than himself, then to two young women, Franziska Matzelberger and Klara Pölzl, who were young enough to be his daughters. Anna Glassl, whom he married in 1873 was by then aged fifty, and it seemed to be a marriage of convenience, she being fourteen years his senior, well off, and with useful connections in the civil service. It wasn't long before Alois took himself a mistress, and by 1880 Anna, who had clearly had enough, was granted a legal separation. Franziska, now the focus of his affection and wary of Alois' wandering eye, insisted that his housekeeper (and cousin) Klara Pölzl - should be dismissed.

In 1882, Alois junior was born, although he was not legitimised until the following year, when Alois senior and Franziska were married after the death of Anna earlier that year. A daughter Angela followed a few weeks after the wedding. In August 1884, Franziska contracted tuberculosis and died at the age of only twenty-four. While she had been sent to the country for convalescence, Alois immediately brought Klara back to look after the children. She became pregnant very quickly after the death of Franziska. As they were second cousins they needed special dispensation from the church to marry, which took four months. Once cleared, they were married on 7 January 1885. Five children followed soon afterwards, of which Adolf was the fourth, born in 20 April 1889. Her first three children all died at various stages of infancy, while her fifth, Edmund, born in 1894, died from measles in 1900 aged six. Paula, her sixth child, was born in 1896, and lived until 1960.

Alois senior has been described as a pompous, strict authoritarian, who demanded respect, while giving little time or devotion to his family. He frequently resorted to beating his sons to ensure unquestioned discipline. At thirteen, Alois junior left the family home, having been found the position of a waiter. However, by 1900 he had been found guilty of theft and jailed for 5 months, followed by a similar offence two years later, for which he received 8 months. On his release, he left for Paris, then London, trying to make a fresh start by securing work in the catering industry.

The domineering Alois senior died in January 1903, and the family relocated to Linz two years later. In 1907, his third wife Klara - Adolf's mother - died from cancer aged forty-seven. The grief-stricken Adolf, who had already failed to secure a place at the Viennese Academy of Fine Arts, determined to return to the city intent on becoming an architect. It did not go well. From early 1908 until May 1913 he remained in Vienna, living hand to mouth, drifting from one menial job to another, unable to get into college to pursue his chosen career. By 1910, after a period of living rough, often in the open, he moved into a men's hostel, while hawking postcards of paintings he had made of views of the city.

So far, much of this detail about the brother's early life is factual and generally accepted by most historians and biographers. It is the next development which has caused the most controversy.

The only source for Adolf's 'visit' to Liverpool is contained in Bridget's *Memoir*. The existence of the manuscript has been generally known since its 'rediscovery' in early 1970s, when the historian Robert Payne, while researching material for his book *The Life and Death of Adolf Hitler*, read through it in the manuscript division of the New York Public Library. This unfinished manuscript, which ends in mid-sentence, was published for the first time in 1979, with an introduction and

The Hitler Family Tree

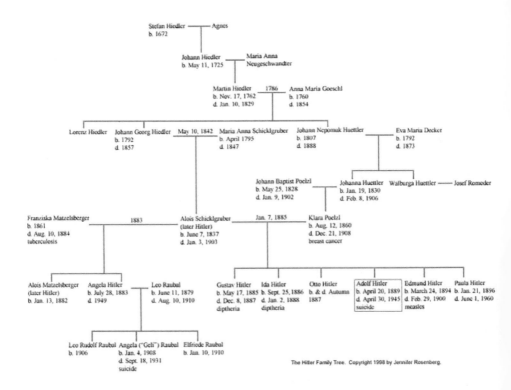

The Hitler Family Tree. Copyright 1998 by Jennifer Rosenberg.

discussion of its authenticity by Michael Unger, then editor of the *Liverpool Daily Post*. It was probably written by Bridget and son William, around 1940-41, perhaps with the help of a ghost-writer, as there are noticeable differences in style contained within.

Historians have little time for the memoir, and have been highly critical of its contents, feeling there are too many discrepancies (not just with the Liverpool episode) to be taken seriously. Indeed, Ian Kershaw, speaking on the *Making History* programme, went as far as calling the memoir 'a work of fiction without a grain of truth'. And here lies the problem. There is no other evidence placing Hitler in Liverpool. Until something else appears to either support or contradict, the controversy is sure to continue.

Filming 'Mission Unfindable' in the Picton Reading Room, Liverpool Central Library. Author Mike Royden is discussing the documentary evidence for the Toxteth Hitlers with presenter Katja Schuurman.

Michael Unger's edition of the *Memoir* was republished in 2011, and while publicising its release, he told JMU Journalism,

> 'My instincts are that he did come to Liverpool. These are also the instincts of some historians, the FBI and the boss of the wartime British spies, William Stephenson. The only doubts that I have had have been dispelled in recent years although some people, journalists and historians among others, doubt it simply because they doubt it. One of my great surprises is how bad the research is of some eminent people.'

Unger's 'instincts' are not enough however, and his views on historians are misleading and unfair. Seasoned historians who deal in convincing evidence can see this *Memoir* is too unreliable to give it credence. Furthermore, research that can take a great deal of time and produces little in the way of tangible material, may have the appearance of no research at all. Not to find material that may well not exist is hardly a failure.

The myth surrounding Hitler's visit was not helped by the novel *Young Adolf* by Beryl Bainbridge. This was a work of fiction, where Bainbridge took the idea of Adolf visiting Liverpool, as recounted in the just-published memoir, and developed the idea further. Later, when it was made into the two-part television drama, it reached an even wider audience. Although she made it clear at the time that it was a product largely of her own imagination, many observers, especially Liverpudlians, accepted the visit as historical fact. Talking to the Washington Post in 1979 about non-fiction, Bainbridge said,

> 'I haven't really got the education for that sort of thing. The bit of what I laughingly call research that I did on young Adolf I quite enjoyed. I felt rather educated rushing around looking in libraries... the part of them [the memoirs] that seems the most real is the part about Adolf coming to Liverpool. It's the most understated, whether it's true or not. There's no proof that he came, but there's no proof that he didn't'.

Good research for a fictional novelist, but trying to blur the boundaries with poor scientific historical research and making unsupported claims to a trusting readership is unforgivable and damaging.

Years later in the Foreword to Gardner's *Last of the Hitlers*, her view of the truth was undimmed,

> '...what rings true, by reason of its mundane content, its very naivety of expression, is her [Bridget's] account of Adolf's arrival in Liverpool'.

This encapsulates the view of many of those who feel this section of the memoir has 'credibility', its very 'matter of factness', not being 'dressed up for effect'.

In fact, it's quite the opposite. The ordinariness of it is quite stark; Young Adolf playing with her child in the kitchen, while chatting about the future of Germany;

> '...he would never hesitate to interrupt my housework to explain how Germany was going to take its rightful position in the world. First would come France, then England. I didn't find this talk very interesting, but whenever I tried to get away he would begin to shout, although I rarely troubled to contradict him. He would whip himself up into a rage and go on until hoarseness or some interruption stopped him. I put it down partly to the pleasure he took in hearing his own voice - another trick he had in common with my husband - and partly to a desire to domineer me'.

A few paragraph later she says,

> '...During his Liverpool stay, Adolf hadn't even picked up enough English to ask directions to the station'.

This topic of conversation seems quite bizarre, given the fact he was an Austrian and was there in Liverpool, according to Bridget, to dodge the draft into the Austrian army. Until one remembers that the memoir was written around 1941 with a complete awareness of Hitler's true intention by then. Maybe it was quite simple and appealing to look back to her little flat in Toxteth and recount where Adolf Hitler first had the idea for world domination. That should sell a few books for William on the lecture circuit.

At the time the memoir was written, it was common knowledge that there was a 'lost year' in Hitler's life. Hitler had never alluded to it, it wasn't in *Mein Kampf* or any other of his writings. Hitler had conveniently glossed over the period, or rewritten it, to provide a more acceptable version of the public figure he now was. His failure to enter the Academy, living rough, the doss houses, and draft dodging, was a phase he felt was not for public consumption. Bridget and William may have been only too ready to fill in the 'missing months' with an alternative story. Those close to him say apart from brief trips to Italy and Paris, he had made no visit to any other country. Furthermore, at no time did he mention to any British people that he met later, that he had ever visited England.

Professor Ian Kershaw and Professor Robert Waite both point to the fact that there are no records in Germany or Austria that point to a visit abroad, while they do place him in Vienna at the time he was supposed to be in Liverpool. According to Kershaw, again speaking on *Making History*,

> 'There is actually an eye witness to Adolf Hitler's presence in the men's home in Vienna in February 1913 at a time when he is supposed to be in Liverpool. Beyond that, the records kept by the men's home were very careful records and they recorded when people were residents and when they left. Adolf Hitler did actually leave the men's home just for a few days, and they

recorded his departure and his return in May 1913, when he left to go to Munich. They again registered his departure. Since the records are so carefully kept, they would unquestionably have recorded a departure of his in 1912, had he been going to Liverpool. What a wonderfully surreal image to think of Hitler standing on the terraces at Anfield, but there isn't a grain of truth in the story.'

The blue half were not to be left out. While researching his book *The Last of the Hitlers*, David Gardner was called by his business partner who had just received a letter from someone he described as a 'complete whacko'; 'some guy says Hitler lived next door to him in Liverpool and they used to go together to watch Everton at Goodison Park. It goes on and on about how he converted Adolf from liking Liverpool when he first came to Britain.' A letter written by the ghost of Shankly no doubt.

Alois left the Liverpool family home for Germany in May 1914 never to return, and he remarried bigamously in 1916 to Hedwig Heidemann with whom he had a son, Heinrich Hitler, (nicknamed Heinz) who was born on 14 March 1920. When war broke out Heinz joined the Wehrmacht and served on the Eastern Front, where he was reported as captured by the Russians. He died in a Russian prison in 1942 after being tortured.

In the early 1920s, Bridget and William moved to live in London. William renewed contact with his father and visited him in Germany in 1929 and 1930, before returning there in 1933 to try to take advantage of his relationship with his uncle Adolf. The dream of a high powered, well paid position did not materialise. It would appear that he was more of a thorn in the side to his uncle who was 'related to the state' only, and who tried to erase his family details, and their potential embarrassing revelations, from all public knowledge.

By 1938, following a summons to Hitler, William was given an ultimatum to give up his British Nationality and commit himself to the Nazi cause. William declined and made a clandestine exit from the country, now fearful of his own safety. Months later in March 1939, he arrived in New York with Bridget, ready to tour the country giving lectures on the subject of 'My Uncle Adolf', the visit being organised between theatrical agents in London and New York. William was now sufficiently at home in his adoptive country that he decided to enlist in the American Forces to fight for the Allies against Uncle Adolf. Meanwhile, the FBI and the OSS were keeping a watchful eye on his every move and spoke to him on several occasions, trying to learn what they could about Hitler and Nazi Germany. Whatever his motives, he was eventually accepted and signed up to the U.S. Navy. In surreal circumstances, as he gave his name to the recruiting officer, he was met with the reply *'Glad to see you Hitler - my name is Hess!'* A great photo opportunity, but the officer was a Gale K. Hess of Chicago. After training he was sent to the Medical Corps and saw action before being honourably discharged in 1946.

In Germany, his father Alois had established a restaurant in Berlin by 1934, which became a popular drinking hole for Nazi soldiers. He kept it open through the duration of the war, but in 1945 he was arrested by the British, although released when it became clear he had played no role in the Nazi regime. Nevertheless, it is reported that he was involved with a right-wing political party into the 1950s, while he also made money signing photographs of his brother and selling them to tourists. He died in Hamburg on 20 May 1956.

Nothing further is heard of William or Bridget Hitler, although John Toland indicated knowledge of them still living in the New York area in the 1970s when carrying out research for his Hitler biography. The trail was picked up by British journalist David Gardner, who spent most of the 1990s trying to find out what happened to William, especially as there was a suggestion that the Hitler name was still alive and well in America. After much research, he found he was too late, discovering instead their final resting place. He wrote,

> 'William died in 1987, 18 years after his mother, in the anonymity he craved for much of his life. His family even considered leaving the grave unmarked, but decided instead to bury him under the false name that had brought him peace'.

In light of the fate of his uncle, and everything the Nazi regime stood for, William wisely felt it advisable to melt away into the background, change his name, and live in obscurity, in contrast to the very public life he had enjoyed on his lecture tours. Clearly, the worry of retribution towards anyone bearing the name could not be ignored. Nevertheless, Gardner discovered William had made a success of his American life. He married a German girl he had met during his time working in Germany during the 1930s, and together they appeared to be the model family; four all-American boys, while he worked in the medical field. Later he set up a blood analysis laboratory, in the home they moved to in the countryside to avoid prying eyes. Neighbours spoke about them as a pleasant family, well respected in the community. There were four sons, Alexander (1949), Louis (1951), Howard (1957) and Brian (1965). Howard was killed in a car crash in 1989, but the three remaining brothers are still living, bearing a double barrel name that gives no hint of their roots. None of the sons married and it is likely that the Hitler name may now finally die out. The fact that William's family have led a relatively normal life in America in the face of their family history is some achievement.

The family understandably refused to co-operate fully with Gardner, nor with the Channel 5 film company. He persisted in trying to shed light on Bridget's memoirs. William's wife Phyllis told Gardner, 'It's all made up', while Alex said, 'We read it and it was the funniest thing I ever saw in my life'.

However, on a later visit when pressed further, Alex went so far as to say it was all true and not only did Adolf visit Liverpool but he visited Ireland too, furthermore, the remaining manuscript was actually completed and the library only had the first half. All of which is unlikely and sounded very much like a sarcastic, angry outburst in reaction to the intrusion into their private lives. There were further contradictions in William Patrick Hitler's life. Not only did he give his first son the middle name of Adolf, but the adopted name he was to use for the rest of his life was the same double barrel name of one of the most notorious anti-Semitic theorists of the far right, and a significant influence on Hitler when writing Mein Kampf. Why use these names?

A family of many contradictions, and a branch that has created the urban myth of Adolf Hitler in Liverpool. Consequently, we may never get to the truth, but to place Adolf Hitler in Liverpool in 1913 is to rely on one piece of very flimsy evidence. Sounds like a Monty Python sketch. Billy Hitler of Toxteth. Adolf in Liverpool. You couldn't make it up.

But did Billy's mother?

Postscript

During the completion of this book, I have had long conversations and meetings with a reputable film company in London, who have made a series of high quality documentaries, plus an award-winning documentary film maker known for his work in American politics, both of whom are working on making films on *The Hitler's of Liverpool*. Whether they see the light of day is not for me to comment on, but is further testament to the continued interest and debate surrounding this urban myth/factual account (delete at your discretion). Both sounded very exciting and the story does deserve a full professional production that would do the narrative and debate justice, rather than the superficial films and reports done so far.

Further Reading

Gardner, David, *The Last of the Hitlers* (2001)
Hitler, Bridget, / Unger, M. ed., *The Memoirs of Bridget Hitler* (1979 - new publication 2011)
Kershaw, I. *Hitler 1889-1936: Hubris* (1998)
Toland, J. *Adolf Hitler*, (1976)

BBC Radio 4
Making History 'Adolf Hitler in Liverpool' Programme 10, broadcast on 2nd December 2003.

On the Net

Royden, Mike, *Adolf Hitler - did he visit Liverpool during 1912-13?*
BBC website www.bbc.co.uk/legacies/myths_legends/eng land/liverpool/user_1_article_1.shtml

Mike Royden's Local History Pages – www.roydenhistory.co.uk